Millennium Management:
Last Chance for American Business

William Lareau, Ph.D.

NEW CENTURY PUBLISHERS, INC.

Printing Code
11   12   13   14   15   16   17

Library of Congress Cataloging-in-Publication Data

Lareau, William.
    Millennium management.

    Includes index.
    1. Organizational change. 2. Organizational effectiveness. 3. Industrial management—United States. 4. Competition, International. I. Title.
HD58.5.L37 1986   658.4'06   86-18247
ISBN 0-8329-0431-7

Contents

This book is dedicated to my wife, Darlene, and all of the other hard-working, competent businesspeople who haven't yet given up the struggle to do a creative and enthusiastic job even when faced with the typical organization's bureaucracy and complaisance. May you keep the embers of American business alive until the fires are stoked again.

Preface

Conduct Expected: The Unwritten Rules for A Successful Business Career (New Century Publishers, 1985) outlined the techniques and strategies for maximizing individual success in a typical business environment. The reality of most business environments requires, among other things, that employees who want to be successful shouldn't rock the boat, give honest opinions (unless they're the same as the official policies), or argue with their bosses. It's unfortunate and sad that such behaviors lead to individual success because they're the very types of behaviors (when practiced by large numbers of people) that stifle a company's effectiveness and productivity. However, a single employee can't do much on his or her own, so there's no reason to have a career destroyed by fighting the system. If you're in such an organization, *Conduct Expected* tells you how to look good and stay out of trouble.

Inside Track: A Successful Job Search Method, published earlier this year by New Century Publishers, is a comprehensive set of applied job-search techniques. *Inside Track* provides job seekers with everything they need to know to get another job as quickly as possible.

Both *Conduct Expected* and *Inside Track* are practical books which serve valuable purposes. Yet they sidestep the most pressing business problem we have in this country: how to remain competitive in an increasingly cutthroat business environment. In *Millennium Management*, I've provided the best alternative available: how to invigorate our business organizations by tapping the tremendous potential locked inside every one of us. Attempting to survive in the typical organization (as outlined in *Conduct Expected*) or looking for another job (as described in *Inside Track*) might help you personally, but it's not going to put our businesses back on top again. It's my hope that enough employees, supervisors, managers, and executives will begin to apply *Millennium Management* techniques so that we can all do less game playing and job hopping. Instead, we can use our energy to kick the stuffing out of competitors.

Introduction

Since business is so fond of talking about it, let's get right to it: the bottom line. American business as a whole is getting its teeth kicked in by foreign competition. For a variety of reasons, some of which are no fault of our own, we're being beaten to the punch in markets which used to be our private reserves. You know it, and you've seen the fear of it which is running through almost every industry in this country. Unless American business does something very different very fast, we'll have lost our chance to remain on top in this millennium; we'll have to wait until the normal cycle of business and history turns once more in our favor. If we leave it to chance or nature, it might be a long time until our turn comes again. We've still got the edge and the resources, if we do what has to be done now, to maintain a good part of what we still have. If we wait until we've suffered more defeats and additional erosion of our markets, we may not then have the resources to meet the larger threats that will follow.

The plain fact is that American business must dramatically and significantly increase productivity in all areas if it's to survive in anything close to its present size and power. Creativity, work output, profits, the development of new technology, and quality must improve in each of our threatened industries (and in some that aren't yet threatened but will be), or we're in big trouble. Yet it's equally plain that most companies have absolutely no idea about what to do next. Executives and managers flip-flop from one fad to another quick fix as they struggle to find something to improve their organizations' productivity. The truth is staring them right in the face, but it's so simple, so straightforward, that it's hard to believe, even to recognize. The unpleasant truth is the worst possible news of all: the supervisory techniques, organizational rituals and processes, and management styles of most businesses operate to smother the creativity, enthusiasm, involvement, and commitment of employees, which are absolutely vital and essential for success in the business world of the twenty-first century. That's the fundamental, bottom-line problem of American business.

The tragic fact is that the typical organization is run with almost no regard for the factors which create dynamic organizations and motivate employees to strive to do a good job. Most organizations have been inadvertently designed to actively stifle the very qualities which a productive working environment must foster.

Think about it for a moment. Most employees, yourself included, know that they have the capabilities to do at least three times as much work, to be five times more creative, and at the same time to enjoy the job more. Almost all employees want to do a good job, want to be able to take pride in the product or service their organization produces, and want to enjoy the personal satisfaction of making a meaningful contribution. Yet countless thousands of surveys across all industries, year after year, discover that the overwhelming proportion of employees only tolerate their jobs at best. More typically, they hate them, feel uninvolved and frustrated, and resent the manner in which supervisors and organizations treat them.

Consider the impact this has on every organization you've ever been part of. Every day, each of us gives up on several good ideas, often before we've completely conceptualized them, because we know there's no point in trying to battle it through the system; we know we'll hear the ubiquitous refrain, "We just don't do it that way." How often do we sit back and wonder what it would be like to work in a job where we could really cut loose? Everyone's looking for one, but how many of us have had such a job or know someone who's found one? Not many. How many times do you avoid mentioning an idea to your boss because you know—absolutely, without a doubt—that he or she will come up with at least twenty negative, self-serving criticisms or comments? How often are you criticized for some insignificant error (such as a typo on a memo you did yourself to get it out quickly) while major, long-term problems are overlooked? How much of your time and energy is wasted every day in attempts to "cover your ass" from the cheap shots of the bureaucracy's minions?

You know, regardless of your level in the organization, that all of these roadblocks and obstacles have dramatically reduced not only your day-to-day efficiency but also your endurance to keep fighting to change things for the better. The implications of your partial surrender to "the way it is" portend future doom for many American businesses and industries. Face it, because you're reading this book, you're one of the few who still care about getting the job done, who are willing to fight the obstacles one more time. For every person like yourself who still nurtures a hope that he or she can make a difference by plugging away, there are countless thousands of good workers who have given up. They no longer try one more good idea, just one more time, before they give up; they made their last stand years ago. They've been hammered down so often that they don't try anymore. Instead, they simply show up for work and do what they've got to do to get through their eight hours of boredom, debasement, childlike treatment, and game playing. And then they go home.

Millennium Management tells you everything you need to know to turn around this sorry situation and get more from your subordinates and your organization than you ever thought possible. *Millennium Management* cuts through all of the nonsense and hot air for which business books are famous. I'm going to give you the tough, hard facts about what you've got to do to get people at all levels to produce more and better and to love it an awful lot more than they do now. I'm going to show you how to get there, whether it's with a small section of hourly employees or an entire high-tech corporation.

I've tried to make *Millennium Management* a complete and comprehensive guide for managers at all levels who have a desperate need to get employees totally involved in the success of their organizations. I think you'll be convinced, after reading *Millennium Management*, that the typical organization isn't even beginning to scratch the surface of the employee productivity challenge. I hope you'll also agree that American business has no other alternative. We've got to turn to our employees and get them more involved, or we're in for much rougher times than we've yet experienced. I've tried, in the limited space of a single volume, to give you what you need to get started. I haven't left out anything essential. I hope, for all of our sakes, that enough of you get tough and do what's necessary to get things in your organizations moving. You're collectively the last hope of American business in this century. Good luck!

CHAPTER 1

The World, Markets, and Workers in the Twenty-first Century

Why are things different now from what they were thirty, twenty, or even ten years ago? How did American business get in this mess? Are we really in a mess? What's the business environment going to be like ten, twenty, or thirty years from now? Are workers going to be different? Are we going to do business differently? And, most important of all, are we going to be saved from further setbacks by a fortuitous turn of events? It's important to deal with these questions right up front. There's been a lot of just plain silly talk about what the next fifty years are going to bring. The popular wisdom is that business, markets, and workers are going to be very different, and those differences will enable the United States once again to come out a winner. But a cold, hard, objective analysis of reality doesn't support such an appraisal.

There's no help for us in the changes now sweeping the business world. As always, the business world, people, and technology will continue to evolve and develop. The changes which took place in the world in the past two-hundred years just happened to work almost magically in our favor. But the changes which are reasonable to assume over the next fifty years aren't going to provide us with similar advantages. Those who succumb to the more extreme, recently popular views of the future are likely to be lulled into a false

sense of security. In that condition, many will follow false hopes, try dangerous tactics, or talk themselves out of doing anything for another ten years.
While that sort of ignorance deserves its own reward, our economy (or your
business) can't afford to have too many people learn the hard way. Let's briefly
examine some of the factors which have been put forth as either the problem
or the solution to our current dilemma. I believe you'll see that we're going to
have to help ourselves out of this jam, and that the only clear advantage we
can seize is to adopt the techniques advocated by *Millennium Management*.

The Problem—Do We Have to Do Anything Differently?

Let's get this one out of the way first. Some contend that the American
economy is about to collapse and leave us mired in the midst of a depression-
type catastrophe. Others claim that we're simply in a transition period between
one era of success and triumph and another, different type of business domina-
tion. The best guess is somewhere in the middle. We're losing a lot of our
market share in many industries, a fair portion of our manufacturing base has
been put out of business, and we're not always first with the latest technology.
Our balance of trade oscillates between outrageously bad and merely terrible,
our unemployment rate continues to ratchet up after every downturn, and we're
faced with growing numbers of low-overhead foreign competitors who are
increasingly willing to take us on in our traditional areas of strength. While our
economy is not going to be driven out of business, we're hurting, and it's not
bound to get better on its own.

People who refuse to recognize this situation often counter by pointing out
that service-sector jobs have generally replaced lost manufacturing jobs, that
much of our trade deficit is the result of currency fluctuations, and that much
of our unemployment is because of unskilled workers who can't adapt to new
industries. There's some truth to all of these points, but they can't explain
away the problem. The simple, unpleasant truth is this: we are having to fight
it out with more and more competitors for a share of finite markets. As
emerging nations develop the market grows, but the competition grows with it.
Each competitor is taking a portion of the available market. This means, all
other things being equal, that we get less. This results in less money (or
exchange value) entering this country to keep the economy moving. The
ultimate impact, with some time lag caused by laws, tariffs, and government
policies and supports, is that we have less money to generate jobs, to pay for
capital expenditures, and to spend on foreign goods. That's the bottom line.
Competitors are nibbling away at our market share, and, unless we do something to reduce the losses, we're going to have to learn to live with less. That's
not the end of the world, but it's bad news for a country which has always
been king of the economic hill.

How Did We Get Into This Situation?

Although it doesn't help, we can take comfort in the fact that it's not our fault that we're faced with this problem. It's also important to recognize that our current situation has been caused by the operation of powerful, inexorable natural forces, not momentary market fluctuations or slight tactical mistakes by business moguls. Once you comprehend the dimensions of the forces working against us, you'll more readily understand why only comprehensive and serious measures can remedy the situation.

Lately, the United States has been the innocent victim of natural cycles of economic growth and development which have gradually turned in favor of others. This country has been blessed with an incredibly lucky two-hundred years. While most of Europe was being weakened by war after war, the United States enjoyed a period of explosive growth into almost endless horizons. The development of the pioneer spirit, the taming of the frontier, the infusion of hard-working immigrants from Europe, almost endless natural resources, the birth of a young and vigorous industrial base, and other advantages put this country in a dominant position early in the twentieth century. The world wars enabled us to come into our full glory. Europe and most of Asia were devastated, and the rest of the world was impoverished or not capable of generating a large industrial base. The entire world was our eager customer. Everyone bought whatever we produced, and we prospered. Their money paid for our science, our schools, our armed forces, our suburban lifestyle. We were on top, and the whole world knew it. But it couldn't last. You can't sell cars and TVs to people, help them develop their economies, show them how to live better, cure their diseases, teach their children technology, and then expect them to remain mere observers of the great capitalistic parade, especially when they've got cheap labor eager to earn money for a better lifestyle than they've ever had.

All at once, they're not just consumers of our products; they're fledgling competitors. Initially, we didn't notice because they sold in their own countries. And at the start they sold only junk or only to fill narrow market niches which were beneath our notice. But they learned fast (remember, we were teaching them all the time). Soon they could do almost as well as we could, but they were able to make products cheaper, and they could market more effectively to their own people. First they drove us out of their home markets (often helped by governments who recognized how high the stakes were). Flushed with success and capital and an even more eager source of cheap labor, they decided to fight it out with us in our prime markets. All of a sudden, we've lost a lot of business, and a lot of money isn't coming to the United States anymore. In fact, now the competition is so good in many industries that our own employees actually go out of their way to buy foreign-made products.

Much of this couldn't have been avoided. If we had been smarter about small cars, electronics, cameras, and so on, we could have retained some of the share we've lost in certain markets. Yet much of the loss was inevitable. You can't create markets for consumer goods without eventually increasing the customers' standards of living to the point where they'll be able to produce those goods themselves. We start by selling things such as records and blue jeans, but then we want more sales, so we sell electronics, computers, and manufacturing technology. Suddenly, the only difference between them and us is language and the cost of labor. Germany, Taiwan, and Japan learned fast, and now Korea, Brazil, and others are doing the same. We taught them how to hold the knife, and they've learned to serve themselves. The problem is that there are a lot more people at the table, and the pie isn't that much bigger. It's only natural for the person who used to get the biggest piece to end up more frequently with less. That's regression toward the mean, that's entropy, and that's why we're hurting.

The challenge to American business is to slow the progression of this entropy process as long as possible and try to ensure that our final, postadjustment share of the market is as large as possible. There's no natural law which dictates that every competitor will possess an equal final share. Natural or circumstantial advantages will lead to a market advantage. If we do something they don't do, if we do something more effectively, if we can boost productivity in a unique manner, we'll have an edge which will enable us to keep a bigger piece of the pie. We're going to lose more in every market than we've already lost, there's no question about it. The competition is still growing in numbers and skills, and we're still sitting on a lot of business simply because we've had it, not because we won it. For quite some time we're going to see almost all of our markets erode further in most industries. The question is how much. *Millennium Management* techniques are something most competitors won't have the will to implement. If enough Americans use them, we'll cut our losses as a country. If your company implements them, you'll come out ahead of your competitors, foreign or domestic. If you use them as a supervisor, you'll get more from your unit or department, your job will be easier, and you'll look like a champion.

"Technology Is a Product"

Technology gets the credit or the blame for just about everything these days. In terms of solving our business problems, however, technology sounds a hollow note. The argument runs, "We don't have to compete along all those different fronts. Instead of making products and fighting for markets, we'll simply be the technological leaders." Forget technology as a way out of this problem. In the past, we were the technology leaders across the entire spectrum of science and industry most of the time. We did set the pace. We don't anymore. Too many other countries have the ability to develop leading-edge technologies in specific markets which suit their purposes. Where it's been in their interests to develop cost-effective, salable technology, we're already finishing second much of the time.

We still provide most of the frontier technology in areas such as computers, medicine, and space travel. The problem is that these areas generally don't translate rapidly into economic advantages (and we're losing our lead in some of these areas as well). In fact, given the manner in which we disseminate technological information and train the competition's scientists, our development of frontier technology is a money loser. In effect, we're using technology as a loss leader, but we don't have any other items for sale in volume to make up the difference. The argument could be made that such research, if we were more efficient in getting the products out the door first, would keep us on top. That's nonsense. Most complex technologies are widely available and are based on many existent subsidiary technologies. It's almost impossible for any one competitor to maintain an advantage long enough to make a lot of money from the technology itself. Once the technology is widely available, the edge goes to the competitor who can most cost-effectively design, develop, market, and service the derivative products. The success of these endeavors is determined by people, organizational factors, and economic variables, not technology.

"Technology Is a Productivity Aid"

Technology, most typically imagined in the form of a computer, is often held up as the magic sword of productivity which will slay the dragon of competition. Computers aren't going to slay anything. In many applications, of course, they're vital and critical tools which save time and money. But computers and other forms of technology have two serious drawbacks as productivity boosters. The first is that they're widely available to anyone who wants them. If your competitors want to put a desktop computer in front of every employee, they will. If you use computers and your competition uses computers, the only person who'll gain an advantage will be the computer manufacturer.

The second problem with technology is that it's just a tool. In most applications technology doesn't define the work itself as it does in genetic engineering, space travel, and artificial intelligence, areas which would be impossible without it. Most often, technology and computers merely present a more efficient (sometimes phenomenally more efficient) way of doing work that depends more on people decisions and actions than on the technology itself. Technology and computers can only work as well as they're told to. If you put a 15K desktop computer system in front of a bored, uninvolved employee who doesn't have any enthusiasm, gets no support from the boss, and believes that it's only a device to get him or her to do more work, what are you going to get? The absolute minimum. If the employee isn't ready and willing to use the computer, he or she is only going to go through the motions, even with extensive training. Contrast that with what happens when you give a computer to an enthusiastic, hard-working, creative employee. This employee dives in with both feet, finds the training he or she needs or gets by without it, and all of a sudden is coming out with new ways of doing things which nobody ever thought about. But that's not the computer; that's just what you get when you provide an involved, enthusiastic employee with good tools. A good employee would be trying to do the same thing without the tools. People, not technology, make the difference.

There's another problem with technology as a productivity aid, particularly in regard to desktop computers, that's gotten so bad it deserves special mention. Each organization only has so much energy to devote to "big deals" or "hot programs." Too much of many organizations' "productivity improvement" energy and enthusiasm is being wasted in frenzied quests to install sophisticated computers on every desk. In a money-is-no-object mode, many employers are installing electronic mail, local area networks (LANs), downloading to mainframes, and other incredibly complex and expensive capabilities on every desk. Vast computer departments spring up to assess each user's needs, establish standards, support software, and update equipment. I've seen companies buy IBM XTs for everyone and then, one year later, sell them all and bring in IBM ATs, for no reason other than to remain state-of-the-art. Between buys, most of the computers sit idle; uninvolved employees aren't going to use something that requires effort if they don't have to. Many executives have been sold a bill of goods about what they're going to get from desktop computers as a productivity enhancer. All too often, what you get are legions of extra computer people on the payroll and hordes of computer freaks spending all day generating graphs that nobody ever needed before, designing spreadsheets nobody ever had to have, and comparing notes about one software program's virtues compared to another. Meanwhile, nobody worries about who's doing the work, developing the next generation of managers, coaching the employees, or providing sections and departments with clear, one-to-one, and small-group leadership.

Don't get me wrong. I love computers. I'm writing this book on one, I use one 40 percent of the time at the office, and I wouldn't want to operate at home or work without one. But when I wanted one at work, I planned and plotted to convince the organization that I could effectively utilize one. I got it because I wanted it. If that organization had dropped one on everyone's desk (which they may end up doing anyway), many of them would sit idle and not yield any increase in productivity. The organization would have spent a lot of money and energy (and have hired legions of computer support people) in the hopes that productivity would increase. That would be a wasted hope unless the employees were involved and enthusiastic.

If you have an employee who wants a computer, get him or her one; anyone with the energy and interest to ask for one will probably put it to all sorts of good uses which don't come to mind at first. But to install them everywhere, in the hopes that computer magic will increase productivity, is a waste of time and energy. Forget all but the essential, process-the-work computers as means of increasing productivity, and pay more attention to getting your people truly involved with their work. That's where you'll get productivity. That's what *Millennium Management* is all about.

"New Products Will Make Up for Lost Markets"

This is a variant of the "technology as a product" argument. It's popularly held that we don't have to worry about the erosion of our markets in traditional areas (e.g., steel, consumer electronics) because we'll always have new products and services to take their place. The prime examples most often held up as proof of this hypothesis are videotape rental stores, mobile phone franchises, computer stores, and the fast-food industry. Without a doubt, each of these provides new jobs and helps keep the money in the economy circulating. However, these types of products aren't going to save us from further losses at the hands of competitors. In terms of foreign competitors, it doesn't matter what we do with our money once it's here. The problem is that too much of our money is going overseas while too little is coming in. Every time a foreign competitor grabs an increased share of one of our markets, it doesn't solve our fundamental problem if a displaced American employee can go out and get a job in a tanning center or at a pizza shop. Differences in pay rates and job security aside, those types of jobs merely circulate the money we already have. We need to increase the relative amounts of money we take in from foreign competitors compared to what goes out. This would increase the amount of money circulating in our economy. Replacing jobs lost to foreign competition with service industry jobs is like giving a transfusion by taking the blood out of a patient's left arm and putting it back into the right.

Of course, the main problem with viewing new products as a differential advantage is that as soon as the new product becomes attractive as a market, everybody will jump in, and we'll be fighting the same battle. A revolutionary new product doesn't make most of its sales in its first year or two. The biggest sales are made when the price comes down, the market shakes out, and the consumers are reassured that the product works and will be around. That's when cameras, VCRs, TVs, and personal computers made their biggest sales. That's usually when foreign competition enters the battle, if they hadn't generated the technology themselves. And that's when they take their typically large share of the market away from us. If we can't beat them in old markets, there's no reason to believe we can do it in new ones.

There's an even more basic flaw to the "continuous new products" view. If you go into any store, of any kind, what types of products or services constitute 90 to 99 percent of the offerings? Not new products, that's for sure. Most of the business in any industry comes from tried-and-true, established, old-technology products or services. There are only so many new products possible in a given time period, and most of them are typically minor twists on old themes. Every industry makes most of its money by selling established products and/or offering the same old service. That's the way it's always been, and that's the way it always will be. There can never be enough new product opportunities to replace monetary loss in established markets. Contentions to the contrary are merely emotional attempts to deal with the fear and frustration caused by the loss of market share in established product lines. Hoping for new market sales to make up for lost ones is foolish for an even more fundamental reason. It takes innovative market research, responsive management, hard-working employees, good basic research, and a willingness to take risks to generate new products which succeed (and even then most will fail anyway). If we had employees at all levels who already had these qualities, we wouldn't have already lost as much as we have. If we want employees with those qualities, we'll have to manage our way to them.

"Automation Will Require Fewer Workers, and We'll Be More Competitive on Price"

There's no help here. Our competitors know as much about automation as we do. They can match us stride for stride in areas in which automation produces better quality or lower costs. In fact, they'll often make out better than we will with the same automation because their lower labor rates bring down their maintenance and repair costs for the equipment. And, after all is said and done, it's the people who decide what and how to automate, where to procure and how to design the equipment, when to do preventive maintenance, and how to schedule production most cost-effectively with the automated processes. If the people you've got aren't going at full throttle, they're not going to be designing, installing, operating, and maintaining your equipment most effectively. Automation isn't a solution; it's merely a tool. Your people are the solution.

"The Evolving Workplace Will Make 'People Management' Unnecessary"

It's recently been profitable for some authors to contend that the "work-place of the future" will, for untold millions of employees, be their own homes. It won't be necessary to have offices, cafeterias, parking lots, and so on. The logical extension of this argument is that we also won't have the productivity problems we now have. Just think, all of the listless, bored, resentful employees we now have are going to work productively and more creatively at home, with nobody to supervise them. Simply working at home is going to turn them into dynamos of creativity and hard work. Come on, let's get serious!

Even forgetting about issues of where they're going to learn proper work habits, how they'll be trained in technical skills, the impact of falling literacy rates on worker availability, and the distractions of the typical home environ-ment, this is the worst idea to come along since tobacco-flavored ice cream. There's no doubt that telecommunications and computers will enable many thousands of additional workers to work at home in the future. But for the vast majority of workers, employment at home will forever be a fantasy.

The work-at-home scenario most often consists of a worker sitting at a computer, processing information via modem or hard line. Most people don't currently work solely with data manipulation via computer as their primary occupation, and they won't do so in the future. If we all worked at home, who would build our cars, truck, planes, TVs, Walkmans, VCRs, appliances, and clothing? Who would research and manufacture our medicines? Who would grow our food and process it? (Even in farming, more and more food is being grown by corporate farm employees who commute.) Who would work in the stores, the police departments, and the courts? Who would repair and build our highways and maintain the infrastructure of our cities? Who would teach our children? Who would work in our theaters and restaurants? Who would play our professional sports and sell us popcorn and hot dogs at the stadium? Who would film our TV shows, repair the TVs, fix our cars? I could go on, but you get the point: for most people, work has always meant going to work some-where else. Most jobs require people to do something with other people or products in person. Many more jobs require large groups of people to work together for reasons of economies of scales. (It's cheaper for 3,000 people to work in one plant building cars than it is to operate 6 plants, each with 500 workers, to build the same cars.)

For at least another few hundred years, and probably forever, most people are still going to have to go to work outside the home. In fact, as you'll find in chapters 2 and 3, the fact that people work as part of a group is more than a chance occurrence; it's something we need and seek. Hating their jobs as they do, many people at all levels derive much more than a paycheck from going to work. They need and enjoy the rewards of social contact. People aren't going to go along enthusiastically with schemes that take away their main source of social contact. Face it, if you can't get your productivity problems straightened out in today's workplace, it's not going to get any easier. In fact, as the next section demonstrates, the odds of getting increased productivity from the employees of the future without doing anything extraordinary are getting worse every year.

"Workers of the Future Will Work Harder and Better"

This is another "no need to worry, chance will bail us out" pipe dream. It's a "people technology" view: since we'll have so many advanced technologies, people will be more advanced, will work harder, and will be more suited to live and work in a technological society. But evolution doesn't work that fast, and the societal forces that shape behaviors and attitudes aren't pushing us in the right direction. The most important determinants of how much and how hard an employee will work are the societal influences which shaped his or her young life. The most important of these societal factors is parental upbringing. If parents (and surrogate parents such as teachers) instill a respect for hard work, an expectation that rewards must be earned, a love of achievement, and a sense of self-worth, you're two-thirds of the way there. The second major factor is the work environment itself. If the job setting provides the things that employees perceive they need to work well, chances are they'll perform exceptionally.

Given the above, how could anyone think that the next twenty to thirty years are going to produce better workers? The evidence argues strongly for the reverse. Consider just a few of the factors shaping the next generation or two of employees.

The functional literacy rate in this country is falling. We've got a large and growing segment of the population that is chronically unemployable and on welfare. Our educational systems turn out proportionately fewer scientists, mathematicians, and engineers than any other "advanced" country, and many of our high school graduates (and not a few of our college graduates) can barely read and write. Are these going to be more productive and harder-working employees than the ones we've got now?

The bigger but more subtle danger is the view of life which society is teaching our children. They're presented with a false and one-dimensional view of life depicted in movies, videos, TV, and larger-than-life hero role models. From these fictional role and value models, our children form their expectations about what life should bring. Their expectations are unrealistic and extreme. For many, the emphasis is now on relaxation, doing their own thing, getting somewhere fast, making it big without too much trouble, and so on. When these workers with high expectations end up in the same boring, stifling, restrictive jobs that today's workers have, how can they be expected to work harder and be more productive?

Earlier generations were raised to put up with all of the nonsense at work and come back for another dose: "Put in your time and keep your mouth shut." I don't believe the next generation or two is being raised to perceive that sort of situation any more favorably than we do. (The next chapter will show how today's employees view the workplace.) They're bound to find the conflict between their expectations and reality much more of a shock. That resentment and disenchantment, coupled with their generally less than Spartan work ethics, poorer education, and so on, doesn't bode well for improved "people technology" in the future.

These societal influences make it even more essential that you adopt *Millennium Management* techniques as soon as possible. You can't do much as a manager or employer about general societal influences, so you'd better do everything you can to ensure that the work environment you provide entices employees to be as productive as possible. In the past the situation wasn't as urgent; workers had been conditioned to put up with more grief. You could afford to let the work environment develop haphazardly. You can't afford that any longer. Now you're going to have to make sure that you do everything possible to get the most out of the employees you'll have to use. If you apply *Millennium Management* techniques, the good employees will flood you with even more creative output and ideas. Better yet, the employees with less apparent potential will generally rise to the occasion and produce surprisingly well.

"The Rapid Pace of Change Makes Any Strategy Risky"

This view is a schizophrenic blend of several of the above reactions: "Things will soon be so different that we can't plan for it. Let's just wait and see." Its proponents argue that since all of the factors discussed above are changing so rapidly, there's not much point in doing anything until the dust settles. There's no doubt that things change continuously in most areas. Yet, while change is sometimes rapid, changes aren't perceived as such unexpected events by those who are wrestling with the anticipated effects. To those who didn't expect change and didn't work on plans to deal with it, perceptions are colored by emotional reactions. Their perceptions of change are charged with surprise, perhaps pleasure, perhaps anger, perhaps sadness.

Consider space flight. It only took sixty-six years from the first short flight in a canvas-covered plane to the walk on the moon. It's pretty amazing when you think of it, but when you actually do a year-by-year analysis, there were no profound, totally unexpected changes for those who were working on airplanes, rockets, and space travel. To those closest to the work, the advances seemed logical, planned, and the result of extremely hard work. Most problems were anticipated, a few weren't, but they were all handled with a consistent, orderly approach. To outsiders, every change seemed surprising, perhaps shocking, and sometimes revolutionary. Any problems appeared bigger and more fearsome than they did to people on the inside. It's always the same when you view changes from afar or from a position of limited information; they seem dramatic and sudden and create all sorts of emotional reactions. Up close, they seem evolutionary and gradual.

The same range of perceptions applies to the business world. We're moving from highly competitive, heterogeneous national economies to a more homogeneous world economy. If you were to view nothing but historical snapshots taken every ten years over the last forty years, the changes would look pretty extreme. On a year-to-year basis, to those who care to look closely, it's clear to see how this company grabbed one market, how that company fell by the wayside, how yet another made dramatic improvements in motivating its employees.

The difficulty is that American business as a whole is still on the outside of the business problems we currently face. Instead of viewing the productivity problem as a challenge to get employees totally involved, many employers are attempting to solve their problem by turning to the types of arguments we've debunked thus far, or sticking with the old ways which won't do the job in the new business environment. They're having an emotional response to the unexpected, and the first thing they do is try to rationalize it away as "the same old game." They've got to realize that the evolution of business isn't a danger; it's an opportunity to gain an advantage in a new situation. But new situations demand new approaches. If we hide our heads in the sand, waiting for things to settle down so we can mark our targets, we'll find, by the time we take our shot, that the targets have moved. Most aspects of business will be forever changing and will be difficult to predict. The things that make people work better and harder won't ever change.

If you begin to implement *Millennium Management* techniques now, you'll develop the type of workforce that will quickly adjust to whatever the future brings. They'll be able to handle any threat, and they'll enthusiastically tackle any problem. The targets may move and the problems may change, but your employees will be willing and able to move faster. That's the only way you'll survive and succeed in the future.

Why *Millennium Management*?

We simply have no other choice. We're facing competition which is growing in numbers, strength, and ability. We're getting beaten to the draw in many of the established markets which provide the basis of our economy. Technology won't save us, because everyone has it, and, all too often, we're not the ones who have it first. We can't expect new markets to take up the slack, because the competition is able to move just as fast as we can. The world of business isn't changing in ways which will benefit us more than our competition. In fact, the changes look to be more damaging to us than anyone else. Workers of the future aren't going to be any better, and perhaps they'll be less potentially productive than the ones we've got now.

It's a critical, tough situation. That's why it's imperative that you begin to employ *Millennium Management* techniques as soon as possible. It's your only option. *Millennium Management* supervisory and management techniques will enable you (and your organization, if enough people practice them) to focus on the single most important aspect of productivity: the commitment and dedication of employees. If they are sincerely involved in the work, they'll rise to the occasion and wreck havoc on your competition. They'll do it because you'll be giving them what they want from work. It's something few employees get from any job. If they get it, they'll work themselves to death for you and love it.

CHAPTER 2

The Factors That Make Employees Love Their Jobs and Work Productively

Employees aren't getting what they want at work, and they're getting more upset about it. That's not a good foundation on which to build increased productivity. If you doubt this, consider the results of only one of the many surveys of employees that prove the point. The Opinion Research Corporation of Princeton, New Jersey, surveyed 250,000 employees in hundreds of companies in 1984. Employees at every level were sampled, from hourly workers to corporate officers.The findings indicated that employees at all levels have a low and declining view of top management, they perceive that the quality of supervision at all levels is declining (especially as viewed by the lowest-paid workers), and they are critical of the quality of their organizations' communications processes. In addition, performance appraisal systems are seen as unfair, and there's a widespread perception that employees who try to perform effectively won't be recognized and rewarded. Further findings demonstrated that first-level supervisors feel that their status and authority are being compromised by the organization and their supervisors. This study is only one (but one of the largest) of hundreds of such studies in every industry which continually and without exception demonstrate that employees aren't supervised effectively, that they know it, and that they resent it. And keep in mind that *employees* doesn't simply refer to the people who report to you ("them"); it includes employees at every level, including yourself.

Just What Do Employees Want?

Just what are employees dissatisfied with? What do they want? Before we discuss specifics, why not test yourself to see how much you already know about what employees want from their jobs? Figure 2.1 presents a list of fifteen factors which influence employees' perceptions about their work. Examine the list, and then, before you read any further, rank each factor in the order in which you think your employees would rate them in importance. If you don't have any subordinates, rank the factors as you believe the employees at the level beneath yours in the organization would rank them. Give a 1 to the item you believe they would rank as most important, a 2 to the item they would rank as second most important, and so on, until you give a 15 to the factor you think your employees (or those beneath you) would rate as least important.

Employees rank these factors a lot differently from supervisors. This same list of factors was ranked by thousands of employees in all sorts of jobs and industries. All of the employees were blue-collar or hourly workers. Each was asked, "Rank the items in terms of their importance to you in your present job." In each company, the employees' supervisors were asked to complete the survey by ranking the factors "as you believe your employees would rank them." Figure 2.2 shows the overall average results of the employees' rankings

		Ranking
a.	Knowledge of what is expected	_____
b.	Help with personal problems	_____
c.	Fair and tactful discipline	_____
d.	Fringe benefits	_____
e.	Personal recognition	_____
f.	Interesting work	_____
g.	Proper direction and training	_____
h.	Good working conditions	_____
i.	Feeling involved	_____
j.	Good leadership by supervisors	_____
k.	Good pay	_____
l.	Feeling of accomplishment	_____
m.	Job security	_____
n.	Company loyalty to workers	_____
o.	Promotional opportunities	_____

Figure 2.1 Fifteen Factors Which Influence Employee Productivity and Job Satisfaction

and the supervisors' estimates of the employees' rankings. The factors have been rearranged to show the employees' rankings in descending order, starting with the factor they rated most important. There's also a column for you to enter your rankings from Figure 2.1.

The results shown in Figure 2.2 have far-reaching implications for every aspect of current supervisory practice and management philosophy. To be blunt, the findings demonstrate that organizations and supervisors don't even know what's important to employees, much less how to give it to them. Is it any wonder that employees are fed up with their jobs? Of the top five factors employees consider most important, not one of them made the supervisors' top five rankings. While employees are most concerned with feelings of accomplishment, personal recognition, leadership, direction and training, knowing what's expected, and fair and tactful discipline, supervisors are focusing on a completely different set of factors. Supervisors incorrectly believe that good pay, opportunities for promotions, job security, and good working conditions are most important to employees. None of the supervisors' five top-ranked factors did better than ninth on the employees' rankings. This indicates that the major thrust of supervisory policies and practices in American business organizations is totally off target. Let's face it; if supervisors can't even roughly approximate the rank order given by the employees, what are the chances that they're actually doing anything to satisfy any of the employees' top five concerns?

		Supervisors'	Rankings Yours	Employees'
l.	Feeling of accomplishment	8	_____	1
e.	Personal recognition	13	_____	2
j.	Good leadership by supervisors	12	_____	3
g.	Proper direction and training	11	_____	4
a.	Knowledge of what is expected	14	_____	5
c.	Fair and tactful discipline	7	_____	6
i.	Feeling involved	10	_____	7
f.	Interesting work	5	_____	8
k.	Good pay	1	_____	9
o.	Promotional opportunities	3	_____	10
h.	Good working conditions	4	_____	11
m.	Job security	2	_____	12
n.	Company loyalty to workers	6	_____	13
d.	Fringe benefits	15	_____	14
b.	Help with personal problems	9	_____	15

Figure 2.2 Employee Rankings and Supervisors' Predictions of Employees' Rankings, of Job Satisfaction and Productivity Factors

These results have been replicated time and time again in all sorts of working environments and with all levels of employees in all types of industries. There's absolutely no doubt that they represent the norm for American business. While the rankings in Figure 2.2 were obtained from blue-collar workers and their supervisors, white-collar workers and middle managers rank these items in exactly the same manner. For several reasons, white-collar and professional types feel even more resentment, frustration, and apathy when they're not given what they want from a job. They're better educated, they have higher expectations, they have a more complete view of the organization's problems, and they work more closely with management. (They're even less inclined to view higher-level managers as especially gifted, "better" people.) Consequently, when they're deprived of fulfillment of the top-ranked factors, they're even more resentful.

Don't try to rationalize that organizations treat different levels of employees differently, that some employees aren't given more of what they want because they couldn't handle it. ("We bear down on the hourly types because we have to, but we treat our managers, technical people, and professionals differently.") The survey results belie this argument. Everyone wants the same things, at all levels, and very few think they're getting them from supervisors and/or their organizations. If you're trying to convince yourself that you or your company is different, you're either a very rare exception or you're avoiding the truth. (How did you do on the survey?) For most supervisors, it's the latter.

It's important to face the cold, hard, bitter truth presented above. You might think that the results of one study which ranks fifteen factors might not be representative of other ways of viewing work satisfaction and employees' needs. But every single theory of work satisfaction and motivation has generated research which predicts and exactly mirrors these results.

Let's take a brief look at three of the more widely accepted approaches to work satisfaction and/or productivity. You'll see that each of them predicts that the top seven items ranked by employees in Figure 2.2 will be most important to employees. When research is done to investigate these theories, it always points in the same direction, backing up the data shown in Figure 2.2. I'm not trying to sell you a theory; I'm trying to show you that the fundamental truth of what employees want is very simple and universal. The names and labels of the factors might change, but the basics are the same.

Maslow's Hierarchy of Needs

Abraham Maslow proposed a hierarchy of five successive levels of human needs. The five levels, from most basic to most difficult to attain, are (in terms of the work environment):

1. *Basic needs*. Pleasant surroundings, no undue work strains, decent pay, good heating and air conditioning, and so on.
2. *Safety needs*. Job security, retirement plans or pensions, fringe benefits, seniority protection.
3. *Belonging needs*. Meaningful interpersonal relationships, team play, feeling part of the organization.
4. *Ego-status needs*. Promotions as recognition, special status, recognition for achievements, being assigned additional responsibilities for taking care of the group.
5. *Self-actualization needs*. Personal growth in the job, creativity, attempting to be the best without concern for recognition of achievement, interest in the work itself.

Maslow contends that an individual can strive for the next level only if most of his or her needs are being met at lower levels. Thus, an employee would not be inclined to worry about or pursue ego-status needs if belonging and/or safety needs were not being met. Also, if needs at a lower level suddenly are not met, the individual will abandon most higher-level need pursuit activities and attempt to fulfill the lower-level needs. If you review the top eight employee-ranked items in Figure 2.2, you'll see that they all represent the belonging, ego-status, and self-actualization levels. These are the higher-order needs that most employees pursue, assuming that their basic needs at lower levels are being met. Since most American companies do a pretty good job of meeting the lower-level needs, employees are most often striving for the higher-order needs. Now look at the factors in Figure 2.2 which supervisors ranked as being employees' top five concerns. Most of them are lower-order needs. Survey studies in hundreds of companies have consistently demonstrated that employees at all levels have much higher unfulfilled needs at the ego-status and belonging levels than at the lower levels.

The implications of this theory are directly relevant to motivating employees toward increased productivity. It should be clear that it's in the best interests of any organization to encourage its employees to work better in teams, to pursue recognition for positive achievements, to attempt to gain more status as a result of contributions, and to be concerned that other employees will speak highly of their contributions. These are the types of efforts that management is always saying it wants. Yet supervisors at all levels are working under the assumption that employees want security and safety needs such as more benefits, more job security, more money, and less risk. These are all factors that cost a great deal but do nothing to satisfy the higher-order needs that will lead to the team play and achievement that increase productivity.

Herzberg's Two-Factor Theory

Frederick Herzberg hypothesized that certain aspects of the work environment act as *satisfiers* and other aspects act as *dissatisfiers*. He contended that these satisfiers and dissatisfiers operate as two separate factors, a satisfaction/no satisfaction factor and a dissatisfaction/no dissatisfaction factor. In order to be satisfied, an employee would have to be *not dissatisfied* on the dissatisfaction/no dissatisfaction factor and *satisfied* on the satisfaction/no satisfaction factor. Figure 2.3 presents a graphic representation of the two-factor theory.

If enough dissatisfiers were removed from the job environment, the employee would no longer be dissatisfied. However, the employee wouldn't be satisfied unless enough satisfiers were also present. The dissatisfiers are such things as poor benefits, bad working conditions, little job security, poor pay, and so forth. If enough of these dissatisfiers are perceived by employees to have been removed, the employee won't be dissatisfied with the job.

However, that doesn't necessarily mean that the employee will be satisfied with the job. In order to be satisfied as well as not dissatisfied, a sufficient number of satisfiers have to be present. Satisfiers are feelings of accomplishment, personal recognition, and so on; the first eight items the employees ranked in Figure 2.2. And these satisfiers are essentially the same as the needs represented by Maslow's belonging, ego-status, and self-actualization hierarchy levels. Both theories predict the same results.

Most companies in this country provide a work environment which has few dissatisfiers. In fact, American industry is forever pursuing new and novel ways to eliminate dissatisfiers. The addition of aerobics classes at work, new furniture, improved pension plans, matching savings plans, remodeled cafeterias, and so on, are all attempts to obtain more productivity through removal of more and more dissatisfiers. The difficulty with this approach is twofold.

First of all, only a very small percentage of employees in typical organizations perceive that there are too many dissatisfiers. This low percentage of

	Absent	Present
Satisfiers	No job satisfaction	Job satisfaction
Dissatisfiers	No job dissatisfaction	Job dissatisfaction

Figure 2.3   Herzberg's Two-Factor Theory of Job Satisfaction

whiners will forever gripe about dissatisfiers, no matter what you do. But most employees are more concerned with obtaining more satisfiers. That's why employees always rate satisfiers as their primary concerns. Removing more dissatisfiers doesn't help at all. In fact, the continual attention placed on removing more dissatisfiers actually causes bigger problems. That's the second problem with this approach.

The difficulty is that if satisfiers are in short supply and the organization concentrates on removing dissatisfiers, the employees will begin to focus extensively on dissatisfiers. They'll be frustrated, and they'll know they can get action on dissatisfiers, so they go for short-term relief. We end up with millions of workers who want to be more productive, want to be more satisfied, but continually push for things that won't give them what they really want. And management, not realizing what's going on, plays into their hands by concentrating on removing dissatisfiers, thinking that the employees will be grateful and will produce more. Both management and the employees get more frustrated and angry because nothing's getting any better despite all the effort.

This view is sometimes hard to accept until you think of how you feel about your own situation in regard to dissatisfiers, which are also called hygiene factors. Consider compensation. To a certain extent, compensation is a dissatisfaction factor (although it serves other purposes as well) which illustrates the role of dissatisfiers in job satisfaction. Think about the last raise you received. Before you got it, you were probably excited, feeling that the additional money would dramatically influence your motivation to work and would make you feel better about every aspect of your job. If the increase was bigger than you expected or a surprise, you were probably euphoric for a short time. A month after you received the raise, chances are you felt exactly as you did before you got it.You quickly adjusted to the new level of compensation, and all of the same old aggravations were just as irritating, perhaps even more aggravating because you had expected things to change. The money didn't effect a substantial and long-lasting change in your attitude and performance because, to the extent that more money is a dissatisfier, more of it (within reason, of course) can't do much to satisfy more important needs such as being involved, recognized, and so on. Of course, some salary increases, particularly those which accompany promotions, can motivate significant changes in perceptions because they signal more than just money; these types of advancements signal reward for achievement, respect for accomplishment, entry into a more highly respected group (the next level of the organization).

Behavior Modification Theory

There are many other theories of job satisfaction and productivity. Every single one of them yields the same conclusions we've already seen. Behavior modification theory demonstrates that even the most severely behavioral approach to productivity yields the same conclusions. It's often thought by many supervisors that behavior modification offers an easy out to the problem of productivity because its language doesn't concern itself with employee perceptions. Behavior modification is often thought to be a hard, objective, "people technology" approach which can be mechanistically applied to get more productivity without having to worry about employees' job-satisfaction factors.

Behavior modification is concerned only with operationally defined behaviors. These are behaviors that are observable, that can be seen and agreed upon by objective observers. Thus, behavior modification doesn't focus on employees' feelings, internal motivations, and perceptions; the only concern is their behavior and how to make them do more of what you want and less of what you don't want.

The fundamental operating principles of behavior modification are *reinforcement* **and** *punishment*. Figure 2.4 displays a conceptual view of these two terms. A reinforcer is defined as an event ("Event X" in Figure 2.4) whose occurrence increases the probability that the behavior ("Behavior A") which preceded it will occur again in the future ("If more Behavior A"). Conversely, punishment is defined as an event ("Event X") whose occurrence decreases the future probability of the behavior ("If less Behavior A") which it follows. An example will demonstrate how these principles work. Let's suppose you're trying to teach your dog to sit when you give the command "Sit." You give the dog a treat each time it sits when you give the command. In terms of Figure 2.4, sitting is Behavior A and the treat is Event X. If the dog is typical, it will soon learn to sit more often, and therefore, by definition, the treat is a reinforcer. On the other hand, if you were trying to stop your dog from chasing the cat, you might swat the dog with a rolled-up newspaper every time you caught it chasing the cat. If the newspaper swats decreased the amount of cat-chasing behavior, the newspaper swats would be, by definition, punishments. This is the main thrust of reinforcement theory.

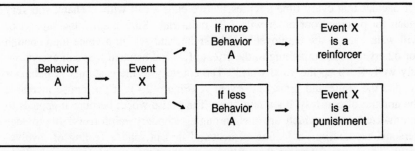

Figure 2.4 Reinforcement and Punishment in Behavior Modification

In behavior modification research with animals, most reinforcers are primary reinforcers such as food, water, sex, removal of extreme cold or heat, and so on. Most punishments involve pain of some sort, most typically a mild electric shock. As you can imagine, it's relatively easy to set up a behavior modification experiment involving animals because it's a straightforward matter to arrange effective reinforcers and punishments.

The situation with humans in the workplace is not quite so simple. First of all, most American employees are pretty well satisfied in terms of primary reinforcers. You can't very well offer chocolate bars or water to employees and expect them to work more productively. Sex as a reward might spur some short-term gains in productivity, but, of course, there are legal and ethical problems in addition to the satiation factor. ("Honestly, Fred, I'm bushed. I don't know if I can handle another reward for productivity today"). You can't offer a slight increase in an employee's pension fund or another fifty cents in the paycheck because most employees don't perceive that they're so deficient in these areas that small increases would make any difference.

Secondary reinforcers are the answer. These include a wide range of things that acquire reinforcing value because they were once paired with primary reinforcers and/or were internalized by the subject.

For example, when you train a dog with food treats, you use expressions such as "Good dog!" at the same time that you give the food treat. (Actually, since dogs are highly socialized to people, you don't need the food in the first place.) After a while, the verbal praise alone becomes a secondary reinforcer which works by itself because the dog associates the praise with you and all of the attention and food. Human beings have a wide range of internalized beliefs and expectations which serve as secondary reinforcers. For example, most of us feel good when we help someone. Our good feelings are internalized secondary reinforcers which we learned as children.

Let's look at an example of a behavior modification effort in a work environment and see how these secondary reinforcers operate. Suppose a supervisor decides to use behavior modification to increase the courtesy which customer service representatives are showing to phone customers. The supervisor decides that every time a representative ends a call with, "Thank you very much for placing your order with J.B. Industries, Sir/Ma'am," the supervisor will walk over to the employee's desk, smile, and say, in a voice loud enough for others to hear, something to the effect of, "You handled that call exceptionally well. Keep up the good work!" The courtesy to the customer is Behavior A, and the smile and praise are Event X (Figure 2.4). If the praise increases the amount of courtesy, it's a reinforcer. The praise works because it appeals to internalized needs which are met through secondary reinforcers. It provides personal recognition, a feeling of accomplishment, and a feeling of involvement. These are the same things that were the satisfiers of Herzberg's Two-Factor Theory, as well as the belonging, ego-status, and self-actualization levels of Maslow's Hierarchy of Needs. They're also the same types of factors which employees always rank as most important. Even behavior modification takes you right back to the top-ranked employee factors of Figure 2.2.

The Bottom Line

No matter where you start your search for the answer, no matter where you turn, no matter what theory you start with, you end up facing the same simple, stark truth. If you want more productive and satisfied employees, you must give them:

- Feeling of accomplishment
- Personal recognition
- Good leadership by supervisors
- Proper direction and training
- Knowledge of what is expected
- Fair and tactful discipline
- Feeling involved

These items are the bottom line for improving productivity. If you provide them to your employees in any reasonable amount, you'll be doing more than 99 percent of all other organizations. And you'll get 99 percent more than other organizations get from their employees. The rest of this book will focus on how you can best provide these factors—these satisfiers—to your employees.

At the same time, the lower-ranked factors (good pay, promotional opportunities, good working conditions, job security, company loyalty to workers, fringe benefits, and help with personal problems) cannot be ignored. We'll devote considerable attention to them, but not because there's a need to offer more of them. As we've discussed, most American companies do enough in these areas already. In fact, in some cases efforts have gone so far as to be harmful. Concentration on these dissatisfiers not only orients employees to incorrectly seek satisfaction by demanding more of them but, even worse, sends damaging signals throughout the entire structure of business. In later chapters, we'll focus on these damaging signals and how you can begin to communicate a more positive message to all of your employees.

Now that there's no doubt about exactly what employees want, let's briefly examine each factor and discuss what they are and why they're so important to employees. Although they are presented separately here, they're actually interdependent and mutually supportive. As the discussion proceeds, I'll point out the important ways in which some of the factors influence others. Keep in mind that *employee* means everyone, from the eighteen-year-old assembly-line rookie to the sixty-five-year-old senior executive. They all have the same types of needs, although their specific requirements will vary according to career status and level of responsibility.

Feeling of Accomplishment

We all like to think that we're competent and resourceful. In our day-dreams we see ourselves as masters of our trade, with the ability to do just about anything. At work, we have a need to demonstrate our abilities and prove to ourselves and to others that we can do the job. We're constantly attempting to control things, demonstrate our value, and exert influence. After years of learning from parents and society that it's good and desirable to be in charge, make decisions, and get things done, we are primed to want to be successful and competent. On top of that, most employees, through personal preferences, prior jobs, and/or education, think of themselves as practitioners of a specific set of skills and experiences which they do well and in which they take pride. We've all been taught to want to attain feelings of accomplishment.

Employees develop these feelings at work by making decisions, analyzing situations and taking appropriate action, and demonstrating their ability to practice their expertise. When they do these things at the level appropriate to their skills and experience, they feel valuable, powerful, and confident. Employees can't convince themselves that they're resourceful and masterful if they're constantly instructed in every little detail or given very little freedom to decide how to perform those aspects of their jobs which they know best. If they're given direction and guidance and then permitted as much autonomy to make decisions as they can handle, most employees will revel in their achievements and come back for more.

Appropriate (meaning more than most employees receive) autonomy to make decisions also causes employees to take more responsibility for every aspect of the work because they have their self-esteem and pride riding on the decision. And because they're taking some of the responsibility, they'll be more careful to ensure that nothing goes wrong. Contrast this with what happens in the more typical situation in which supervisors call all the shots, tell employees just to do their jobs, and micromanage every detail. Since the ideas aren't at least partially their own, employees are not concerned with seeing that things work out. They just want to get enough done to stay out of trouble.

For example, many assembly-line supervisors believe that assembly-line workers can't think for themselves. As a result, supervisors hardly ever attempt to give the workers autonomy or avenues for gaining a sense of accomplishment. After all, they reason, how much leeway for independent decision making is there on an assembly line? Not as much as in the front office, perhaps, but the employees don't expect that much. A little bit would go a long way. The supervisor might suggest that the employees get together and discuss how they'd like to schedule breaks and vacations. The supervisor might ask the employees to come up with a way to handle problems created by absenteeism, or how to solve a nagging quality problem. Once it's partly their problem, the employees have a stake in solving it.

Personal Recognition

The need to be recognized as unique and valuable individuals is universal. Every employee wants to feel that he or she has an impact and is appreciated because of his or her specific contributions. The only way this perception can occur is if each employee gets regular and personal feedback on his or her performance. I'm not talking about formal performance reviews, which, as typically practiced, are worse than useless. They create problems, disrupt morale, and don't appraise anything (see chapter 8). We're concerned here with frequent, informal, one-to-one feedback about how the individual employee is perceived by the supervisor. All too often, supervisors act as if employees simply operate on autopilot for days and weeks at a time, doing the work mindlessly without needing any encouragement or contact. They're not. Every minute, they're thinking about whether they're measuring up against their own internal standards, wondering what the supervisor is thinking about them and the department, and wondering how the section or department is doing. Without feedback, they're forced to make assumptions based on what they know. Since most organizations don't disseminate enough information, employees usually make incorrect or biased assessments. If they don't see the supervisor all day, they assume, "He doesn't care about us down here working our guts out for him." Or, if they only see the supervisor when there's a problem, they infer, "Typical. We never see her when things are going good, but let one problem pop up and she's down here in an instant."

People want to know how they're doing because they most often assume they're doing well. They'd like to get the pat on the back they feel they deserve. And if they aren't doing well, they'd prefer to be told before they make themselves and their work group look worse. Of course, they want to be told in a constructive manner (direction) rather than getting body-slammed (controlled and abused). Just because things are going well doesn't mean that everybody knows it, and it doesn't mean things will continue to go well. Big problems start with small misinterpretations of instructions and minor, incorrect assumptions made because the supervisor wasn't around to answer a small question. Ten or fifteen small, incorrect assumptions later, the problem is big, the employees thought they were doing a good job but weren't, and, like magic, the supervisor appears to supervise the problem through control and abuse.

It's absolutely essential to pass along positive individual feedback ("I want you to know that your work lately has been great and that I mentioned it to the boss—thanks") and group feedback (short, "we're coming along fine in making our goals" meetings). If given correctly, this feedback serves several vital purposes. It makes the entire group feel like winners. It shows that their leader (the supervisor) recognizes their value. And it demonstrates to the good workers that their efforts earn them praise. They'll do more to earn more. Chapter 5 describes these feedback techniques in detail.

Leadership

As you'll discover in the next chapter, people have a very strong compulsion to form groups. One of the most consistent characteristics of groups is that each one has a leader. It's no different at work. Employees want consistent and dependable leadership because good leadership enables groups to function more effectively and harmoniously. Good leadership is much more than de facto supervision. The sad fact is that most supervisors function as appointed title holders rather than true leaders. A good leader clarifies important issues to the group, maintains group harmony by ensuring that all members know what the rules are, and serves as a spokesperson of the group's interests to other groups. The group leader also serves as a catalyst to assist the group in accomplishing its goals. Because we're social creatures, we've been raised to recognize these benefits of leadership, and we seek them out whenever we form groups. At work, the leadership role is even more critical for the group because so much rides on the leader's activities. A good leader will make the group and each individual employee look good to the organization and to himself or herself.

Proper Direction and Training

The need for direction is one of the few employee needs that supervisors readily admit and attempt to provide. Unfortunately, they confuse direction with control. There's an important difference. Direction implies goal setting, explanation of limits on authority and responsibility, feedback on results, support if required, and the freedom to decide on those operational details which aren't etched in concrete by the organization. Control, on the other hand, means just that; the supervisor dictates every aspect of the work, and the employee simply follows orders (or else). Employees want, seek, and enjoy direction because it provides the means to get their work done efficiently, to demonstrate their skills, and to feel good about themselves. Control works to limit employees' concerns about whether or not things work out.

For example, a supervisor orders an employee to generate a few graphs on her PC. The supervisor needs the graphs for a monthly report to his boss. The supervisor tells the employee what data to put on the graphs and sends the employee away. When the employee comes back with the completed graphs, the supervisor whines, "No, this isn't what I wanted. I need them larger. And why didn't you use three colors instead of two? Do them again." So off goes the employee to try again. Is this direction? Of course not. It's control, and bad, sequential control at that. The supervisor had no right (if he expects to motivate the employee to want to do a better job in the future) to send the employee off on a half-defined task. If supervisors can't specify exactly what's required, they have to be willing to take what they get or they'll alienate their employees after a few instances. If you're going to resort to control, at least do it right, and outline every aspect and detail. If you always know more about the work than the employee, you'll do great if you always have the time to explain everything. Since supervisors don't usually know as much about every aspect of the work as the employees, and also don't have the time to explain every detail, control doesn't work as well as direction, particularly if the job involves any judgment calls by the employee.

Direction is the only alternative. The employee is told what the desired result should be ("A really striking set of graphs for my monthly report to make us look good"), is given general guidelines or an example ("Use a lot of color and make them big—here's some from a report the boss liked"), and is told when the job has to be done ("Try to get them done by this afternoon so we can make sure they fit in with my other material"). Proper direction enables the supervisor to work on other tasks while the employee is independently making decisions, doing the work, learning, and feeling involved. This approach gets more work done and makes the employee feel important. Every employee wants direction like this. While some may need or want more direction than others, no employee wants to be controlled.

Proper training is important for several reasons. Employees generally know when they're not doing a good job, and they usually have a pretty good idea about why they can't do better. If they don't have the skills to do the job, they're bound to make a lot of errors and receive a lot of negative attention from their bosses. When they get in trouble because they don't know how to do the job, resentment and hostility are the result. All too often, this is the problem with most supervision or management seminars. Supervisors are packed off for a few days and are supposedly trained in supervision. But when they get back to the job, they still can't supervise properly, and they know it. The supervisors are expected to be better, they're not, management is disappointed, the supervisors get caught in the middle, and they resent it. This resentment, even if it's not consciously recognized for what it is, leads to all sort of counterproductive behaviors and attitudes. It's the same at all levels. Employees know when they're not properly trained to do the job, and they hold management responsible, particularly when they're criticized for poor performance. Of course, training alone can't guarantee more productivity unless enough other factors are also satisfied. But without proper training, even the most dedicated and motivated workers are going to have problems.

Knowledge of What Is Expected

Goal setting is very important to everyone. We all feel more comfortable when we know why we're doing something and where we expect our efforts to take us. This goes a little further than direction, although direction and guidance are part of it. Here we're talking about goal setting and planning in terms of general responsibilities and duties. Employees want to know the big picture, how and why their contributions fit into the larger scheme of things. This type of information allows employees to feel as if they can make judgment calls when there's some doubt about what to do. If they understand the whys and wherefores of their jobs, they're reassured that they won't make any serious miscalculations in their individual work. For example, suppose it's not entirely clear to a baker whether it's quality or sales that's really important to the company. One day, the manager stresses quality as being most important, but as soon as the big orders come in, all of a sudden it's not a good idea to take the time to turn out the best quality. Without knowing exactly what's expected in both a general strategy and a day-to-day operations sense, the baker has no way to make accurate judgment calls for himself. In this type of situation, employees read the wind and bend according to its direction on a given day. This invites mistakes and errors, as well as resentment when the employee gets in trouble for misreading the signals.

All too often, as part of the currently popular fad of company culture programs, organizations are putting together mission statements that are supposed to help every employee understand exactly what to do. Unfortunately, these mission statements typically end up as all-encompassing motherhood-and-apple-pie manifestos. For example, one organization drafted the following mission statement:

> It is the goal of XYZ to become the market leader in its industry by producing a wide range of state-of-the-art electronics products which will be of the highest quality and which will sell at a lower cost than the competition. XYZ shall also be a leader in the service of these products. XYZ is firmly committed to the development of its human resources as the only way in which the above goals can be attained.

Why don't they cure cancer and bring about world peace while they're at it? This organization had no hope of attaining even one of the above goals, but nobody in the inner circle who developed the statement had the nerve to say so. There was a feeling that if they kept telling it to the employees it would do something to inspire more work. Of course, this mission statement was greeted with hoots and snorts down in the ranks, because the employees knew that nothing had changed; they'd still have to carefully read the organizational wind every day and on each issue to determine which way to bend in order to stay out of trouble. Employees want and need to know what's expected, in meaningful and applied terms which relate directly to their jobs. Then they can work to gain the recognition and feelings of accomplishment which we all seek.

Fair and Tactful Discipline

Discipline is a strange business topic. If mature adults with proper work motivations are properly directed and led, there should be relatively little need for discipline. Fair and tactful discipline is cited by employees as a major need primarily because they're very often subjected to arbitrary and unfair discipline. We're not talking here about reprimands for not coming to work or coming in late. Everyone knows that these things are obvious mistakes which will get them into trouble (although the employees are aware of the arbitrary nature of enforcement—how often does an executive get into trouble for coming in a little late?). The discipline problem, in the eyes of the employees, is that employees are blamed for errors which occurred not because the employee deliberately did something wrong but because something in the system went wrong. For example, I worked with one manufacturer whose spray painters were routinely sent home for days without pay because of a sag or run in their work. Yet for fifteen years these "discipline problems" had been producing 95 percent perfect paint jobs with outdated equipment. When so-called discipline is applied in these cases, it only serves to harden employee attitudes about management and to destroy their resolve to care about doing a good job. When such mistakes occurred, the correct approach would be to view them as system errors which could be jointly solved by management and employees through problem solving, coaching, and/or training.

Another discipline problem involves fairness and appropriateness. Most instances of discipline and employee complaints don't involve being sent home or fired but merely being reprimanded unfairly. One minor but typical case involved a supervisor who had single-handedly turned around a nightmare of an operational department. After improving production by 50 percent and simultaneously cutting personnel costs by 20 percent, this supervisor was called in by her boss and berated for fifteen minutes because of a single misspelled word on a handwritten note that the supervisor had sent to the boss and was not intended to go any further. Making it worse was the fact that the boss was almost functionally illiterate regarding grammar and syntax in her own work but for some reason had learned to spell. While the employee got no praise for a miracle turnaround that was the talk of the company, she was castigated for a single inconsequential misspelling. That's the type of arbitrary and petty discipline that motivates employees' concerns for fair discipline.

Most employees freely admit errors and are willing to work hard to correct them if they're treated appropriately. In the above case, nothing should ever have been said. On the other hand, if a letter were sent to an important client with a major typo, it would be appropriate to point it out and ask the employee to be more careful next time. If the significant errors were to continue, then perhaps training or closer direction and guidance (reviewing drafts) would be in order. This is proper discipline (and direction). Ranting and raving, insulting putdowns, and harassment are not discipline; they are emotional outbursts which alienate employees and do nothing to improve the situation.

Feeling Involved

Employees want to feel as if they're an integral part of getting the work done. They need to know what's going on, why they're doing what they're doing, and how any forthcoming changes are going to affect them. And they need to believe that their role is important. All too often, supervisors expect employees to know what's going on simply because the supervisor knows. Presumably, important information will find its way to the employees who want to know. But it never does. The grapevine is great for rumor and scandal, but it's notoriously inefficient for keeping employees informed about business details. And that's what they want most. When the employees have a clear picture of what's going on and how they fit in, they have a clearer picture of why they must do things in a particular manner. They also feel as if they have a stake in making things work.

Employees yearn to be involved for several reasons. They're constantly observing events and making assumptions about what's going on behind the scenes; this is natural curiosity. When events influence them and they aren't involved in the decisions and don't know what's going on, they're anxious. Think of how you feel when a big meeting takes place and you're not invited. You wonder what's going on and what you're missing. You wonder why you were left out, even if it isn't any of your business. When employees are left out of day-to-day involvement in all of the big and little decisions that affect their jobs, they begin to feel resentful, anxious, angry, and then indifferent, particularly when they're given orders to do work which they had no part in planning.

There are several important aspects of being involved. One relates to feelings of commitment to the group. As employees learn more and more about their department's operations and interactions with other groups, they begin to identify more strongly with the group. As a result, not only are they in a better position to make judgment calls about work actions simply because they have more facts, but they're also more committed to making the group look good. You'd be surprised at the hunger for information which employees at all levels have, information not only about their department but about everything that's going on. You may have a hard time believing that entry-level bank tellers would be interested in hearing about changes in the bank's computer center, but they are. They might not remember most of what they're told, and they might not even care about the details. But they will remember that you took the time and trouble to include them. They like to feel that they're in the know. It makes them feel as if they're a part of the bigger, more prestigious organization (the entire bank) than just the branch where they work. It's the same in every business.

Another critical aspect of involvement is participation in group rituals and decision making. This is particularly critical at the smaller work-group levels. Employees generally have extremely perceptive understandings about the level of participation in decision making that's appropriate for them to expect. They know where they stand and how much input they should be permitted. Unfortunately, even the little bit they expect and would cherish is hardly ever solicited. It's essential that you include all of your subordinates in your decision-making processes. You must tell them what's going on and, for those actions or problems on which you'll be working, ask for their suggestions. You're not asking them to tell you what to do, and you're not suggesting that you couldn't do it yourself. You're demonstrating to them that you value them, respect their views, and wouldn't do anything important without at least asking their opinion unless it was an emergency. Often many of them won't have any suggestions. Although you may occasionally get some surprisingly useful advice, that's not the point. You want them to know that if they have an idea at any time, you're open to it. You want them to perceive that you value them and trust their judgment. If you involve them in this manner, they'll begin to see every action of theirs as something that's important to you. They won't let you down very often.

Daily contact between the supervisor and each employee is important to feelings of involvement for several reasons. First of all, regular contact with the supervisor reinforces feelings of group cohesion. The supervisor is the group leader, and his or her proximity strengthens feelings of group identification and loyalty. Secondly, and even more essentially, the contact gives the supervisor an opportunity to clarify the central values of the work group. By distributing pats on the back and giving direction to employees, the supervisor is reducing the odds that employees are going to make erroneous assumptions about how to do things. Without daily contact of a meaningful nature, the supervisor comes to be viewed as a mere figurehead of the organization and not as a leader of the group. Without the supervisor as a group leader, the employees must fill voids in their assumptions with their best guesses about what's important. Best guesses are sometimes far off the mark. Worse yet, if a supervisor doesn't come around regularly, it's a cinch that most of the visits will be motivated by problems, and that's very damaging. The supervisor only shows up when there's a foul-up. Nobody needs to be seen as that type of leader.

32

Is It So Much to Ask?

Is it unreasonable for employees to want their jobs to provide satisfaction of the factors we've discussed? Given the way most organizations operate, employees aren't going to get what they want. They already know that, and they do what they have to do to get through the day without it; they hunker down and throttle back their energy and enthusiasm, which they attempt to displace to after-work activities. They're a little frustrated, but they'll survive. The question is, will businesses survive without giving them satisfaction? I don't think so. Without the active participation of all employees, there's nowhere else to look for substantial gains. We all know how much harder we'd be able to work (and would want to work) if our organizations satisfied even part of our needs. The chapters which follow will outline techniques and strategies for providing these satisfactions that employees want and businesses must have.

CHAPTER 3

Organizational Dynamics: Relentless Mechanisms That Few Harness

There are powerful, hidden forces at work in every organization. These forces influence every action, perception, and decision of the organization's members. If these unseen powers are working in your favor, efficiency, productivity, and morale will improve dramatically. If they're working against you, there will be more mistakes, less teamwork, and lower morale. Incredibly, very few organizations make any conscious attempts to control these forces. Because they can't be seen and can't be tallied on the balance sheets, these powerful forces are almost always left to operate haphazardly. Those who fail to take advantage of these forces are making a big mistake. Properly influenced, these hidden forces can be the source of the single biggest boost in productivity available to any organization. Left to follow their own predictable course, the hidden forces will consistently compromise your efforts to provide a working environment most conducive to productivity.

The hidden forces are organizational dynamics, which influence and/or determine much of the behavior performed by the members of a group. Organizational dynamics influence group members' perceptions and expectations about an organization's capabilities, personality, goals, and method of operation. These expectations and perceptions exert significant influence on every

34

judgment, behavior, analysis, and emotional response that occurs in an organization. Properly directed, organizational dynamics can be oriented to send a positive signal which will bring out the best that the employees have to offer. More typically, the organizational dynamics are not directed, and employees are shown, in hundreds of ways, that their best efforts will be frustrated and lost through petty conflicts, departmental rivalries, and the organization's inherent mistrust of individual initiative.

Even though few people in an organization may actively notice the operation of organizational dynamics, everyone feels their effect. For example, we've all heard a variation of the observation, "This is a very conservative company. We like to move slow." Employees in these companies know that rapid change isn't welcomed, that you don't rock the boat, and that policies and procedures are followed very closely. This type of belief or expectation influences all of the employees in a very subtle and powerful manner. The employees then behave in a manner which further reinforces their expectations. It's not the effect on individual employees that's important; it's their pervasive influence over most of the people and processes most of the time which accounts for the powerful influence of organizational dynamics. It doesn't matter if 2 or 3 or 7 percent of an organization's employees behave contrary to the influence of the organizational dynamics. It's the 98, 97, or 93 percent of the employees who are influenced which will determine what works and what doesn't.

The Silent Hidden Power

I don't know what there was about the place. All the time, you felt like you were walking on eggshells. Nobody ever said anything about not, well, not speaking out when you didn't agree with an idea or a proposal, but you always had the feeling that you'd better not. I never heard of anyone getting in trouble for arguing, but I also never saw anyone try to argue while I was there. You just got the feeling that it would be a real bad idea. One time I remember real well, after about a year, I was in a meeting on a Saturday morning and the VP came up with the most stupid proposal I had ever heard. I could tell, from looking around, that a lot of the other guys felt the same way, you know, the slight roll of their eyes when you'd look at them. But the Assistant VPs loved the idea, and nobody, none of the other five of us, said a word. We knew it was a mistake and it would bomb, but we knew, or at least felt, it would be a bigger mistake to say anything. I left there after two years, and it was only when I got to the new job that I realized how oppressive the pressure not to say anything had been.

Former insurance industry manager

It's not enough simply to supervise your employees effectively. If you want maximum productivity, it's absolutely essential that the organizational dynamics be turned in your favor, to work with you rather than taking their normal, typical, and natural contrary course. Proper supervision and one-to-one management techniques aren't enough to do the job by themselves. You're going to have to exert whatever influence you have to bring the organizational dynamics under the control of management.

Organizational Dynamics Defined

Organizational dynamics is a name for the collective operation of a number of factors and processes which influence the behaviors, expectations, and beliefs of people in groups. These factors are universal among human beings. Whether they're innate (due to genetic influences) or learned is a moot point. They're so pervasive that we must accept them as a constant of human interaction. When these factors are discussed in reference to small groups of people (meaning two to twenty people), they're often called group dynamics or small-group dynamics. When they're discussed in terms of their effects on larger groups, such as companies, they're generally referred to as organizational dynamics.

Group dynamics are processes which influence the formation, operation, and maintenance of relationships among individuals in a group. Since almost all work processes and decisions are intimately involved with the relationships and interactions between members of small sections and departments, group dynamics influence every aspect of an organization's work. With a group, a number of quite predictable things will almost certainly happen. For example, it's almost a given that office workers will, all other things being equal, like people at nearby desks and in nearby sections better than employees who work farther away. This simple and predictable human tendency, called propinquity, leads to all sorts of expectations and assumptions which influence how people work with one another.

An organization, such as a company or division, is composed of numerous groups, such as maintenance, "mahogany row," the personnel department, and other groups which aren't so obvious in structure. A group of groups tends to operate and maintain itself in a predictable manner. For example, as an organization grows and evolves, the groups within it tend to limit the flow of information between groups. A proper understanding of what's really going on at work requires an appreciation of this and many other processes of organizational dynamics.

On the following pages I will discuss various important aspects of group and organizational dynamics. Each topic will be presented in two sections. The "What you need to know" section will summarize basic information from the thousands of research articles and hundreds of volumes which have been written about each topic. The "Implications" section will then point out the most critical impacts and influences which the group or organizational dynamic has in the work environment. I think you'll begin to see that there's a lot more going on at work than getting the product out the door. In fact, a lot of what's going on is actually working *against* getting the best product out the door.

Norms, Roles, and Goals

The basic building blocks of group dynamics are norms, goals, and roles. Group dynamics result from their operation.

Norms
What you need to know

The norms of a group are the rules by which the group operates. Every group has a set of established norms. The group members may not be able to recite them, but they follow them and know when they're being broken. People are incredibly accurate and perceptive when it comes to observing and recognizing norms. We develop these skills because each of us belongs to at least three to six groups (nuclear family group, husband-wife group, bowling group, card-playing group, work group, fraternal group, extended family group, church group, etc.). As we move in and out of these groups during the day, we're expert at quickly and accurately recognizing which group norm is relevant and then switching our behaviors to match those group norms so that we'll fit in properly with the group. In the golf group, it might be considered perfectly acceptable (and even expected and encouraged) to tell off-color jokes, but when the setting moves to the church, the same people quickly adjust to the norms against telling such stories. Nobody has to say anything, but everybody knows.

Although we can expertly switch our behaviors to match vastly different norms of various groups, the norms of any one group are remarkably resistant to change. This is because each person in the group has a vested interest in maintaining the group as it is. The current norms, whatever they might be, are well known and understood, serve to increase the members' feelings of security when they obey the norms, and enable members to win rewards and acceptance from other group members by obeying and reinforcing the norms. Attempts to change norms have to fight all of these contrary influences. Thus, group norms don't change unless many members at once perceive great threat or potential gain. This is why it's so difficult for any one person to influence the norms of a group.

At work, many norms are spelled out. In most organizations, the rules for filling out expense reports are well defined, letter and memo styles are established, and how meetings are run, if not written out, could be clearly explained by almost anyone to a new employee. These well-defined norms aren't the most important ones. The norms which influence the more important productivity factors, such as what you have to do to be recognized for achievement, involvement, creativity, risk taking, commitment, and so on, are generally unspoken. In fact, employees in most organizations would have a difficult time explaining the accepted company position on risk taking in their jobs.

In the absence of specifically explained and explicitly supported norms, each employee develops his or her own interpretation of the norms of the work group he or she is in. Through day-to-day contact and feedback from each other, the group's norms eventually stabilize themselves somewhere around the average interpretations of all of the members, with some distortions caused by the influence of more powerful or influential group members (the boss has more influence than the average employee). In this manner, each work group establishes its own set of norms for every type of behavior and attitude. While a few members may not agree completely with the group's norms on a specific topic, they don't violate many of them openly. For example, it might be the group norm not to push the boss about a new idea; once you get a no, you give up. A specific employee, understanding this norm, may actively violate it by attempting to hard-sell the boss two or three times. If this were to happen frequently, the boss might get upset (perhaps without knowing why), and the

---

Norms at Work

When I first came to work here, I had never worked very late at the office before in other jobs. Sure, sometimes I'd stick around in a pinch, but I've never had any trouble getting my work done. But I noticed that everyone was hanging around at the end of the day for another hour or so just for appearances. At first, I'd hang around for a few minutes to shoot the bull, and everybody would be real friendly until I'd start to cut out and then they'd be a little cool. I noticed after a while that a lot of informal decisions would always be made after work in these groups. So I started hanging around, first because I didn't want to get left out on anything important and then because everything seemed to be friendlier all day if you were in the late group. I never even noticed it was so bad until my wife got upset. I was staying at work for almost two hours extra every night just to be in the "in" group! I really resented the time it took, but I knew I'd look real bad if I didn't stay. I stopped staying, but I think it's hurt me with this company.

Construction industry engineer

38

other employees might begin to make comments to each other and to the norm violator, whom they may begin to treat differently. Generally, this type of pressure eventually brings the employee into line or forces him or her to leave.

It's been well documented through research and observation in business environments that active participation in establishing and supporting a group's norms will increase a member's respect for the norms. If the members are encouraged to participate in establishing the norms, whether they're informal social norms or productivity requirements, they'll be more committed to them. We'll examine this process more fully later in this chapter.

Don't underestimate the incredibly pervasive influence of unspoken norms. There are active, well-established, and scrupulously followed norms for things about which nobody in the group ever thinks. Take creativity. Some work groups have strong norms against daring new ideas. In these groups, members have found by trial and error that new ideas irritate the supervisor, create a lot of negative attention in the form of nitpicking quibbles, are subjected to detailed searches for minor flaws, and result in additional work to generate responses to attacks. In these situations, everyone quickly learns that you get a lot more points by stepping all over a new idea and taking cheap shots at it (which support the group norms) than you can by trying to push a good idea through the system.

This type of norm doesn't have its most damaging effect on a specific idea which surfaces and gets the treatment. The far more serious damage is done when an idea pops into an employee's mind and is then dismissed almost out-of-hand because the employee knows the norms and doesn't want to rock the boat. After working in the organization a while, this type of mental screening process about all norms becomes almost automatic. As we discuss the operation of other group dynamics, you'll see why the screening process is almost always unfavorable for new ideas, changes, or individual initiative.

Implications

If you don't actively define norms which can be followed by each group member, they're going to follow their own subjective norms. These internal norms don't often give you the type of performance you need (as most people will take the safest and most self-serving alternative if they have any doubts about what works). And if you don't actively demonstrate by means of your own behavior that following the norms earns rewards, nobody will pay any attention to what you say.

Goals
What you need to know

Every group, even an informal one such as a bowling team, has goals which define the reason for the group's existence. The bowling team's goals might be to have fun and perhaps win a trophy. In the work environment, most defined groups have formal goals, many of which are documented in detail. Procedures for maintaining accounts payables and receivables, budget tracking, and the like, would no doubt be spelled out quite specifically for the accounting department. However, as with norms, the most important goals of a group are not always spelled out. The unspoken goals are those the group members have developed after observing what works and what doesn't work to win them rewards and avoid problems. The result is a series of unspoken or informal goals to which the group devotes considerable attention.

In an informal group such as the bowling team, the unspoken goal may be to pretend to be big drinkers and talk a lot about "throwing down a six-pack," but with the understanding (an unspoken norm) that it's all in jest. The person who actually did get drunk would be in serious trouble with the group for pursuing a goal which wasn't on the agenda.

At work, the unspoken goals typically revolve around the style in which the work is done, the amount of conflict between people and departments that's acceptable, and the types of gains groups attempt to obtain through competition with other groups. These unspoken goals come into existence to satisfy the needs (as discussed in chapter 2) of employees which aren't being met by defined goals. In effect, in every group there are two sets of goals, those which are formal and well known, and the informal, often more strongly pursued goals.

It's easy to find examples of companies in which informal goals are the first priority. Whenever internal politics are played viciously with no quarter given, the formal goals of the organization have taken second place to the unspoken goals of interdepartmental and interpersonal competition for promotion and status. While these highly competitive and cutthroat environments are the most easily recognized examples of informal goals being ascendant over the organization's formal goals, they're not representative of those most damaging to productivity. The more common situation is where the informal, unspoken goals of many groups, and perhaps most of the organization, revolve around staying out of trouble and not rocking the boat. These types of goals evolve over the years as employees in various groups discover that management doesn't want to hear about problems and doesn't take implied criticism kindly (as when someone suggests that there's a better way to do something), and that nobody is going to act on any new ideas anyway. The formal goals of the organization may say that innovation and creativity and state-of-the-art technology are the company's stock in trade, but everyone knows that's only annual-report verbiage. In these types of organizations, the employees know that you go through the motions of pursuing the formal goals but the important thing is to pursue the goal of staying out of trouble. You can spot these organizations in an instant because there's always a lot of joking about "covering your ass." They may call it a joke and they may chuckle a bit, but everybody in the organization knows it's not a laughing matter if you leave yours uncovered.

Implications

You can't afford to have employees wasting their energy in attempts to pursue informal goals which are opposed to the organization's goals, especially since most informal goals involve keeping out of trouble and maintaining the status quo. If you're going to have to get new ideas and come up with better ways to do things in order to survive, you've got to cut down the amount of effort which employees divert from the formal goals of the organization. The only way to do this is to define and establish goals which allow them to meet their personal needs (those discussed in chapter 2) *while* they're pursuing the formal goals. To do this you must demonstrate that working toward the defined goals generates both individual and group rewards. In essence, you're attempting to make both sets of goals the same.

Roles
What you need to know

Roles are specific, predictable sets of behaviors (and the accompanying perceptions and beliefs they support) which are performed by group members who serve a specific function in the group. There are a limited number of roles in any group, and they're typically defined very specifically and consistently across groups. For example, almost all groups have one member who functions as a leader and another member who functions as a social facilitator (attempting to keep things calm and peaceful).

There are three basic types of roles in the work environment. The first is the *enacted role*, the role the group member is actually fulfilling (as might be evaluated by an objective outside observer). The second type of role is the *perceived role*, the role the person believes he or she is performing. There's no shortage of employees in every company who believe that they're working productively but whose enacted roles (what they're actually accomplishing) fall far short of the mark in terms of objective analysis. The third type of role is the *expected role*, the set of behaviors group members expect from a person fulfilling a specific role.

The amazing power of roles to shape behavior is demonstrated by a famous experiment in social psychology. A group of normal male college students was selected to take part in a one-week experiment. The group was randomly divided by coin tosses into two groups, the prisoners and the jailers. The students were taken to a mock prison setup in the basement of one of the college buildings. The only instructions they were given were to tell them what group they were in and that they would be in the experiment for one week. The experiment had to be terminated early because the jailers began to brutalize the prisoners by doing such things as herding them out of their cells for frequent inspections. At night, when the researchers weren't around, the jailers even made the prisoners walk blindfolded to the bathroom. Several of the prisoners, when visited by friends or family members, broke down and cried about the treatment they were receiving. Simply because they had been assigned the role of jailer, ordinary college students became authoritarian brutes. And assigning the role of prisoner to the same type of normal students turned them into docile, compliant sheep. The groups could have spent the week of the experiment as one big, happy group without any jailer or prisoner behavior. The mere titles of the roles triggered all sorts of expectations in both groups.

The roles of people at work are more complex and have many more assumptions and expectations surrounding them than the one-dimensional roles of jailer and prisoner. Work roles motivate much stronger behavior. If the role of an employee is to just do the work and leave the decisions to management, most employees will become accustomed to the role and, if not comfortable in it, at least secure in knowing how to maintain day-to-day interactions. Once employees settle into this or any other unproductive role, it's very difficult to get them to change; they don't know how to act in a different role, the new behaviors haven't been practiced, there's no group support system set up to reward the new roles and norms, and there are usually not many people around to act as role models. While it's easy to reason that employees should welcome opportunities to participate more fully in decisions, they become accustomed

---

Trying to Change Roles

It was hard to believe. In fact, I still find it amazing how my staff resisted my efforts to make them take more responsibility for decisions. No matter what I did, they still kept coming back to me to get my OK or to ask me to make the choices. I told them they could hire whoever they wanted, and they still brought the candidates to me. I told them that as long as they were on budget, they didn't need my approval to buy normal supplies. What did I get? You guessed it. Every purchase order for every pencil still ended up on my desk for signature. The only thing that made me not give up on them was the demands on my time from the new business we bought. I couldn't make all the decisions. I now see that as the best thing that ever happened to me or the company. It took about a year before everybody was making their own decisions. It was really amazing. I know now it was because I didn't let them have the freedom before, and they didn't know how to handle it. It's really amazing when you think about it, isn't it? Grown, well-paid businessmen who have to be forced to take the ball and run with it.

President of a machine tool company

---

to past practice and will often strongly resist changes which would provide them with considerable satisfaction of their needs for achievement, recognition, and so on. It takes considerable and consistent effort to get them to change their ways. That's the price that must be paid for years of encouraging subservient employee role models.

If there is a discrepancy between the perceived, enacted, and expected role behaviors, this is termed *role conflict*. The most widely known type of role conflict in business occurs when the employee's perceived role of "hard worker" conflicts with the expected role which the supervisor wants to see. This type of role conflict often leads to the classic "things aren't working out" exit interview. The tragedy is that the employee in this type of situation has typically never been given a specific and detailed set of norms which define what the supervisor expects from a "good" employee.

Role conflicts hurt groups in many ways. They always create lower morale, reduced efficiency, and interpersonal conflicts. The most deleterious and common type of role conflict in terms of productivity is a simultaneous conflict among all three roles. The employees are doing what they think they should be doing (perceived role). Most of this work is done to obey informal norms and in order to work toward informal goals, which aren't usually in synch with formal group and organization goals. At the same time, they're probably not getting the job done the way it must be done to get the company where it needs to be (the enacted role isn't on target). As a result, they're usually perceived as poor employees because they're not living up to the expected role which management wants (and which itself may not be on target with what's needed).

This energy-draining role conflict occurs because employees aren't kept up to date on the vital information they require to feel involved, supervisors aren't giving specific and regular feedback, and the leaders of the organization haven't been successful in establishing fairly uniform norms and goals for all groups. Since there are three sets of norms and goals involved, the organization's goals and norms (even if they're accurate) get very little attention and in fact may suffer from being directly opposed by the informal goals and norms of many of the groups.

Implications

The goal is to create an environment in which the three roles are very close to one another in terms of the behaviors and expectations they foster. When this occurs, and when the same type of unification effort is made concerning goals and norms, most of the work that takes place will be done in support of the organization's goals. This can only happen if you share as much information as possible about what's needed, what's going on, and what everyone expects. You've got to adopt the attitude that employees at all levels can never be provided with enough information about what's going on. Aggressive dissemination of information ensures that employees will make few factual errors in perceiving the organization's norms and goals. And it also ensures that employees will have few opportunities to make unfavorable assumptions because they don't have enough information. If the shared information is orchestrated in the proper manner (by means of the *Millennium Management* techniques discussed in chapter 7), it will also serve to move the norms and goals of every group and individual closer to those of the overall organization. That means less conflict, less wasted energy, less frustration, and greater productivity.

Group Processes

Norms, goals, and roles are the three main characteristics of groups. Their generation and maintenance drive other group processes which regulate the activity of groups and organizations. There are several group processes and phenomena which are extremely important to an understanding of how work groups and organizations function.

Group Formation
What you need to know

The formation of groups happens spontaneously and automatically. In fact, it's a rare collection of people who won't form a group (meaning that roles, norms, and goals will be established) when they spend some time together. The largest number of people who can effectively function as a small group is about fifteen. Once the number of people in a group gets larger than seven, the odds increase that subgroups will form. Smaller groups make it easier for the members to communicate regularly with all members, to know each other well enough to maintain group bonds, and to clearly exert the influence of their roles over the other members. In a department of twenty to thirty employees, there many be anywhere from four to seven or more subgroups. This is a problem if it's left to operate on its own, because the norms and goals of each subgroup don't usually parallel those of the department or section.

At the beginning of this chapter I mentioned propinquity, which is the strong tendency of people to like or feel more comfortable with people who are nearby as compared to those who are more distant. Propinquity arises from our social heritage of feeling safer in groups and of not having to worry continually about our safety when we're among people we know. For example, you may not know anything about a neighbor other than the fact that he lives nearby. For all you know, he could be a child-molesting ax murderer. Yet, when you drive by, you might wave or smile if you see him out in his yard working. You've accepted the neighbor into your neighborhood group. If you see a stranger in your neighborhood, it's a different story. You look; you wonder who it is and what he or she wants. The same forces, but much more compelling, operate at work. Because subgroups work together every day, they begin to trust one another (or at least feel more comfortable with each other) more than groups and people with whom they have less contact. They begin to support the subgroup norms and goals more strongly than those of the department or the organization. In that the typical subgroup has limited information about what's going on, they commonly develop norms and goals which are off-target in terms of what the organization or department needs. Yet, since members identify most strongly with the subgroup, it's those off-target norms and goals which get the most attention. This happens every day in every department in every company.

There's nothing you can do to stop subgroups from forming within departments and sections. In fact, the subgroups serve a vital function in providing employees with appropriate groups with which they can identify and to which they can actively belong. If subgroups didn't exist (this never happens), the large size of most departments and sections would make it impossible for individuals to be part of a group which they could get their arms around. In such a situation, individuals would have nowhere to turn for comfort when frustrations and setbacks occurred. The result would be even more turnover and even lower morale.

Implications

The key to properly harnessing subgroups is to provide sufficient feedback, information, and guidance so the norms and goals of the subgroups are more closely attuned to those of the department and the organization. At the same time, you must provide as much satisfaction of individual needs as

---

A Different Company

Things were different when the company first started. There were only about ten of us in the office, and we all knew what was going on and could pick up the loose ends at a moment's notice. Now, we're all spread out all over the place and people don't try to help out as much. I actually had some supervisor tell me the other day that the shipping department had more important things to do than locate an order for us up here in sales. Can you believe that? It's like he's working for another company.

Sales manager for a plastics manufacturer

---

possible so that it becomes difficult for employees in subgroups to rally around norms which are counterproductive to your departmental or section goals. If you're beginning to sense that there's a central theme concerning information, communication, and feedback which runs through all attempts to properly control and orient group dynamics, you're absolutely correct.

Group Cohesion
What you need to know

Groups maintain their roles and norms and pursue their goals in direct proportion to the members' perceptions of the value and status of the group. The more the group is viewed as a winner by its members, and the more benefits they perceive they obtain from being a member of the group, the harder they'll work for it and the greater they'll value their membership in it. In fact, the higher the perceived status of a group, the more sacrifices people will make to be admitted to the group. Countless research studies have demonstrated that people value membership in a group in direct proportion to the difficulty of gaining admittance into the group.

Several basic conditions must be satisfied before a group can develop an effective sense of cohesion. The group members must have a clear and consistent view of the goals of the group, they must have regular and consistent contact with one another, and they must believe that each of them stands to benefit if the group benefits. To the extent that these three basic conditions are satisfied, the group will be cohesive.

Attribution theory is an entire branch of social psychology which explores the mechanisms people use to determine the causes of their behavior and that of others. It's a very important aspect of group cohesion. The fundamental attribution concern about any behavior is whether it is primarily caused by the characteristics of the person who commits the behavior or by the social situation in which it occurs.

The bottom line about individual and group attribution is that people and groups attribute the good things they do to internal factors ("We did it because we're good people"), and they attribute their bad, questionable, or incorrect behaviors to external factors ("How could we help it? Those idiots at corporate were the ones who started this policy"). When these attribution effects work on individual sections, departments, and subgroups, they serve to deny the reality of the situation by causing interpretations of the facts which make the group look good and not responsible for anything bad that happens. The result is that groups begin to develop norms which create reasons why "it's not our fault" and why "we could do better if those *other* guys would . . ." The result is a strengthening of group bonds which interferes with the primary mission of the organization or department.

46

Implications

Even a bunch of losers must be made to see themselves as winners if you want them to work harder for the group. That's why it's important to make sure that solid, factual, good news about your department or organization is trumpeted to everyone. It will make the group seem more successful, and members will identify more strongly with its norms and goals. If the group believes that it's a bunch of losers or if they perceive that others view them as losers, they're not going to work as hard. Employees want to be winners, and if they're led to perceive themselves as winners, they'll begin to believe that their group is a high-status group. They'll value the group more, work harder to attain its goals, support its norms more strongly, and struggle to make the group and its leader look good.

Just as critically, every attempt has to be made to characterize errors and mistakes as system flaws which "we can all fix if we work together" rather than as "someone's mistake." Assigning blame for errors, unless they are caused by a chronic poor performer, only serves to harm the group by reducing its perception of its own value and status. Worse, it hardens subgroup and section or department group norms which attribute the real blame ("if management knew what was going on") to someone else. Nobody at any level ever thinks they're personally at fault, so it's a waste of time to find out who did it so you can blame them (unless it's malicious or chronic). And it's a waste of effort to try to blame someone in any type of complex system where the employees are reasonably intelligent; it's almost impossible to find the "blamee" because everyone is smart enough to keep the blame moving to the next group until the angry person tires of the search and gives up. If the blame is eventually pinned on someone, it's usually some poor wretch who's so far down the line, that he or she doesn't have anything to do with the problem. The more effective approach is to work on solutions to problems which don't cause groups to feel threatened and demeaned. They'll then worry about fixing the problem instead of working to deny that they're involved or responsible.

Compliance with Group Norms
What you need to know

Every dimension of group processes serves to strengthen members' obedience and compliance with group norms. The influence of group expectations on the behavior of an individual member is extremely strong. We all like to think we are our own person, but the truth is that very often we are more the group's obedient member. That's one of the hidden dangers of group influences on an organization; nobody likes to admit that they're influenced by anything besides their own choice. As a result, when decisions and behaviors are molded and shaped by unfavorable group forces, very few people will step back and notice or admit that they're being strongly influenced by forces other than objective, scientific, individual choice.

Another famous experiment provides a powerful demonstration of a group's influence on the behavior of members. In this experiment, subjects sat in a room with a small group and estimated which of three lines was the longest as various arrangements of lines were presented. Unknown to the subject, all of the other people in the room were in league with the experimenter. These collaborators deliberately gave wrong answers according to a prearranged script. In experiment after experiment, using different types of subjects and different assortments of collaborators, many different researchers have always found the same thing: from 20 to 40 percent of the subjects would give an obviously wrong answer rather than go against the majority. And this was a group of strangers who had no personal or business ties! The only inducement to go along with the crowd was every person's natural tendency not to defy an unspoken norm, even in an informal group.

There are times when groups permit members to violate norms without loss of status. People who have great power or influence with the group or who have served the group well are allocated "idiosyncrasy credits"; they're given some leeway to violate norms. The amount of leeway depends on their previous contributions and/or current status. Thus, sometimes a very outspoken employee is permitted to violate the group norms because he or she might have made a killing on the Jenkins deal the year before or is considered to be "our secret weapon." Thus, his or her violations of the norms are viewed as earned idiosyncrasies which will be tolerated, and perhaps even cherished, by the group as long as the violations don't exceed the earned credits. If you look carefully at the work groups in your organization, you'll see that any long-term violators of group norms are generally perceived as having made significant contributions in the past or are viewed as special in some other way. They may look like they're violating group norms, but they're only serving the group in a different, just as structured and predictable, role.

Occasionally a group will have a "court jester" role in which a member is expected and encouraged to act outrageously. This is the type of employee who frequently says critical and shocking things about the organization and/or management that would end most careers. The court jester has become a character ("Well, you know crazy Bob") who isn't taken seriously. The jester isn't violating the norms the group has set up for him or her. In fact, if the jester were to become serious and abide by the other members' norms, he or she would be treated with suspicion and would get a lot of negative attention.

New employees, not having had the time to do anything special, have to come in with very high status if they expect to violate group norms and get away with it. Nonextraordinary members are not given any leeway by the group and can't be expected to defy group norms very often. Even creative, enthusiastic employees who are brought in to change things, after being

Group Signals

I have to tell you, I have a different view of myself after what happened in that meeting. I've always thought of myself as a rugged individualist type who wasn't influenced by anything, but now I'm not so sure, maybe I'm just getting older or maybe wiser. I was presenting my proposal for the new order processing system, and I noticed that the president was smiling as he whispered something to one of his MBA assistants. I kept talking, but I had a sudden flash of insight as I looked around the room. I saw, or I thought I saw, a lot of half smiles, sort of condescending, "here we go again" looks from some of the people. I was always coming up with new ideas, and many of them were accepted, but I knew, I mean I really knew right then what was going on. They thought my fervor and enthusiasm were cute or something, maybe too naive for their sophisticated blasé attitudes. Well, right then I said screw them all. They'd never know the difference anyway between a good idea and a bad one, so let someone else give them bad ideas and get laughed at. That was four years ago, and I haven't tried to push a single new program that requires their approval.

Management information systems director of a major brokerage house

pounded down many times by supporters of the group norms, will often begin to push less hard, will begin to self-censor their more radical ideas, and will more often come to support the very group norms they were brought in to change.

Implications

Groups exert a great deal of influence on members' compliance with norms and role. The biggest part of this influence is driven by the group leader. An even greater influence is possessed by those higher up the chain of command.

Management's greater perceived power sends strong signals about what's expected and rewarded. An employee depends on the boss's approval and the blessing of the organization's leaders for the opportunity to earn his or her livelihood. Given these influences, how hard do you think the average employee at any level is going to fight for the correct action if it's counter to the currently popular wisdom of those in power? The group wouldn't let them even if they wanted to. And, if it's been noted that risk takers (as opposed to those who merely talk about risk) are quickly put in their place, how many risks (group censure or disapproval) do you think the average employee is going to take to try to push a new idea through or fix a problem? Remember, the 20 to 40 percent of the subjects who went along with the wrong answer had no other pressure on them than the innate human preference not to violate group norms. Group members at work have their personal anxiety, livelihood, and professional status on the line. With all that at stake, the percentage of people who go along with the majority or with the leader's perceived position is always going to be much higher than 20 to 40 percent; it will be more on the order of 70 to 90 percent. Unless you do everything in your power to demonstrate that you sincerely value participation from everyone and that you want to hear opposing, new, or different ideas before you act, most employees will accurately read the subtle signs of group norms and will go along silently with the path of least resistance.

Organizations

In a manner of speaking, organizations are not natural. Prior to the last ten thousand years there was little need for a large group of groups to get together to work on complex, long-term, special projects. This is a very important point. Group dynamics evolved because they worked in favor of survival; groups served to protect individuals and allow them to have offspring. In a sense, group dynamics evolved along with our brains and bodies. Organizational dynamics are another story.

Until the establishment of agriculture and herding, humans probably existed mainly in large family-related groups or tribes which survived by foraging. There was no need to form large organizations. Once agriculture and livestock were discovered as ways to provide food, it was necessary for lots of people to gather in one place in order to do the work. Hence the arrival of complex organizations. From the first crude farms of ten thousand years ago, we've come a long way in terms of the types of organizations we establish and work in. These days it's not uncommon for fifty thousand people to get together in one large office building as part of a single organization.

The important point is that the dynamics which run our organizations have not naturally evolved in the same manner as group dynamics. Evolution hasn't had time to do anything in the ten thousand years since we started to establish organizations. Our intellects have created the need for organizations. The only way we can build enough cars and process enough insurance claims is with large organizations. But simply because we need them and have established thousands of them doesn't mean that they're supposed to run efficiently.

It's very dangerous to assume that the manner in which organizations function is designed or somehow preordained to work efficiently. Organizational dynamics are not wired in to anything. They simply happen as a result of many groups of groups having been thrown together. Most of what happens is counterproductive to getting work done efficiently, because organizations operate to smother opportunities for members to obtain satisfaction of their basic needs. If we want to make organizations as efficient as we require, we have to do a lot more than just let them operate on their own.

While organizational dynamics aren't natural in the same sense as group dynamics, they are more predictable. Groups can behave in markedly different ways, because one or two strong members and/or a unique working environment can dramatically alter the group's behaviors compared to another group in the same general situation. Organizations aren't as diverse as groups in their range of characteristics and operations. The influence of each group in an organization is moderated and counterbalanced by the actions of the other groups in the organization. The summary effect of many groups in concert almost always acts to even out the possible range of actions. Therefore, while organizations aren't natural social structures, they're quite predictable regarding how they evolve and operate.

Types of Organizations
What you need to know

Organizations are generally classified as being somewhere on a continuum which has *classical theory organizations (CTOs)* on one end and *nonclassical theory organizations (NTOs)* on the other. Don't let the word *theory* mislead you. There are no true theories about organizations, and the few that do exist aren't useful to people who are battling it out in the trenches of business. Most theories of organizations are merely descriptions of what goes on in various types of organizations.

CTOs are the organizations we most often think of when we think of business. They're characterized by a pyramid management structure which has one leader at the top and increasing numbers of managers at each descending level. Other characteristics include narrowly defined jobs, functionally defined departments (finance, maintenance, etc.), close supervision (each manager supervises a relatively small number of employees), and lots of controls, rules, and regulations. CTOs operate with the basic philosophy that employees don't like work, must be made to work, aren't capable of thinking creatively, and are only at work for the money. It's well established that as organizations embody more CTO characteristics, employees like their jobs less, feel as if they get less recognition, and feel more controlled.

The vast majority of business organizations are and have always been CTOs. It's the premise of *Millennium Management* that we now have to modify the underlying CTO philosophy that drives many of our day-to-day supervisory actions or we're doomed to continuing low productivity compared to what we've got to have.

At the other end of the continuum are the NTOs. These are characterized by few layers of management, many employees reporting to any one supervisor, broadly defined and continually changing job duties, project-oriented work groups, and an emphasis on employee involvement in decision making. The underlying philosophy behind NTOs is that employees want to do good work, need only direction rather than control, and can be responsible and creative if properly motivated. It's been repeatedly demonstrated that employees are happier and more productive as organizations enact more NTO practices. Unfortunately for the average employee, there aren't very many NTOs around. Think tanks, some research settings, and perhaps some smaller advertising or consulting concerns are about the only types of industries where NTOs can be found in any numbers.

The reason for the small number of NTOs is twofold. First, NTOs in their usual configuration aren't as efficient in producing large amounts of a product or in operating a continuous process (such as an assembly line) as are CTOs. If you're not going to go to a great deal of extra effort to carefully design a work environment with NTO characteristics, it's easier to let organizational dynamics take their course and create a CTO. In a CTO all you have to do is tell people what to do and where to go and then direct your energy at keeping them there and correcting mistakes.

The second reason for the small numbers of NTOs is more serious in its long-term impact on productivity: the attitude most managements have toward their people. The sad truth is that the majority of supervisors and managers in American industry (and everywhere else) are firm believers in the underlying philosophy of CTOs; they honestly believe (but don't publicly admit) that workers are basically lazy, stupid, uncreative louts who must be watched closely and firmly controlled. If not, why do many large office settings in industries such as insurance still use bells to tell people when to start working, when to stop working, when they may go to the bathroom, and so on? Why must middle managers making $50K per year get three signatures to approve a ten-dollar lunch expense? Why must a supervisor of forty assemblyline workers have to ask for permission to buy coffee and donuts for his or her weekly meeting with the troops? Don't tell yourself that these are all examples of necessary financial and management controls; they're not. They are merely manifestations of an attitude that says, "If we let them get away with one thing, just one little thing, they'll ruin our business. They just can't be trusted." We can no longer afford to think of our most valuable asset in this negative manner.

Implications

The simple truth is that if you demonstrate to your employees that you don't trust them and that you don't believe they want to do a quality job for you, they won't. The good employees will feel denigrated and insulted, and their work groups will have low morale and little self-respect. The poorer workers, in the absence of strong peer pressure to work and produce, will turn management's "can't trust them" attitude into a self-fulfilling prophecy; you'll get exactly what you expected. With our desperate need for better quality and higher productivity from every employee, I don't believe any organization can afford to send that message to its employees. If you're allowing your organization to function unchecked with the policies and procedures of a CTO, that's exactly what you're telling every employee every minute of every day of the year.

The key is to incorporate as many characteristics of NTOs into each section/department/group of your CTO as possible. The basic structure of a CTO is essential for running large organizations. There's no other efficient way to organize a lot of people to do very specific and complex things. Yet people are happier in NTOs because they more closely approximate a small-group environment and because they're provided with more avenues for developing self-respect and obtaining personal recognition. Through the correct type of communications practices and small-group supervisory techniques, it's possible to run a CTO which will be perceived to a certain extent as an NTO by the employees. That's the purpose of *Millennium Management* techniques. Obtain the best of both, the operational cost-efficiency of a CTO with the employee involvement of an NTO.

The Cycle of Organizational Growth
What you need to know

As they grow, organizations tend to move from the NTO end of the continuum to the CTO end. The reason is a direct result of group dynamics. When an organization is very small, perhaps ten to fifteen people, it's one large group rather than a group of groups. There may be subgroups, but it's easy for everyone in the organization to interact on a daily or hourly basis. This interaction serves many vital purposes. It enables the group leader to clearly and directly communicate the organization's goals to every employee. Better yet, the leader is actually present to display appropriate role model behaviors and to give firsthand positive reinforcement for performance. The most powerful influence is the fact that the group leader and the organization leader are one and the same. All of the group members know that they are in with the top man or woman and that they're important, valued members of the organization (or else they wouldn't be around as a drain on the young organization's resources).

As the organization begins to grow, it hires more people and begins to expand its quarters. It becomes a bona fide organization (a group of groups), and strange, not-so-good things begin to happen. All of a sudden, the organization's leader isn't the group leader for all employees. In fact, if the organization begins to expand quickly, the organization's leader soon functions as a group leader of only a very small and select group (the executives). When goals are passed along to the employees, they arrive by indirect means, filtered by several layers of management. Aside from the loss or distortion of information which this communication route causes, the urgency and personal nature of the information is gone because it's not perceived as vital to each small group's welfare. Pretty soon, there are separate departments for shipping, administration, personnel, sales, and production. Within each section or department, various subgroups spring up as the employees seek membership in groups which have some personal meaning to them and which will help them maintain their self-respect. In order to control all of these people and departments, the organization begins to institute rules and regulations to ensure that everyone's treated equal and that nobody gets away with anything. Pretty soon, what started out as a classic example of an NTO becomes a CTO. While this type of development is sad to witness if you've been in on the early stages of the organization's growth, it's a fact of organization development which almost always occurs.

Once an organization has reached a fairly stable size and structure, the actual growth in the number of its employees may slow down, but the organization doesn't stop evolving. Once the flush of growth has subsided, the curse of organizational middle age arrives: bureaucracy. As several recent presidents haven't understood, bureaucracy isn't the result of wanton waste and sloppy management by greedy politicians and inept middle managers (although those types don't help). Some degree of bureaucracy is a natural, normal condition for organizations, much like some degree of arteriosclerosis is to be expected when people age; it may not be healthy, but you expect to find some.

The Bureaucracy Wins Again, and Everyone Loses

I was working in a Fortune 20 organization where my colleagues and I in our plant location put together a proposal to get corporate funds of $20K for a small, do-something-nice-for-the-employees program, a health fair, at our facility. Nobody in the corporation had ever done one before. We wrote a proposal and submitted it. The fact that a facility producing over $700 million a year had to ask permission to spend $20 thousand says a lot by itself. After eight months of submitting endless revisions of the proposal and justifications, we were finally visited by a team of corporate representatives who told us that "the new guidelines" required us to complete sixteen different proposals in order to conduct the same type of health fair! Some of us even laughed out loud when they told us that. We were also told, however, that if we submitted the proposals, we could get a total of about $60K if we asked. Hell, the trip expenses for the visitors had to be $5K by itself. We let the idea die after that episode.

Personnel executive in a chemical processing plant

Bureaucracy occurs because groups and individuals, lost in the maze of sparse and secondhand information about the organization's goals and norms, and frustrated in their search for satisfaction, begin to pursue their own goals with their own norms. You begin to see empire building at the expense of the organization's profitability (although every step is always supported by arguments to the opposite effect). It may not even be conscious, greedy empire building. In many cases, the people involved actually think they're doing the best thing.

If you don't do anything aggressive about bureaucracy, it continues to develop as more and more groups and individuals begin to see that the best way to carve out a little bit of personal satisfaction and power is to fortify their own little corner of the organization. Anyone who can write a proposal can come up with countless reasons why even the most abhorrent bit of bureaucracy is absolutely necessary for increased productivity. In any organization, there are always enough foul-ups and mistakes to provide fodder for the bureaucracy builders. And in the typical organization, there's generally not enough opportunity to gain status and recognition by pursuing the goals that the organization must attain. The consequence is that groups and individuals who have the energy and ambition to get somewhere do the only thing that looks like it will bring recognition and feelings of accomplishment; they bite off a piece of the organization and build an empire.

Implications

Because organizations of any size (or complex/large-number production requirements) will always operate at the CTO end of the continuum, it's absolutely essential for you to manage your individual employees with as many NTO techniques as possible. Fortunately, employees give more weight to events that are closer to them in geographical and/or interpersonal terms. If you, as a supervisor, treat them in an NTO manner, they'll come to view the entire organization as being more of an NTO than a CTO. They'll not only work better for your group, but they'll be less frustrated by organizational practices and less likely to divert their energy to productivity-damaging informal goals. As a manager who may have influence over more comprehensive organizational communications and systems, you'll find that any efforts directed toward breaking down group jealousies and barriers will reap returns many times over.

Improved communication between all levels of personnel and departments or groups will help by substituting some portion of the organization's goals and norms for those of the various groups. This will serve to decrease the amount of conflict between groups and the organization as a whole. If you don't take action to move the norms of all of the people who work for you closer to your organization's goals, the bureaucracy will continue to thrive, driven by the misdirected energy of your most creative and talented people. Your employees don't have the resources to simultaneously protect themselves from the energy-draining exercises forced on them by the bureaucracy, to figure out what the organization wants, to try to meet their own group's norms, and at the same time to take care of the job.

Summary

This chapter has detailed the processes which operate to establish and maintain groups and organizations. You've got your hands full if you attempt to tame these forces to work for you rather than against you. The organizational dynamics, if left to follow their natural path, will work against productivity every second. If you can afford this liability, you're one of the few lucky ones.

If you decide you've got to have every last bit of productivity from your group, section, department, or organization, you can bend organizational dynamics to your will. They're not immune from control efforts. By applying the correct set of techniques, you can turn a surprising amount of their power in your favor. Harnessing organizational dynamics, even to a limited extent, will yield benefits which will startle and amaze you. Your employees, whether you're supervising a few line personnel or an entire Fortune 500 company, will work harder, waste less effort, be more productive, and like their jobs more. You'll have the ultimate satisfaction of knowing that you did something few leaders have the guts or the intelligence to accomplish. You will have tapped the last great resource of productivity available for your organization.

CHAPTER 4

Millennium Management: What It Is and How It Works

This chapter will explain the operational approach of *Millennium Management* and how that approach will be presented in the remainder of this book. We'll also explore some related issues such as the relationship between so-called Japanese management and the strategy and techniques advocated by *Millennium Management*.

The Importance of Perceptions

Before we discuss how *Millennium Management* works, let's talk for a moment about perceptions, those of managers and those of employees. Throughout this book, you must understand one point very clearly: your perceptions as a manager or supervisor of what your employees think or want doesn't matter. It's irrelevant if you think all the employees love their jobs and it's not important to them if you think you're giving them all lots of feedback and praise. Your perceptions don't matter. The only perceptions that are important for productivity are the employees' perceptions. If the employees perceive that they're not being treated fairly or aren't being included in the decision making, it's immaterial whether the supervisor thinks they're all one big happy family. If the employees' perceptions are unfavorable, regardless of the reality, you're going to have problems, and you're not going to get the productivity you need. This is a critical point for two reasons.

First of all, it's a given that managers and supervisors assume they're doing better than they actually are. If you ask even the most abusive, restrictive, and interpersonally unskilled supervisor how good he or she is on a scale of 1 to 20, you never get an answer lower than 10 or 12. Because they've had the job for a while, haven't been fired, and probably haven't ever been corrected in regard to their poor supervisory technique, they think they're doing great. Yet, if you were to ask for ratings from the employees who work for the same supervisor, you'd get laughs and sneers, and 4's to 6's, if not 1's and 2's, on the 20-point scale. I've worked with supervisors who, when faced with overwhelmingly bad survey results from all of their employees to such questions as "How much confidence and trust do you have in your supervisor?" (see appendix A for this survey instrument and directions on its use), argued that the abysmally low average answer was due to a boss the employees had ten years earlier. In the absence of (and even sometimes in spite of) objective analyses of their performance, supervisors almost universally rate themselves better than they are. And since most organizations are opposed to objective attitude surveys of employees, management and supervisors are seldom faced with the cold, hard, unadorned truth about their effectiveness.

This self-deceit is critical because, operating as it does on all levels, it enables management to talk itself into thinking that any problems must be the fault of employees. Managers reason, "Who else could be at fault if all of us great people have been to countless management seminars and are now being participative, understanding, enlightened leaders? If we enlightened, informed leaders can't get results out of the employees, it must be because they're just lazy and unmotivated." I've encountered this attitude in countless companies. Know it and believe it: every management team in the world paints a more attractive picture of itself than reality supports. Corporate presidents and line supervisors are no different. In fact, the self-deceit gets worse as you go up the ladder, because there are fewer and fewer people who are willing to put their careers on the line by suggesting that things aren't great. Top management always has a much more favorable picture of the organization than is actually the case.

The second vital point about perceptions is more subtle: management must concern itself not with the actions they're taking or how the employees ought to react but with the employees' perceptions of what's going on. In other words, it's not as important to deal with the reality of the situation as it is to focus on the perceptions the employees have of that reality. If your employees have negative perceptions of a good situation, you're in trouble even if you're doing a lot of the right things. All too often management starts out by trying to change employees' perceptions of supervision and the organization but gets frustrated when progress is slow or problems arise. Then they stop focusing on changing the employees' perceptions and return to operating according to their estimate of how the employees ought to feel. Once they return to worrying about their interpretations of the situation rather than employees' perceptions, they're in trouble.

You must accept your employees' perceptions as the issue to be dealt with, regardless of how you view the situation and irrespective of the "rightness" of what you're already doing. For example, take the subject of work pressure. I recently conducted a series of interviews in a large manufacturing facility. Almost without exception, every department and section perceived tremendous work pressure. This led to tremendous resistance whenever it was necessary to reassign workloads or add new work elements. The employees perceived that they were already working at a fever pitch. This perception (measured by surveys) was shared by executives, middle management, line supervision, and hourly employees. Yet you could walk around any department almost anytime and find people wandering around, visiting, discussing sports in small groups, even reading newspapers and doing crossword puzzles on the manufacturing floor between units coming down the assembly line. The reality was that the actual work pressure wasn't high (compared to many other work environments). However, the employees perceived it as high for a number of valid reasons. They perceived that they had no autonomy, no participation in decision making; they perceived little innovation; and they perceived that they had little or no supervisor support. In that situation, every single management action was perceived to be a request for more work. The result was that employees felt overworked, believed they were overworked, and weren't going to gracefully or enthusiastically accept more of anything. In fact, the problem was management's inability or unwillingness to permit real participation and involvement by most employees. In that facility, to improve the situation, it would make no sense and do no good to attempt to convince the employees that the work pressure wasn't high. They perceived it as high, and that's the reality you'd have to deal with; their perceptions determine what they're willing to do and how they'll interpret everything you do.

A final point about perceptions will help you understand why *Millennium Management* techniques place a great deal of emphasis on communication and information transmission to and from employees. Perceptions are heavily influenced by an individual's assessment of a situation's significance to his or her interests. If something looks like there's something in it for us, we tend to look upon it more favorably. A vital part of leading employees to this favorable impression is to provide them with information which makes them feel as if they are part of a larger group than their work group. Limited information results in limited, self-centered, narrow, and restrictive perceptions about what's in a particular person's own self-interests. Increased information, even without any editing or slanting, results in more of a group-oriented, less self-centered appraisal of "good." It's this "we are a group" perception that's so critical to providing an environment conducive to productivity. The smooth communication of lots of information is critical to influencing perceptions in a positive manner.

Between a Rock and a Hard Place

Managers and supervisors in Western countries face a dilemma when they attempt to lead their organizations. The culture of Western civilization emphasizes independence and creativity. The role of the individual in shaping events is a central theme touted in movies, literature, and business itself (e.g., stories about self-made millionaires, crucial last-minute decisions which form empires, etc.). Each and every low-level employee, middle manager, executive, housewife, and student is constantly barraged with cultural messages which proclaim the value and nobility of independent thought and action. Individual initiative and struggle against restraint are seen as the ideals. You might well say that such cultural norms provide the foundation for Western society itself. *Millennium Management* techniques tap this cultural resource by enabling supervisors and managers to function as truly effective leaders of employees who already possess these underlying norms.

Yet, as we've seen in the last two chapters, most business organizations are structured and led in a manner which directly conflicts with this powerful and pervasive belief in the nobility of individual effort and responsibility. Consider the situation in the typical organization. Management makes all the decisions; employees are forever reminded, by every little control and regulation, that they're not trusted; and every action they take must be approved by at least three levels of management. It doesn't stop there. As they struggle to protect their empires, even senior managers are perceived as paper shufflers who refuse to stand up for anything, middle managers are typically told how to do their jobs, and employees at lower levels are viewed as mindless automatons and treated accordingly. The entire structure of the organization and the resulting style of leadership at all levels operate according to parameters which are absolutely contrary to the cultural norms of Western society and its heroes. And you expect your employees to work with fervor in such an environment? No way!

As we've seen, employees who are controlled and frustrated by management, the bureaucracy, and unskilled supervisors have no stake in making the organization work. (Survey results such as those in chapter 2 don't come from happy, involved workers.) They believe the system is deliberately frustrating the individual creativity and personal initiative they've been brought up to believe in and which they accept as the way it should be. Any management system, any type of leadership style, or any type of corporate culture program which doesn't actively accept and nurture the Western world's value of individual initiative isn't going to be more effective than the mediocre results we've gotten so far. Without such an orientation, any culture goes directly contrary to the basic cultural norms of Western society and can't possibly be effective in inspiring the employees with creativity and initiative. The only leadership style and corporate culture which will allow for superior results in Western nations, particularly in the United States, are ones which emphasize personal creativity and initiative. *Millennium Management* does this by giving employees more of what they've been raised to expect and want in a work environment.

"Japanese" Management

There's a lot of talk these days about Japanese culture and its superiority to ours in certain areas, particularly in business. There's a lot of faddish cultism here, as well as a fair amount of whitewash about some of the more unsavory elements of the Japanese system. In reality, there are statistically very few Japanese companies which operate as we've been led to believe by the media and Japanese PR types. For every Toyota and Mitsubishi there are hundreds of sweat shops where the employees are treated in ways which would violate our laws. Much of the ""Japanese advantage" is built on the backs of poorly paid workers. And even in the successful companies where employees are decently paid and treated with respect, there are unattractive mechanisms at work, such as the pressures brought to bear on dissenters by shop stewards, the company, and colleagues. That pressure to conform and the reason it works are the "strength" of Japanese management where it's actually practiced. This strength is considerably different in character from the inherent strength of Western culture's individuality and initiative.

The Japanese culture emphasizes the value of the group over the individual. There are exceptions, but the welfare of the group, its safety, and the primacy of society over the individual are the basic norms. This isn't something that's shouted from the rooftops, but it's a pervasive element of many Far Eastern cultures, and it affects almost every aspect of their societies. It is established powerfully and consistently that personal advancement and initiative are laudable values but that first, before the individual, comes the welfare of the group. Displays of personal daring and courage are held in high esteem in Japan, but not for the same reasons as we favor them. Our typical hero, in fantasies and in the media, stands alone, protecting his or her values. The typical Japanese hero stands up to protect the welfare of the group as a whole.

This "group first" norm has been consistently inoculated into every aspect of Japanese society for many hundreds of years. Right from the first day a new business in Japan opens its doors, it has an innate advantage over an American counterpart. There is much less conflict between the cultural values the average Japanese employee learns as a child and the cultural norms he or she encounters in the work organization. The structure of the typical classical theory organization (CTO) requires every individual to make many sacrifices of individual achievement and impulse so that the organization's norms and regulations will operate effectively. The typical Japanese worker is more inclined to make these sacrifices; he or she isn't quite as frustrated as the typical American employee. The result is less friction between individual employees and management, fewer misinterpreted communications between groups of workers, and the improved morale of working in a system which everyone values and understands. The workers still want the same things that all workers want (recognition, sense of achievement, and so on), but they perceive that they can earn rewards more quickly by first making the sacrifices that working in a large organization requires. Westerners, brought up on a diet of stand tall, do it on your own, don't take any stuff, and John Wayne and Clint Eastwood movies, are faced with much more of a conflict between their personal norms and those of the typical organization. Instead of working alone, everything is done in groups, it's hard to assign responsibility for successes and failures, and employees are treated like children. This results in the formation of the unfavorable informal norms and goals we discussed in chapter 3.

That's why so-called Japanese management works so well in Japan. When it's tried in this country, with American employees, it can't work as well as it does in Japan because we don't share the cultural norms which the Japanese grow up with. But it does work much better than our typical approach. Strangely enough, it works well for the same reasons that *Millennium Management* works: it presents the employees with an extremely consistent and homogeneous set of work norms which all levels of management and supervision continually reinforce. The Japanese system works here not because it's innately superior but simply because every aspect of the organization focuses its energy to ensure that all employees clearly understand every nuance of the organization's norms and goals.

If an American organization were to implement an entire spectrum of *Millennium Management* practices, it would have a considerable advantage over anything the Japanese, or anyone else, could produce. Our cultural norms for valuing individuality and taking initiative are a powerful force. That force is just what we need to unleash in our organizations. We're not getting anywhere now because we allow normal organizational dynamics to run their typical course and frustrate our employees' best qualities. At the same time, we often permit the situation to further frustrate the best of what our employees could give us by adding additional regulations and allowing bureaucracy to run wild. If, on the other hand, an organization were to work hard at sending strong, clear signals to every employee about the ways in which initiative would earn rewards, and provide good one-to-one supervision at the same time, that organization would set free a pent-up tide of productivity which would be awesome to behold. The organization would be setting up conditions which would capitalize on the strong cultural norms with which we've all grown up. That's what *Millennium Management* does.

Millennium Management Isn't an Easy Way Out

As you've seen in the first three chapters, the factors which motivate employees and the processes that operate in organizations and groups aren't any different now from what they've ever been. And they're not apt to change much in the next thousand years. If you don't accept this point, you'll be afraid to face the truth: getting more productivity from your employees is going to be hard work, perhaps the hardest you've ever done. There are no magic palliatives or secret tricks to improving productivity. If you think there's a new way or a new management technique that will pull your fat out of the fire without hard work, you'll be inclined to talk yourself out of trying *Millennium Management* techniques. Think of all the fads and gimmicks that have come and gone in every place you've worked. Did any of these programs really do much? There have never been easy, convenient ways to improve productivity or motivate employees. Most so-called new theories or approaches to productivity or motivation are simply new jargon or a simplistic rehashing of one limited technique or another.

Millennium Management does not pretend to be a new or revolutionary theory or approach to management. The things which make people and organizations work effectively have never changed. What you've got to do to get more out of your employees is deal with the issues and factors discussed in the

---

What's Next?

Frankly, sometimes I get a little discouraged. This organization has tried everything, with a capital E, to get some spirit into the workforce and increase productivity. We've tried everything. Some of it's been pretty ridiculous although it seemed to be the thing to do at the time. We've bought so many programs that our managers laugh when another one's introduced; they know it's just another four-day wonder. We've tried almost anything. We sent twenty of our top people to a wilderness camp so they could learn to depend on each other by climbing trees and crossing rivers. Yet the employees, and the supervisor too for that matter, don't do anything differently. I don't know, sometimes I think we're all so frustrated that we'll try anything so we can convince ourselves we're working on it. Every time I see a consultant come out of the president's office, I worry that we've just bought another one.

Executive VP of a utility company

---

earlier chapters. *Millennium Management* is a comprehensive presentation of strategies and techniques for dealing systematically and aggressively with every possible factor which can be influenced to improve productivity in an organization. I'm going to show you how to put together a set of mutually supportive strategies and techniques of supervision and organizational manipulation which will make you (and your organization, if it wants to go along) a winner.

The key to successful productivity is to implement as many *Millennium Management* techniques as possible, given your level of influence. Some of the techniques will appear obvious. Remember, I'm not trying to sell you a new theory. Every one of these techniques works. What I am trying to sell is an appreciation that maximum productivity requires a comprehensive and systematic application of techniques which address the entire spectrum of supervisory and organizational leadership.

The Two Main Thrusts of Millennium Management

In order to maximize productivity, you've got to aggressively direct your efforts at two principal targets: the supervisor-employee interface and the leadership component of organizational dynamics.

The Supervisor-Employee Interface

The supervisor-employee interface consists of all of the one-to-one interactions and communications between a boss and his or her direct subordinates.

In terms of increasing productivity, supervisors are the most powerful influence in every organization. A poor supervisor can quickly turn a group of good employees into a rabble of grousing, bitter malcontents. A good supervisor, even in an oppressive environment, can motivate his or her employee to do outstanding work. Yet the entire spectrum of supervisor-employee interactions gets less attention than any other aspect of business. There are endless seminars about quality, company culture, executive stress, and technical skills, but there's hardly ever any significant attention focused on helping supervisors do their jobs better. Sure, there's training going on, but the majority of it concentrates on telling supervisors what they should be doing and then sending them back to the job to try and do it by themselves. Nobody ever observes them or gives them guidance or feedback on their performance in satisfying their employees' needs for recognition, achievement, information, and so on. (We'll discuss the limitations of typical training programs in chapter 9.) Most supervisors are assumed to be doing a good job if they can get the day's work done and account for all of their people. As you saw in chapter 2, that type of impoverished approach can't do much for real productivity gains. Most supervisors don't have bosses who could give them such feedback on their performance even if the boss was willing to spend the time; most bosses haven't had any in-depth instruction themselves about how to properly supervise employees. The subject of how to effectively motivate, relate to, communicate with, and direct subordinates is not taught in business schools, and it's not something that companies make a sincere effort to teach their supervisors. They introduce them to the topic, but after that it's every abusive and/or withdrawn supervisor for himself or herself.

It's been difficult for organizations to deal with this type of problem because they haven't understood its significance to productivity. Supervisors themselves, and the supervisory function itself, at every level, have always been the unglamorous stepchildren of business. To be brutally frank, most organizations consider their first-line supervisors to be nothing but slightly better-behaved rank and file, sort of members of management but not considered part of the management team. At the same time, the workers themselves are typically viewed as little better than an unclean caste by management who contend, "They're paid to work, so why should we have to coddle them to get work out of them?" It's not popular these days to admit this belief, but I've been hearing it from numerous managers at all levels in every size of organization from Fortune 10 to five-person companies. It's merely one of the countless instances in which different group norms lead to negative views of other groups. Given this attitude, is it any wonder that little significance is accorded to the supervisory-skills aspect of management?

Even if organizations believed that employees were worth good supervision, there's reason to believe that there would be very little emphasis placed on providing employees with the factors reviewed in chapter 2. To most managers, supervisory skills are considered common and almost natural. Entry-level management types are presumed to be professional supervisors when they're hired. They might be perceived to be a little green and in need of seasoning, but they're presumed to already know the basics of how to supervise and motivate employees. This situation is analogous to that of pre-twentieth-century armies in which gentlemen and nobles were automatically assigned officers' rank because they were presumed to know how to lead. Military history books are packed with examples which demonstrate the disastrous consequences of that type of assumption. Just where those gentlemen of yesterday and today's supervisors are supposed to have received leadership training, including instruction in proper supervisory techniques, isn't clear.

Because it's easier to hope it's been taken care of by someone else, or to assume that any sharp young tiger inherently knows how to supervise, the techniques and skills of effective one-to-one and small group supervision have been woefully ignored. The employees' crisis of confidence in their supervision, tracked by survey after survey, is built on this neglect.

Chapter 5 will present, in detail, the techniques which are absolutely essential to effective one-to-one and small group supervision. These are the hands-on techniques and behaviors which will enable a supervisor at any level to give each employee more of the recognition, satisfaction, and achievement that they want out of their jobs. At the same time, these techniques will enable the supervisor to more consistently influence the work group's norms and goals so that they're more in line with those of the organization than those of the informal group.

The Leadership Component of Organizational Dynamics

The leadership component of organizational dynamics is the process by which organizational leaders (at any level) attempt to infuse the entire organization with spirit or galvanize them into action. Most efforts to change company culture allude to this process. Organizational leadership is the influencing of work-group norms and goals by a manager who is not the actual supervisor of the work groups at that level. In other words, it's a process by which a non-group leader attempts to exert influence as a leader through means other than one-to-one supervision and direction. Let's refer to this process as norm and/or goal inoculation. In effect, the organizational leader inoculates his or her norms and goals into each work group and hopes that they influence each small group's values to line up more closely with those of the overall organization. To the extent that the small group's goals and norms (and role definitions too, for that matter), come into line with those of an overall department or the entire organization, there's less conflict, less wasted energy, and fewer miscommunications.

Organizational leadership isn't limited to the organization's de facto leaders. For example, take a department manager with three section heads who do the actual supervision of the employees. Since this manager isn't the actual leader of any of the employee groups, he or she must use inoculation techniques if the department organization is to be maximally effective. It's not enough for this manager to simply supervise the section heads and hope that things will work out. Even when positioned only one level of supervision above the employees themselves, there's too much opportunity for goals and norms, not to mention operational information itself, to become distorted. Even if the supervisors themselves are outstanding in providing for the needs discussed in chapter 2, it's critical that the department manager work hard at norm and goal inoculation. Otherwise, the employees will begin to perceive their individual section goals as being distinct from those of the department itself, and they'll come to view the pronouncements of the department head as official fluff rather than vital goal and norm information. Remember, in the absence of information about what's going on, employees will make assumptions which are unfavorable. The organization leadership's use of inoculation techniques minimizes these damaging effects.

As the organizational leader becomes further separated from the employees by intervening levels of managers and supervisors, it becomes increasingly difficult to practice effective norm and goal inoculation without taking special steps. There are too many opportunities for distortion as the message moves down the command chain. Unfortunately, this type of long-distance inoculation process is the most important in a large organization. The fact is that the organization's top leaders have the clearest picture of where the organization is going and how they'd like to get there. If this picture is accurately and consistently communicated to all the employees, there's less occasion and less reason for informal goals and norms to develop. What happens in the typical organization is that there's no effective inoculation going on, and the crystal-clear message that started out from the head shed arrives at the lower levels in a form which even the executive who originated it wouldn't recognize. Through a variety of *Millennium Management* techniques, it's possible for an organization's leader to inoculate his or her message into the organization so that when a message arrives, each employee interprets it by means of norms and goals which are closely related to those which the leader supports.

Most organizations fail in their attempts at norm and goal inoculation because they make only halfhearted attempts. As the distance (in terms of management levels) between the would-be message-sending manager and the employees increases, it's essential to increase proportionately the number of inoculation channels used and the strength of the signal sent on each. For example, one of the *Millennium Management* inoculation techniques is the executive press conference. In a small organization of 100 to 150 employees, an executive might attain sufficient norm inoculation by holding a press conference every few months, coupled with lots of in-person visibility. Any one of a number of inoculation techniques might be substituted for the press conference and yield effective results. In an organization of 2,500 employees, on the other hand, the top executive would almost certainly have to employ simultaneously a wide variety of *Millennium Management* inoculation techniques. A coordinated effort involving luncheons, press conferences, in-person visits, strike forces, and so on, would be necessary to overcome the organizational distance. Few executives, on their own, realize the importance of this inoculation process, and most therefore don't do anywhere near enough.

More damaging yet, these executives assume that their subordinates are taking care of events in their own organizations. Typically, they aren't doing anything more than managing the day-to-day operations, leaving the organization dynamics to flow where they may. In a large organization, every manager must practice inoculation techniques of his or her own, so that the lower-level employees receive a consistent message from at least two sources: the organization leader and the supervisor. When a truly effective effort at norm inoculation is underway, the inoculation process is performed by each successive layer of management so that the signals perceived by the employees are strong, numerous, and consistent with those that started out at the top of the organization. This ideal situation is a reasonable goal for any company, but few have the will to pursue it.

Chapter 6 presents the mechanics of *Millennium Management* planning, which involves all employees in every aspect of the organization's goal-setting process. Chapter 7 outlines a variety of techniques for using the organization's vast array of formal rituals, communication channels, and ceremonies to send strong norm inoculation signals to every corner of the organization. Chapter 8 outlines the basic requirements of a compensation and performance appraisal process that will reinforce all of the norms for individual effort and initiative which all of us were raised to value. Chapter 9 describes how training efforts can best be designed to support norm inoculation efforts and supervisory skills building. Finally, chapter 10 tells you how to put it all together and get to work.

Each of the norm inoculation techniques requires a great deal of effective one-to-one supervisory work at all levels. The planning process techniques, as well as many other programs and strategies of norm inoculation, are not presented as an element of supervisory techniques, because such inoculation processes must generally be approved and initiated by higher-level managers. Every supervisor, at every level, must perform the functions outlined in chapter 5 if he or she is to be effective. At the same time, an individual supervisor's application of specific techniques from chapters 6 through 10 will depend on his or her special situation.

CHAPTER 5

The Role and Behavior of a Millennium Manager as Supervisor

The supervisor is the most influential figure in the life of an employee. If a supervisor provides an employee with the opportunity to earn as much satisfaction as possible from the job, the employee will work productively even if the overall environment is unfavorable. The best results are obtained if the supervisor and the organization are simultaneously practicing effective *Millennium Management* techniques. If the organization is practicing effective norm and goal inoculation techniques, an effective supervisor will discover that his or her efforts will create faster and more profound results. The supervisor won't have to fight for every small gain of commitment from the employees. Conversely, if a supervisor is aggressively implementing proper supervisory techniques, the organization's norm inoculation efforts will be more accurately and quickly interpreted by the employees and more enthusiastically pursued.

Both main thrusts of *Millennium Management*—one-to-one supervisory techniques and norm and goal inoculation techniques—must support each other if an organization is to obtain maximum productivity from its employees. The organization must make it easier for the supervisor to be effective by implementing many of the programs and techniques we'll discuss in later chapters. And the supervisor must use the incredibly powerful influence of a small-group leader to serve as the last booster station for the messages which are sent down the line by the organizational leadership. The payoff for the supervisor is that the clear messages from the top of the organization will also enhance the effectiveness of the supervisor's one-to-one relationships with his or her subordinates. If a supervisor performs these two functions, the employees will be getting more of what they want, they'll know where it's all going, they'll view the supervisor as a trusted small-group leader, and they'll produce.

What Is Supervision?

Insofar as *Millennium Management* is concerned with people skills and employee motivation rather than technical skills such as financial forecasts and facilities planning, I'll be making the assumption that your organization possesses an acceptable level of technical expertise in its field. Technical skills aren't usually the problem. The reason employees aren't giving enough productivity is not because organizations don't have adequate technical skills; our employees aren't doing as well as we require because we're not supervising them and communicating with them in an effective manner. This chapter is going to focus exclusively on supervision as the interpersonal behavior interface between supervisor and employee. This interface consists of the behaviors which supervisors perform in order to obtain work from subordinates. Clearly, many supervisors have a lot of their own work to do in addition to managing their subordinates. There are few supervisors, especially in office environments, whose duties don't include report generation, analyses, committee work, and the like. Let's define these non-subordinate management tasks as technical and administrative duties. I'm going to assume that supervisors can adequately perform their technical and administrative tasks; we've got bigger and more important fish to fry.

Who Motivates Whom?

Before we delve into the techniques which comprise effective supervision, let's deal with the issue of where motivation comes from. A statement you hear often these days is, "You can't motivate employees; they have to motivate themselves." Like most dangerous information, this expression has just enough truth in it to be dangerous. It's popular with management because it puts the onus for lack of motivation on the employees rather than where it belongs: on management. After all, as one manager told me, "If the employees aren't as productive as we'd like, it must be their fault, because employees have to motivate themselves. What can I do? If only we had better people."

The kernel of truth that makes this observation dangerous is that any conscious behavior is self-initiated by an individual; there are few things anyone can make us do unless they threaten us with bodily harm. Most of what we do, even if we don't like it, we do consciously and deliberately. In that sense, it's correct to say that employees motivate themselves. Yet, in the real world, things aren't that simple. If you starve a person for five days and then place them in front of a smorgasbord of gourmet food, can you honestly claim that you didn't make them eat? Maybe someone who's on a diet or has incredible willpower could resist the food. Most people would stuff themselves. You wouldn't have made them eat, but you'd have set up such a favorable set of circumstances that the overwhelming majority of people would dig in. In practical terms, you made them eat.

The situation with regard to motivation to be productive is not different. Just as most starving people would dive into the smorgasbord, so too will most employees respond to proper motivational cues in the work environment. The overwhelming majority of employees have psychological and social needs which are even more powerful than hunger (if they're not starving). (Remember Maslow's hierarchy—you only pursue the higher levels if the lower needs have been fulfilled.) Just as it's natural for people to eat if they're hungry, it's even more natural for them to do better work if the work environment satisfies their job-related needs. These needs were discussed in chapter 2 and are the very same needs that supervisors weren't able to rank accurately. If you provide a working environment and a supervisory style which provide for at least some satisfaction of employees' work-related needs for achievement, recognition, and so on, the employees will respond by working harder and better. You will have made them work harder; in effect, you motivated them.

If, on the other hand, your organization and your supervisory approach do not provide for the basic needs of employees, you can't expect the employees to motivate themselves. Why should they work for something they believe they're not going to get? Don't contend that you don't motivate employees. You, as a manager or supervisor, have incredible power to motivate increased productivity from employees.

The Ten Basic Functions of Supervision

There are ten basic management functions which a supervisor must perform in order to get maximum productivity from his or her employees:

1. Coaching
2. Encouraging joint goal setting
3. Providing feedback
4. Providing personal recognition

5. Encouraging joint decision making
6. Conducting participatory problem solving
7. Encouraging individual development
8. Providing appropriate training
9. Conducting group maintenance activities
10. Providing unconditional support

These ten functions comprise the main operational activities of a supervisor who is attempting to get the most out of his or her employees. While each is operationally distinct in terms of what it looks like in action, they are not completely independent factors. For example, an effective coaching session involves elements of both feedback and personal recognition.

It's important to understand the relationship between the ten basic functions and the perceived needs of employees. In chapter 2, we saw that employees rank their perceived needs in the following descending order:

1. Feeling of accomplishment
2. Personal recognition
3. Leadership
4. Proper direction and training
5. Knowledge of what is expected
6. Fair and tactful discipline
7. Feeling involved
8. Interesting work

These are the first eight of the fifteen ranked factors; they are the satisfiers (in Herzberg's theory) which employees perceive that they're lacking. The other items were dissatisfiers which aren't in short supply in most American organizations.

The relationship between the ten *Millennium Management* supervisory functions and the eight satisfiers ranked highest by employees in chapter 2 provides the basis for a great deal of insight into the proper allocation of effort by a supervisor. Figure 5.1 displays this relationship.

The righthand side of Figure 5.1 presents the ten *Millennium Management* supervisory functions. The eight top-ranked job satisfaction factors which were presented in Figure 2.2 and listed above are displayed along the top. The numbers 1 to 8 above the satisfaction factors are the employee rankings of the factors (with 1 being the most important). The relationship between the two sets of variables is demonstrated by the ratings in the body of the table.

Each of the ten supervisory functions is rated as 0, 1, 2, or 3 on each of the satisfactions factors. If the supervisory function is directly and intimately involved in meeting employee needs for the satisfaction factor, it's given a 3.

| | 1 | 2 | 3 | 4 | 5 | 6 | 7 | 8 | |
	Accomplishment	Personal recognition	Leadership	Direction & training	Knowledge of expected	Discipline	Involvement	Interesting work	Totals
1. Coaching	1	2	2	3	3	3	3	1	18
2. Goal setting	2	0	3	1	3	0	3	2	14
3. Feedback	1	1	3	2	2	2	1	0	12
4. Recognition	2	3	2	0	0	0	3	1	11
5. Decision making	2	1	1	0	2	0	3	2	11
6. Problem solving	3	1	1	0	0	0	3	2	10
7. Individual development	1	2	2	2	0	0	1	2	10
8. Training	1	1	1	3	0	0	1	1	8
9. Group maintenance	0	0	3	0	1	0	1	1	6
10. Support	0	1	3	0	0	0	1	0	5
							Grand Total		105

Figure 5.1   The Ten Supervisory Functions and Their Relationship to Employees' Top-Ranked Job Satisfaction Factors

Thus, "providing coaching" is rated a 3 on job satisfaction factors 4 through 7. The behaviors required to provide coaching to employees is intimately and primarily involved with influencing employee perceptions that they're receiving proper direction and training, knowledge of what is expected, fair and tactful discipline, and feeling involved.

A supervisory function is rated a 2 if it is very important to the employees' perception of the job satisfaction factor but is not its central and primary component. Thus, the coaching function is rated a 2 on both the "personal recognition" and the "leadership" satisfaction factors. A supervisor's coaching behaviors will strongly influence a subordinate's perception that he or she is being personally recognized and his or her views of the supervisor as a leader but not as strongly as satisfaction factors 4 through 7.

A 1 rating is assigned if the supervisory function is involved, but not critically, in influencing employees' perceptions of a particular job satisfaction factor. The coaching function was given a 1 on both the "feelings of achievement" and the "interesting job" satisfaction factors, because coaching influences employees' perceptions of these satisfactions but not dramatically.

A 0 is assigned if the supervisory function is comparatively unimportant in influencing employees' perceptions of a satisfaction factor's fulfillment. For example, the supervisory function "encouraging joint goal setting" is rated 0 on the satisfaction factors of "personal recognition" and "fair and tactful discipline" because goal setting has little influence on employees' perceptions of these two satisfaction factors in comparison to the other supervisory functions. Keep the words *in comparison* in mind; these rankings are relative to each other. To some extent, each is related to the others to some degree, and they're all important.

The totals in the righthand column of Figure 5.1 are ratings of the comparative importance of the supervisory functions in providing employees with fulfillment of the eight satisfaction factors. The bottom righthand box presents the grand total weight or score of all ratings on all employee satisfaction factors.

Providing coaching clearly emerges as the most critical supervisory function, with a total score of 18. Proper performance of the coaching function contributes significantly to each of the eight satisfaction factors. This makes intuitive sense in that coaching procedures provide opportunities for doing so many good things with subordinates. While coaching, the group leader is in a one-to-one situation with the employee, is giving feedback, is demonstrating that he or she is the leader, is giving the employee specific and special attention, and is providing the employee with an opportunity to participate in negotiations of future behaviors.

Encouraging joint goal setting ranks second, with a total score of 14, primarily on the strength of its three ratings on the "leadership," "knowledge of what is expected," and "feeling involve" satisfaction factors.

The last of the top three supervisory functions is providing feedback, which rated 12 points. While feedback is an essential element of every supervisor-subordinate exchange, there are a number of distinct feedback behaviors that constitute this specific supervisory function.

The "big three" supervisory functions account for about 42 percent of the total ratings of all supervisory functions.

The next four supervisory functions fall in a group with ratings of 10 or 11 points. Providing feedback, providing personal recognition, encouraging joint decision making, and conducting participatory problem solving provide significant fulfillment of particular satisfaction factors but don't each deal with as broad a range of the satisfaction factors as did the top three. As a group, these four account for 40 percent of total ratings, just a little less than the total influence of the big three.

The last three supervisory functions—providing appropriate training, conducting group maintenance activities, and providing unconditional support— are the specialized functions. Their ratings are comparatively low, but not because they're unimportant. As a group they account for 18 percent of the total ratings. These last functions of a supervisor pick up the loose ends which the first seven functions don't catch. They also define highly specialized supervisory behaviors which, like the spices in a stew, may not be large in quantity but are important for overall balance.

The ratings of the supervisory functions in Figure 5.1 provide a convenient means of determining how much supervisory effort should be devoted to each function. All other things being equal, more important functions should be given more attention. The relative importance of each function can be determined by adding its points across all satisfaction factors and dividing this total by the grand total of 105 which is shown in the lower righthand corner of Figure 5.1.

Figure 5.2 presents the results of such an analysis for each of the supervisory functions. The second column, entitled "Function %" displays the comparative importance of each supervisory function. For example, the 17 percent shown for coaching was obtained from Figure 5.1 by dividing its total of 18 points across all satisfaction factors by the grand total 105 points. This calculation was made for each function. All entries in Figure 5.2 and later figures are rounded off to the nearest whole number (some column and row totals may be off by 1 or 2 as a result). Figure 5.2 is based upon a 40-hour work week. The top heading displays the various percentages of a supervisor's work week which might be devoted to subordinate management duties. The body of Figure 5.2 presents the number of minutes which a supervisor should devote to each supervisory function.

For example, if a supervisor spends 50 percent of his or her time on subordinate management tasks (with the other 50 percent being spent on technical and/or administrative duties), Figure 5.2 suggests that a total of 206

Functions	Function %	Percentage of 40-Hour Work Week Dedicated to Supervision							
		10	20	40	50	60	80	90	100
1. Coaching	17	41	82	165	206	247	329	370	411
2. Goal setting	13	32	64	128	160	192	256	288	320
3. Feedback	11	27	55	110	137	165	219	247	274
4. Recognition	10	25	50	101	126	151	210	226	252
5. Decision making	10	25	50	101	126	151	210	226	252
6. Problem solving	9	23	46	91	114	137	183	206	228
7. Individual development	9	23	46	91	114	137	183	206	228
8. Training	8	18	37	73	91	110	146	164	183
9. Group maintenance	6	14	27	55	69	82	110	123	137
10. Support	5	11	23	46	57	68	92	104	115
Supervisory Time (Min)		240	480	960	1200	1440	1920	2160	2400

Figure 5.2   Recommended Allocation of Total Time (minutes) Per Supervisory Function For Various Percentages of a 40-Hour Work Week Devoted to Supervision Duties

minutes per week should be devoted to coaching, 160 minutes to goal setting, and so on down to a suggested 57 minutes for providing support.

This means that with 50 percent supervisory time, the supervisor would be required to spread the 206 minutes of coaching with all employees. For ten employees, the 206 minutes would allow just over 20 minutes per week per employee for coaching.

There are several startling implications which should be obvious to every reader after even the most cursory glance at Figure 5.2. The first is that few, if any of us, are receiving the type of supervisory support which Figure 5.2 suggests. The second is that few of us are giving that type of support to our subordinates. Remember, when we talk of supervision, we mean boss-subordinate relations at all levels, not just on the shop floor. In order for each of us to perceive that we're receiving satisfaction on all of the top-ranked job satisfaction factors, all of us must be given the support and direction suggested by Figure 5.2. Let's face it, we're not giving it and we're not getting it, either.

Many of us will contend that our employees and/or ourselves "don't need" so much coaching and/or goal setting time by countering with, "That's fine for new employees or slow learners but my staff doesn't need that type of supervision and I certainly don't." This is the shoddiest form of flimsy excuse and it stems from a very unhealthy and ignorant attitude about supervision. Most of us, and our employees, have a negative view of supervision which portrays the majority of boss-subordinate interactions as bad. In other words, the less time we spend with the boss or our employees, the better we (and our employees) feel. This is our heritage from decades of using supervision to reprimand and control employees. If you're going to get more productivity out of your employees, you've got to stop viewing the 10 supervisory functions as aspects of reprimands and/or controls and begin to view them as important, participatory activities.

Each supervisor and subordinate may not need to give or receive as much time as indicated for every function, every week. But if less of one is required, the time can be profitably spent on another function. For example, employees who are well settled into their responsibilities and who have few new duties may not require as much coaching. Their well-trained status makes them ideal candidates with whom to spend more joint decision-making and/or more problem-solving time; the supervisor can benefit from their expertise. Admit it, though; just now, when you thought that you might not have to spend as much coaching time with a subordinate as Figure 5.2 indicated, you felt relieved, as if a burden had been removed. And you probably weren't anxious to quickly review the list of functions to see where you might be able to apply the extra time to other functions. Again, this is the negative attitude about supervision which makes it impossible for ourselves and our employees to get what we need from our jobs so we can all be more productive.

Many supervisors, upon viewing the body of Figure 5.2, contend that they "just don't have the time." They make excuses such as, "I've got more to do than hold hands with my employees, I've got a *job* to do." This is, once again, nothing but guilty squirming. Note that the times we discussed above were for a supervisor who devoted only 50 percent of his or her time to supervision, or 1200 minutes per week. That leaves one half of the work week for technical and administrative duties. There's plenty of time for the "other" things. Suppose a supervisor were to contend that he or she can only spend 20 percent of the work week on subordinate management functions. As Figure 5.2 demonstrates, that's a total of 480 minutes of supervision time. With 10 employees, this computes to 8.2 minutes available for coaching (the 82 of Figure 5.2 divided by 10) per employee, 6.4 minutes devoted to joint goal setting, and so on. Let's face it, few supervisors spend that much per employee even when they don't have any administrative and technical duties. And few supervisors, particularly those who have large numbers of employees (5 or more), have other duties that consume more than 50 percent of their time.

It is undeniably true that supervisors at all levels are not spending quality supervisory time with employees. Most supervisors don't aggressively supervise their employees by productively working with them. Rather, they wait until there's a problem and then attempt to fix it, often by reprimanding the employee and issuing warnings that it better not happen again. The supervisor then returns to the "wait mode" until the next difficulty occurs. In the absence of problems, this approach appears to work because nothing obviously bad is perceived to be occurring. Yet, because this type of supervision deprives the employees of opportunities to get what they want most from the job—the fulfillment of the "big eight" satisfaction factors—much damage is being done. It's just not visible. If you want the most from your employees, you'll have to supervise them aggressively according to *Millennium Management* guidelines. The next sections outline techniques for each of the ten supervisory functions.

Coaching

Coaching is the direction of subordinates through ongoing feedback sessions which are conducted individually or in small groups. A series of coaching sessions revolves around a particular process, program, or project on which the employee is currently working. Coaching which isn't directed at a specific activity isn't so much coaching as it is a group maintenance or personal recognition function. These are important functions, but they won't do what coaching does. The goal of coaching is to improve employees' abilities to do a task better and/or to teach them new skills and approaches. Discipline falls into this function when it's handled properly. In most cases, proper coaching of an employee's initial episode of poor performance will get the employee back on track before formal disciplinary procedures (warnings, suspensions, etc.) are necessary.

Coaching is the most powerful supervisory tool; that's why it attained the highest score in Figure 5.1. Coaching allows a supervisor to simultaneously accomplish a number of critical tasks and satisfy several important employee needs. Coaching provides significant satisfaction of needs for four of the top-ranked employee satisfaction factors: proper direction and training, knowledge of what is expected, fair and tactful discipline, and feeling involved. Coaching also provides moderate perceived satisfaction of employee needs for personal recognition and leadership.

Coaching improves the quality of the employee's work by ensuring that he or she doesn't get off-track, make mistakes, or waste efforts on dead ends or unproductive techniques. It also provides an avenue for the supervisor to influence the employee's norms for performance and, at the same time, establish a personal bond of loyalty with the employee. The most powerful impact of coaching is its value in increasing the employee's sense of self-esteem and pride in doing a good job. Effective coaching allows the employee to give the supervisor and the organization what it wants. This keeps the employee out of trouble and in the positive glow of the supervisor's respect and approval.

Coaching requires a regular series of meetings with employees, both one to one and in small work groups (two to five). Larger meetings aren't effective as coaching sessions, although they can be effective as informational and norm inoculation mechanisms. Coaching sessions must involve behavioral specifications of what the supervisor wants and the specific conditions necessary for acceptable performance. The first coaching session in a series must provide the employee with the following information:

1. An exact description of the assignment or activity
2. An explanation of why it's important
3. The reason why the employee is being selected
4. An expression of confidence in the employee's ability, involving mention of a related past success
5. A specific description of what the product must be
6. An explanation of the types of support and resources which will be provided
7. A request for the employee's commitment
8. A timetable for the next step
9. A check of the employee's understanding of what's been said, best accomplished by asking the employee to describe what he or she is going to do and how and when it must be done
10. A reiteration of confidence and a further mention of the next step

The following is a sample of a supervisor's remarks in an initial coaching session. The numbers in parentheses indicate which of the above points is being covered.

(1) "Good morning, Bob. I've been asked by the department manager to put together a report on all of our clients who buy more than $100,000 per year. I'd like you to handle it for me."

(2) "This report will be used to target the clients for more marketing effort so we can expand our product base, so it's very important to the company."

(3) "I am very pleased with the work you've been doing in straightening out our delivery routes."

(4) "It looks to me like you'll be able to do a good job for me on this project."

(5) "What I want is a list which shows each client with over $100,000 in annual sales over the last twelve months. I'd like each client

shown on a separate page. For each client, I'd like to see the sales broken out by month and by individual product lines.

(2) "That will enable us to see who's buying what and when."

(6) "I've checked with the accounting department and they can give you the reports for the last twelve months tomorrow morning. If you have any questions, just ask."

(7) "Can I count on you to help me out on this?"

(8) "I need to give this report to Mr. Bronski next Tuesday, so I'd like to have you bring a rough draft to me this Friday."

(9) "Just to make sure we're clear on this important project, why don't you read back the notes you've taken?"

(10) "Bob, I think you're going to do a great job on this report, and we'll be able to use it to really make some big sales gains. I'll look forward to seeing your rough draft this Friday."

That's all there is to a basic coaching session. It's simple enough, but how many of us have ever given or been given such an effective, concise description of a work assignment? If the project is simpler and the employee more skilled or experienced, it may not be necessary to give as much detailed description of the product (point 5), especially if it's routine. But never short-change any of the other steps. They're important not only to ensure that the work gets done but also to demonstrate to the employee that you care enough about his or her performance and success to take the time (although it doesn't take much time).

The points to be made in each successive follow-up coaching session on the same topic are as follows:

1. A compliment on some aspect of what's been done so far, unless it's so worthless that you can't find even one good thing to say

2. A specific explanation of where it does or does not meet your specifications

3. If it's not satisfactory in some respect, an inquiry about why (there may be a good reason)

4. A description of what needs to be done differently

5. A description of resources and support that will be made available

6. An expression of confidence in the employee's ability

7. A timetable for the next step

8. A request for the employee's commitment

9. A check of the employee's understanding of what's been said

10. A final expression of confidence and a mention of the next step

The following are samples of a supervisor's dialogue in a well-done follow-up coaching session. The numbers refer to the above points.

(1) "Bob, this report looks pretty comprehensive. I can see that you put a lot of work into it. Most of it looks great, especially the extra notes for each client about any sales promotions that were in effect when they made the buy. I hadn't thought of that, and it's important."

(2) "There's not enough detail on product-line break-outs for the months of November and December. As I mentioned, we're going to need all of those data."

(3) "Is there any reason why you couldn't get that information?"

(4) "I didn't realize that we didn't have product-line computer reports until this past January. You'll have to go into the files and pull the paper for each client. It's a chore, but we don't have any choice."

(5) "That's going to be a lot of work, so I'll have Smith give you a hand for a few hours this afternoon. I'll have her come by your desk after lunch."

(6) "So far, I'm really impressed. I think the boss will be very happy with this report."

(7) "Since we're a little behind, I think you'll need to get this to me in almost final form by Monday afternoon at 2:00."

(8) "Can you handle that for me?"

(9) "Give me a brief description of the changes you're going to make and how you'll use Smith to help on this."

(10) "I'll tell you, I'm really impressed with this so far. I'm looking forward to seeing the report on Monday morning."

A session similar to the above should be conducted after a subordinate completes each reportable phase of a new project or process. Don't think that you can prosper by short changing employees on coaching and get away with it. It's a supervisor's single most important function.

Encouraging Joint Goal Setting

Joint goal setting is the establishment of a subordinate's performance targets (goals) by means of discussions and negotiations between the supervisor and the subordinate. Goal setting is much like coaching, except that coaching deals with discrete projects and processes which are imminent, while goal setting involves the planning and assignment of the types of projects and processes on which the subordinate will be working in the near future.

As shown in Figure 5.1, goal setting is the second most important supervisory function. It provides significant satisfaction of perceived employee satisfaction of leadership, knowledge of what is expected, and feeling involved. Goal setting also provides moderate satisfaction of employee needs for feeling of accomplishment and interesting work.

Goal setting is a critical element in building commitment among subordinates. Any work assignment, no matter how difficult, will be perceived more favorably if the subordinate has some advance warning and has been given the opportunity to give his or her input. Foreknowledge of and participation in the planning of future events eliminates the shock of any unpleasant assignments and increases anticipation of favorable events. More importantly, participation in setting goals increases the employee's commitment to them. If this is done with each subordinate, the overall effect is to build a strong feeling of teamwork and commitment among the group about the goals.

There are two elements of effective joint goal setting. The first is person-to-person sessions. These are the one-to-one and small-group meetings in which the employees are informed about the goals of the organization and the supervisor and in which their personal goals are discussed and negotiated. The second element is the distribution of information about how the group, the organization, and other departments of interest are doing in terms of their goals.

One-to-One and Small-Group Meetings

Effective goal-setting meetings with subordinates involve the following steps:

1. The goals of the organization, the supervisor, and the department are detailed so the employee gets the big picture and understands why he or she is going to be assigned various tasks.
2. The supervisor outlines the minimum level of support which the subordinate must provide.
3. The supervisor asks if the employee has any suggestions concerning new or different ways to attain the assigned goals and/or any difficulties with them.
4. The supervisor responds to each suggestion and explains why it is or isn't acceptable.
5. The supervisor sums up the goals which have been negotiated.
6. The employee is asked to summarize his or her understanding of the goals and to outline a plan for achieving them.
7. The supervisor asks for the employee's commitment.
8. The timetable for the next step is established.

The above items can't generally be done in one session. Typically, steps 1 through 3 are conducted in one meeting and steps 4 through 8 in a second meeting. There may be considerable time between these meetings if the job duties are complex or the employee is also a supervisor. In many cases it may be necessary to repeat steps 3 through 8 more than once if there are points of dispute or complexity. Let's look at some sample dialogue which a supervisor of sales might use in a goal-setting session with a salesperson. As before, the numbers in parentheses refer to the above points.

(1) "Sally, I've just gotten next year's goals for this division from the head shed. The company is shooting for a 20 percent increase in sales. I've been told that I have to have an increase in our bread sales of 25 percent and an increase in our frozen cookie sales of 15 percent."

(2) "As far as I can tell, that means that you're going to have to come up with another fifteen accounts like the ones you've got now."

(3) "Do you have any suggestions about strategies or alternatives for reaching this goal? Given your territory, are there any insurmountable problems? Why don't you think on it for a couple of days, and we'll get together on Friday morning and talk it over. I'm sure we can come up with a winning plan."

These three steps are usually handled in one session, after which the employee is asked to work up a few ideas. It's ridiculous for a supervisor to expect any type of decent input on the same day. The employee needs time to explore alternatives and think about problems which need to be addressed. All too often, supervisors simply tell subordinates, "I want your goals for the year by tomorrow morning," with no discussion, no background, and no direction. Is it any wonder that most business plans are left to dry rot shortly after they're typed?

The following are remarks the supervisor might make at the next goal-setting meeting.

(4) "I like your idea about concentrating on building sales within our existing customer base. Unfortunately, that's not going to help you much in your territory as most of your potential accounts are small specialty shops. We've got to get about 20 percent from everyone on the average or the president will be out here in a second. What I'd like to see are some ideas on grabbing more of the trendy little café business. What do you think about working your ideas for a mailer and a follow-up campaign into that area?

(5) "OK, so what we've got is the following . . ."

(6) "Now, suppose you go over your plans one final time as you see them, and then we can get to work on them."

(7) "You've come up with a great plan. Can I count on you to get it done?"

(8) "Let's get together in two weeks to see how things are going and to see if we need to refine anything."

At all times, the supervisor must be willing to accept the subordinate's suggestions if they are anywhere near as good as the supervisor's ideas. This is the 90/110 percent rule, which states that if you permit a subordinate to use his or her own ideas that are only 90 percent as good as yours, you'll end up getting 110 percent more results in the long run. Only some degree of ownership builds commitment, involvement, and responsibility.

Information Distribution

The second aspect of joint goal setting requires the supervisor to continually provide each employee individually and the work group as a whole with plenty of information concerning their own, the section's, the department's, and the organization's progress toward goals. Some of the general information will be passed along during routine meetings and coaching sessions, but you can't simply assume that the employees will know how everything is going through indirect sources. You want them to take their own goals seriously, so it's essential to couch some of your feedback specifically in terms of the goals. This is best done in formal one-to-one or small-group meetings if a few employees are working together closely on a task or project. If there's bad news about an employee's performance, he or she should be given the feedback privately, before you speak to the group. Don't give goal-related feedback in a very informal session, such as when you encounter an employee in the hall; it will seem like it's not that important. Set up a specific time and introduce the topic formally.

The points you want to cover in the one-to-one meeting are:

1. Briefly reiterate the goals.
2. Describe how the employee stands in terms of the goals as of the meeting date.
3. If the employee is on target, give plenty of praise and encouragement. If not, ask the employee why the goals are not being reached. Listen carefully; there are usually valid reasons.
4. If you need time to research the employee's responses, set up another meeting. Otherwise, tell the employee what you think needs to be done and invite his or her responses.
5. Ask the employee to describe the changes he or she will be making to get back on track.
6. Ask for the employee's commitment.
7. Set up a timetable for the next goal-review meeting. Once a month is a good interval, long enough to get a good picture of progress but soon enough to catch any problems. Of course, if the project is short-term, you may have to conduct weekly review sessions.

Small-group and departmental information on the group's and the organization's goals should be simultaneously and continuously presented by means of memos and charts sent to employees or posted on bulletin boards. We're talking here not about the types of information which will be discussed in chapter 7 (formal organizational communications) but about specific goal-related information. For example, a group of manufacturing workers should be provided with weekly, or at the very least monthly, charts and tables concerning important quality information (defect, reject, scrap, and repair rates/costs) as well as information on turnover, absenteeism, productivity, costs, and so on. The information must deal directly with the goals of the group and not simply be general data concerning the company as a whole. The information must also be designed so that it's meaningful and can be understood by the employees. Supervisors should design their own methods of presentation and should be responsible for regular updates, as well as for seeing that all of their employees understand the information and have their questions answered. This is where much of the recommended goal-setting and feedback (the next function to be discussed) time is spent by a good supervisor.

Providing Feedback

While most of the other functions involve some degree of feedback, here we're speaking of a very particular type of feedback. First and most important is feedback which involves employees' suggestions, observations, complaints, and plaudits. Quite simply, the supervisor must always get back to the employee about any issue the employee has raised.

The second aspect of the feedback function concerns general information about every aspect of the organization's operation of which the supervisor is aware and which is not gossip or hearsay. This is information which might not be directly related to coaching, goal setting, and so on.

Providing feedback is the last of the "big three" of the supervisory functions. The feedback function provides significant satisfaction of employee needs for leadership. It also provides moderate satisfaction of employee needs for proper direction and training, knowledge of what is expected, and fair and tactful discipline.

One of the major complaints of employees, particularly those in large organizations, is that they never get answers or feedback to their questions and suggestions. Most of the time the reason for the lack of response is unintentional; the supervisor was too busy, didn't have time, or forgot about it after having every intention of looking into it. The effect on subordinates, especially if the environment is nonparticipatory, is not so innocent. Subordinates in most organizations perceive their role as being less in on things and less valued by the organization because of their comparatively low status. Whenever they don't get feedback to one of their concerns, they make the worst possible attribution of motive. In the case of a supervisor's lack of feedback, they assume the supervisor doesn't care or doesn't value their input enough to remember to follow up. This severely restricts the supervisor's effectiveness as the group's leader, hurts his or her personal relationship with each employee, and reinforces any negative feelings about the organization which the employee might be harboring.

Think of how you feel when you see a group of supervisors at the next level above you go into a room and close the door. Admit it, you spend just a moment wondering if there's something going on that you don't know about and about which you have something to say. If you're honest, you'll admit that you're a little angry at being left out and not being considered important enough to be in the know. When subordinates don't get feedback on small day-to-day issues, they have this same reaction, only it's more powerful because of their closer ties with their supervisor and their comparatively lower status. In order to avoid this problem, the supervisor must demonstrate consistently that he or she is committed to keeping subordinates informed and up-to-date on all vital and trivial (but relevant) issues, questions, and concerns.

In order to fulfill this function, the supervisor doesn't have to develop a repertoire of interpersonal skills such as those required by the coaching and goal-setting functions. The main operational requirement of providing feedback is careful, almost compulsive recordkeeping and followup. Whenever an employee raises an issue or asks a question, the supervisor must make a note of the day and time, the employee's name, and the issue. It's important for the employee to see the supervisor write down the information. In Western culture, if something's really important, we write it down. It's important to show this type of concern to employees. The organization can help supervisors establish a tradition for this practice by purchasing special notebooks for this purpose which are small enough to be carried in a pocket. After they've been in use for a while, the mere appearance of the notebook when the subordinate is talking will serve to demonstrate that the supervisor is taking interest. I'm currently working in a large manufacturing facility which has developed an informal system of this type. The "notebook" is a few pieces of standard paper, folded lengthwise and left sticking out of a pocket. Most of the supervisors and middle managers carry them around. When the paper and a pen come out of the pocket, every employee knows the issue is important.

Of course, to the point of writing down the information, no feedback of consequence has occurred (unless the supervisor is sending bad signals with body language and comments). The supervisor must research the question or comment, write the answer in the notebook, and then return to the employee within a reasonable time to give him or her the feedback. I recommend the following type of interaction:

> The supervisor walks up to the employee on the job, takes out the notebook, and says: "John, last Tuesday about 11:00 A.M. you asked me about the new

form for reporting cash shortages. I checked with the district office, and it looks like the idea we sent over got turned down. Looks like we'll have to handle it ourselves."

At this point, the feedback should be used to start a combination joint decision-making session and goal-setting session. You can see that each of the functions naturally supports, facilitates, and leads into others. Most items should be followed up within a few days, and all within a month. The important thing is to follow up every item until the employee gets an answer. If it's taking a while, that's OK, but the employee should be given interim feedback:

"John, last Tuesday about 11:00 A.M. you asked me about the new form for reporting cash shortages. I checked with the district office and they didn't have an answer, so I'll check with them again next week. I just wanted you to know that I'm working on it."

The mere fact of the supervisor's concern and followup will win points even without a definitive answer. In the above case, the supervisor would make a note of the interaction and then pursue the followup. Every day, each supervisor, at every level, should devote some time to researching items (generally only a few phone calls are required to deal with most items) and checking the notebook for open items. If something's necessarily been left open for a long while, it's essential to inform the employee periodically that you're still on top of the situation. Supervisors who religiously follow this practice are viewed as strong, concerned leaders.

The second and less important aspect of providing feedback is to make as much general information available as possible. The subordinates must be led to view the supervisor as a primary source of useful information about the organization and its current events. A supervisor should make a habit of passing along items of information from his or her supervisors and from the organization's executives. If something is in the wind, the supervisor should see that his or her subordinates are informed first. This reinforces the supervisor's role as an authority figure and leader.

The best mechanisms for this type of feedback are regular group meetings between subordinates and supervisors and occasional memos or notes distributed to all employees. Chapter 7 recommends that the organization establish a formal requirement for regular sectional and department meetings. In the absence of such a policy, a supervisor should hold his or her own sectional meetings. The meetings should be as short as possible, free of filler speeches, and should not be used to exhort the employees to do more work (the other functions will take care of that concern). The meetings should be used to keep people informed of recent and upcoming changes and news. If meetings can't be held during work time because of process constraints, they can be held on a voluntary basis (perhaps the organization can spring for donuts and coffee) five to ten minutes before work begins or during a break.

These meetings should be supplemented by occasional memos or notes from the supervisor, photocopied and sent to all subordinates. The content of the memos should include general news about the department and the organization, progress toward goals, actions taken on employee suggestions, and any other information which the supervisor believes the employees would like to know. Supervisors should distribute at least one such memo every two weeks and never more than three or four per month.

Providing Personal Recognition

Personal recognition is provided when a subordinate perceives that the supervisor values him or her as a unique and worthwhile employee. When this process occurs, it provides significant satisfaction of employees' needs for personal recognition and feeling involved. The personal recognition function also provides moderate satisfaction of subordinates' needs for feeling of accomplishment and leadership.

Personal recognition, at its most basic and important level, conveys to each employee an awareness that he or she is valued, not so much because of specific contributions or a job well done (which is part of the feedback and coaching supervisory functions) but because of what the employee uniquely brings to the job; it's a perception that you're appreciated because you're you and because you're part of the group.

This is a very subtle function but extremely important, particularly in larger companies. One problem which individuals encounter in large groups and organizations, as we saw in chapter 3, is that it's extremely difficult to buck the system. In a large company, the norms and goals are typically restrictive and controlling. There's a universal tendency in that type of environment for individuals to feel confined and disconnected, to perceive that they're a faceless cog in a big machine. With that perception, an individual isn't going to be taking many risks or trying new ideas, won't have as much pride in the group's performance, and won't be as concerned with doing a great job for an organization which doesn't appreciate him or her. A supervisor who performs the personal recognition function consistently can encourage an employee to perceive that he or she is recognized as an individual, is valued as a unique personality, and that it's the individual, not the system, which is important to the supervisor.

This is an easy and straightforward function to perform. The supervisor must demonstrate to the employees his or her belief that the employees are not a group, "the guys," "that bunch in the plant," or "the rank and file." The supervisor must lead the employees to believe that he or she values them as individuals. You'd never think of referring to your family as "that bunch at the house," because you know them personally and have personal feelings for them. While your feelings for even the best employees aren't as tender as those you might have for your family, as a supervisor you've got to treat them as individuals about whom you are concerned if you want them to worry about doing more than the average for you.

The techniques of personal recognition are:

1. Always address employees by their first names if there are no outsiders around. When there are visitors from outside areas, use Mr., Mrs., and Ms. as appropriate.

2. Talk with every subordinate at least once a day for a minute or two even if there isn't a pressing subject. This will build a leader-subordinate bond and a personal commitment that will make it difficult for the employee not to want to watch out for the supervisor. This time can be used as general feedback time.

3. Never bark orders at employees, such as "Jones, come into my office" or "Jenkins, pick up that broken part off the floor." Instead, use "Bob, would you please come in here for a moment?" and "Sally, do me a favor and please pick up that part, will you?" Everybody will know it's still an order, and everyone will still know who's the boss. The courtesy demonstrates that the boss cares about the employees' self-respect. Many supervisors erroneously believe that lower-level workers don't expect refined and polite treatment because they're "rough types" and/or uneducated. But everybody wants to be given respect. The people who generally get the least of it will respond best to it.

4. When completing a conversation with an employee, thank him or her for taking the time and effort to talk with you. It doesn't have to be lavish, perhaps only "Thanks for coming by" (even if you asked them to come in), but it's just another indication of your esteem.

5. Always use employees' names on any good news items that are circulated to other groups or managers. Don't write, "A bunch of us down here did this." People love to see their names. They'll appreciate the fact that others are noticing their contributions, even if the issue appears insignificant to you.

6. If an employee makes a suggestion you like, make sure that you mention the employee's name and give him or her full credit for it. You still get credit for anything your people come up with, but you'll get a lot more work from everyone if they know you're not hogging the kudos. Use the feedback function to let the employee know that you sent his or her name up with the idea (and your support; you don't want them to think you're letting them take the risks). It's a good idea to post a copy of any note or memo you send with the employee's name on it and also mention the idea at any meetings or small-group gatherings where the subject is appropriate. Once the

supervisor is perceived to be someone who recognizes individual contributions, all subordinates will work for their share of the honors.

Encouraging Joint Decision Making

Joint decision making is the cooperative selection of alternatives by a supervisor and an employee. It doesn't imply a democratic choice process (although on occasion it could be), and it doesn't mean that the supervisor is surrendering his or her authority. What it means is that the supervisor is actively utilizing the input and knowledge of subordinates when decisions must be made.

While the functions of goal setting and coaching clearly involve elements of joint decision making, this function outlines a process for handling all situations in which there's an alternative among courses of action which will affect subordinates.

Employees will be committed to making a program work only if they perceive a potential personal gain from it and/or they have had a part in deciding what to do. In effect, if they need the product of the decision or own a piece of it, they'll fight for it. As we saw in chapter 2, the only thing most employees think they're getting out of a job is money. If they're not getting any satisfaction of their more important needs, they go through the motions just to get paid. In that condition, it doesn't make any difference whether they do things inefficiently or efficiently as long as they stay out of trouble. To them, one authoritarian management program is the same as any other. However, if they're involved in the decision-making process, it's a different story. If they participate, a little bit of their pride and ego is involved, and they won't want to settle for less than something that will make them look good. You must involve them as much as possible.

A supervisor can effectively perform joint problem solving only if he or she makes a commitment to involve employees in some manner in every decision which affects them. This means that no decisions should be made autocratically unless there's an emergency. This doesn't mean majority rule or voting or endless delays. We're talking about appropriate levels of joint decision making depending on the subject matter, time constraints, and so on. There are several levels of effort for involving subordinates in joint decision making.

Level 1

This is the situation in which a decision has already been made for the supervisor by the organization. If the organization as a whole were practicing joint problem solving, there would be few surprise decisions announced without some degree of advance notice and participation. In this case, the supervisor should announce the decision to his or her employees and explain the reasons for it in as much detail as possible. This should be done regardless of the organization's own announcements. The supervisor is trying to present himself or herself as the group leader, and these types of events reinforce that image. This type of announcement also provides an opportunity to take some of the steam out of the employees' complaints, if any, about the policy. The announcement of the decision can be made individually to each employee, to small groups, or to the supervisor's entire section, as time and operations permit.

Level 2

This level of joint decision making is appropriate when upper management or operational constraints have dictated that a certain type of change will occur, but the exact manner in which the change will be implemented hasn't yet been decided. For example, management may decide that it's necessary to relocate a department to another floor of the building. Once the decision to move has been made, it's essential to use this level of joint decision making to involve the employees in making decisions about the operational details. At this point, the supervisor should perform the following steps:

1. Announce the decision which has been made and the reasons for it. This is best done in one large group, if possible, so that everyone gets the news at the same time and in the same language.

2. Outline the types of decisions which have yet to be made, and ask the employees to make suggestions. One good way to do this, particularly if there's initial low participation because of past friction, is to ask for volunteers to form a committee to handle the project. Announce that if no one volunteers for the committee, people will be selected to serve on it. (Participatory management means that everyone must participate, whether they like it or not.)

3. Explain how the process will work. Ideally, the employee group will make suggestions, perhaps even come up with a plan, and then the supervisor will present it to management. It's essential that the supervisor share all relevant information with the employees so they don't waste time working on suggestions which cannot be implemented because of factors unknown to them.

4. After management has made its decision, meet with the employees to announce the decision and explain the reasons behind it. It's a good idea for a member of upper management to attend this meeting and handle questions.

Level 3

This is the most intensive level of joint decision making. Here, the employees are given a range of alternatives or possible courses of action, one of which will have to be implemented, and are asked to work out their recommendations and justifications. This type of joint decision making has to be condoned by top management. Otherwise, the decisions are usually made before the lower-level employees hear about it. The steps are the same as those for level 2, except that the first meeting is used to outline the range of alternatives which appear to be relevant. The employees may come up with more. Typically, this type of process will require several iterations; once the major alternative has been selected, further level 2 decision making must be conducted.

Conducting Participatory Problem Solving

There's a fine line between participatory problem solving and joint decision making. The problem-solving function involves many of the same steps as joint decision making, but the subject matter of the discussions is different. Participatory problem solving is the cooperative resolution of acute or long-term difficulties which haven't been remedied by standard efforts. It's one thing to involve employees in decision making on nonproblematic decisions; it's much harder for most organizations to approach problems without assuming employee guilt of some kind or blaming them for not working hard enough. Therefore, this function must be viewed separately. Participatory problem solving operates on the assumption that the majority of problems occur as a result of unfortunate combinations of factors, none of which is deliberately caused or consciously allowed by employees.

As pointed out in chapter 1, the employees we've got now are the ones with whom we're going to have to work. In chapter 2, we saw that most employees want to do a good job but don't believe that organizations permit them to contribute. That means we must send the most positive messages at all times and not waste time and worsen the situation by trying to determine who's responsible or at fault for a problem. What's important is to get everyone involved in fixing it. If you try to fix blame, you'll find out that even the laziest, most uncreative employee can come up with all sorts of creative reasons why he or she isn't at fault. It's no use even to worry about who's at fault. Worry instead about approaching problems as challenges which can be solved by the employees.

When a problem occurs, or when it becomes enough of a bother to require action, it's critical that the supervisor take the following steps:

1. Announce that the problem is serious and that the group will be working on it. This should be done in a single group meeting so the

importance of the problem is obvious. As you can see, many of the functions involve these meetings, which serve many joint purposes. Announce that the supervisor will be coming around to every employee to get their suggestions on how the problem should be solved. Ask for volunteers to work on a committee to come up with a recommendation. If no volunteers surface, appoint a few to work up a proposal.

2. Visit with every employee for a few minutes, tell them about the problem, ask for their input, and, if possible, give them an appropriately detailed (for their level of skills) description of the problem and any relevant information about it. Ask them to think about it, and tell them you'll be back in a few days or a week.

3. Visit with each employee again and determine their input. Write down what they say. This is similar to the feedback function. Tell them you'll get back to them when you've considered everyone's input. See what the committee has come up with. Determine what you think needs to be done.

4. Go back to each employee, read them what they told you in the previous meeting, and tell them what course of action you've decided upon, given the committee's input and your analysis.

5. The next time you have a meeting, announce the proposed course of action, even if the result was that nothing could be done. Thank everyone for their help, and give the names of the people who served on the committee and anyone who came up with an exceptional idea.

You may have to repeat steps 3 and 4 a few times if the problem is complex. Each contact with an employee in this type of process only reinforces good things. And don't worry about time constraints for these visits; you'll be spending less time in the long run because you'll solve many of the problems on which you're wasting all of your time now.

Encouraging Individual Development

This supervisory function is the mechanism by which the supervisor conveys to his or her subordinates the perception that individual status and success are critically important to him or her and the group. This is a subtle function, closely related to training and to personal recognition. Through this function the supervisor conveys to each employee that it's important for him or her to continually learn to do more, to assume new responsibilities, and to increase his or her area of expertise so the employee will be poised to seize future opportunities as they arise. This function is the antithesis of allowing employees to settle in to their jobs.

Change is the bottom line condition of life and business. All of us evolve physically and psychologically as we age. Businesses do the same as market conditions force changes. At the same time, many employees, particularly in large organizations, tend to become static in their view of jobs and duties. This is partly a result of the comfort we all take in routine. But part of this settling in is caused by the almost universal impression of individuals in large organizations that one person can't change anything. The supervisor must do everything possible to eliminate this perception. Many of the supervisory functions attack this problem in various ways, but it's important to give it some specific attention and effort. If employees are encouraged to perceive that their development and change into more accomplished roles is valued by the supervisor, they'll begin to become more involved in all aspects of their jobs. A certain sense of adventure and excitement will be kindled as they see that there are new things to do and new ways of doing the same old job.

The hands-on techniques for this function include the following:

1. Cross training, allowing employees to learn each other's jobs, is an effective means of developing an employee. It also provides for redundant personnel skills in case of absences.

2. Delegation of responsibilities to employees is important. Many of the duties which a supervisor finds boring or tedious would be viewed as a challenge and an honor by an subordinate. This would free the supervisor to spend more time performing supervision functions and would increase the employee's feelings of achievement and self-esteem.

3. Assignments to head up special projects or teams will do most to make an employee feel valued. If you're forming any committees or teams, always appoint someone to be in charge, unless the group has formed themselves and selected a leader before coming to see you.

Whenever you perform one of the above actions, always announce it to the employee on a one-to-one basis, explaining that you're taking the action because you feel it's a good opportunity for the employee to develop his or her range of skills and at the same time contribute to the group. Always point out that you've picked him or her because of outstanding performance (but if it's not true, don't say it). The one-to-one interview comments are much the same as those shown in detail for the goal-setting function. Then, the next time you have a group meeting, mention the committee and the team. Then point out the team leader and say a few nice words about your confidence in that person.

Providing Appropriate Training

A supervisor provides appropriate training by seeing that his or her employees get all of the training they require in order to excel in their jobs. This may seem like an obvious supervisory function that's routinely taken care of in most organizations, but it's not. Generally speaking, if an employee has been doing a job well enough not to be fired, it's generally assumed that the employee knows exactly what to do and that any problems in output are the result of employee deficits. This is a logical error of the highest magnitude and is the source of endless problems. Employees know when they're not up to speed in their job skills, even if they won't admit it, and they resent being held accountable for errors they can't avoid.

For example, consider the spray painters mentioned in chapter 2. They were continually being punished for errors in their work even though they had never received any formal training in their craft. Over the years, on-the-job training was used to pass the skills from one person to the next. They were doing a very good job in general, but there were occasional errors for no apparent reason (other than plain and simple mistakes). The general consensus among supervisors was that differences in humidity, temperature, paint batches, brands, and so on, were the cause and that the employees should have known how to compensate for them. The employees also believed that the same causes were responsible for the problems, but they didn't know how to compensate for them. In the classic tradition, management would come down hard when the problems occurred and would suspend the workers or reprimand them, on the assumption that the employees were causing the errors through inattention or on purpose. The employees were resentful and angry because they had no idea what to do; they felt they were doing the best they could but knew they didn't have the necessary skills. This was a classic case of a lack of necessary training. If management would have sent these individuals for a few days of technical training in their craft, there would have been fewer problems, both with the paint jobs and with employee concern for trying harder. Each time this training was proposed, management would cite lack of time for training, no substitutes to take the places of those in training, the expense, and so on. Yet there were always enough people to cover the jobs of those who would be suspended without pay for a few days, and there was always enough money and time to continually repaint the jobs done improperly.

This attitude is a problem even when the employees don't know they have a deficit. I once worked with a man who generated large numbers of computer reports for his personnel department. As I became more familiar with the computer system he was using, it became clear that he was woefully unskilled and unknowledgeable about the capabilities of the system. He was doing things the long way, entering data multiple times when transfers could have been made, and so on. His supervisor didn't know anything about computers, so he didn't know there was a better way. As a result, my acquaintance was grinding away, wasting huge amounts of time and energy that could have been profitably applied to doing a better job and making him feel better about his work. Proper attention to the training supervisory function would have rectified both this problem and the painters' difficulties.

Aside from the benefits of increased technical skills and job-related knowledge, individual development reaps great returns in employee pride and self-esteem. When they see that the organization cares enough to send them to training in their areas, employees begin to view themselves and their jobs as more significant.

The essence of this function is for the supervisor to constantly review employees' performance and job-related responsibilities and aggressively search for ways to improve their job-related skills. On the average, at least 2 percent of all employees should be enrolled in some type of job-related developmental activity at all times. This is the equivalent of about 40 hours of training per year per employee. If you're doing less than this for each of your subordinates, you're not doing enough. Several very successful organizations devote at least 80 to 120 hours per year per employee to personal development and technical training.

The questions the supervisor must ask as he or she reviews each employee's performance are:

1. Has the employee been to a technical workshop in his or her area in the last three years?
2. Does the employee have problem-solving skills?
3. Does the employee have obvious interpersonal skill deficits which are creating problems in team situations?
4. Is the employee making errors in a consistent manner which could be related to a skills deficit?
5. Are there impending changes in technology or processes which will affect the employee?
6. Does another facility or industry have a better way to do the employee's job or process which the employee could profit from knowing about?

You're not looking for an excuse to send employees to any type of training just to do training. Chapter 9 will point out the folly of that approach. However, you must aggressively search for training needs. In the typical organization, employees are reluctant to suggest training because they're afraid supervisors will think they're just trying to get out of work or are admitting that they're not good enough at what they do.

Conducting Group Maintenance Activities

This function is targeted at increasing the positive feelings each subordinate has of the supervisor's work group. To a certain extent, the performance of the eight functions already discussed will do this, as the inevitable group activities which take place will serve to make everyone in the group feel more accomplished and successful. Yet more must be done.

Just as there's a tendency for an individual employee to get lost and feel unnoticed in a department or section, a group can also develop a similar set of perceptions. Organizations invariably homogenize their treatment of various work groups. Everyone ends up perceiving that they're all the same, just another department number lost in the organization's computer. Much of this results from legal constraints on equal pay, equal benefits, and so on. Little attention is paid to generating differential identities for groups other than at the facility or division level (and even then, care is taken not to offend the poor performers by lauding the outstanding locations). A natural artifact of this situation is that the individual work group is lost in the shuffle unless the supervisor of that work group makes a strong effort to establish positive team spirit. Performance of the other functions will make everyone feel better about themselves and their jobs. Performance of the group support function will provide a supervisor's employees with a convenient and natural place to put all of those feelings, a positive team spirit and identity.

There are a number of hard and fast rules and techniques which must be used to maintain positive group spirit and feelings of pride. They include:

1. The supervisor must always talk positively about the group to every level of management and to the group itself, no matter what the occasion. If there's a problem, "We can fix it." If someone makes a disastrous mistake, "Even world champions make a mistake every now and then. We'll see that it doesn't happen again." If someone criticizes the group, defend it: "I'll put my people up against yours anytime." This will do two things. First, it will eventually get back to the troops, who will be pleasantly surprised and proud of the supervisor for sticking up for them. Second and more importantly, if the supervisor continually talks positively about the group, he or she will begin to think positively about them. This will lead to more frequent and pleasant interactions with the employees and will lead the supervisor to expect that the group will be successful. This type of expectation is contagious.

2. The employees must be influenced to think of their section or department as a group. The supervisor can do this through section meetings, short memo/newsletters about the section (as in a feedback technique), and special badges for the group, such as departmental signs, caps or shop coats for line personnel, customized calendars, memo pads, and so on. The goal is to make the subordinates think of the group as a functioning team.

3. The supervisor must look for ways to promote the group to upper levels of management. Whenever there's a good performance by the group or an individual in it, the supervisor must see that the appropriate levels of management are made aware of it. The communication

must always mention the group's achievements as well as those of the individual. After the upper levels have been informed, the supervisor must then let the work group know of the mention, preferably by announcing it in a group meeting and/or by posting a memo.

4. If the group has done something special or has had a particularly good period of performance, the supervisor should give the entire group a boost by asking one of the higher-level executives to drop by and congratulate the employees. Few executives are asked to do this sort of thing, and they generally love it. It makes them feel as if they're in touch with the troops. They're usually not, of course, but that's not important. What is important is that the entire group will feel flattered and special.

Providing Unconditional Support

This last function, while not ranked high on the tally in Figure 5.1, can kill a supervisor if it's not done. Unconditional support means that, in every instance, the supervisor must assume that his or her subordinates are in the right until absolutely proven otherwise. Behaviors which support this assumption must be in force at all times, no matter what happens.

Very few supervisors perform this function. There are two reasons. First, because of a sense of insecurity about their position should they argue with someone who's casting aspersions on their people, they give in and go along with the accuser. Second, and worse, most supervisors consider their employees to be not too smart, not quite as good as they are, and therefore probably guilty. For example, a colleague of mine (let's call her Darla) once worked as a supervisor in a large chemical processing operation. She had done wonders in turning around a bad situation and was recognized throughout the company as someone who could get results. Yet her boss always sided with anyone who had a gripe. If there was a difficulty with personnel over an employee who wasn't working out, Darla's boss would accuse her of having an attitude problem. If an employee went to personnel and complained about being given a written warning, Darla got a lecture about being more considerate. No matter what happened, Darla was assumed to be incorrect. Despite a bright future with that company, Darla soon left because of her boss's lack of support. The quickest way to kill an employee's enthusiasm and initiative is to not stick up for him or her when the chips are down. That's one of the primary traits expected of a group leader: unconditional support for every member of the group. It's really one of the most important things a supervisor can do.

Much unconditional support is provided through the performance of many of the other supervisory functions, but this aspect is a set of discrete attitudes and resultant behaviors. Some supervisors perform many of the functions discussed earlier but don't realize how extensively they compromise all of their good efforts by not providing unconditional support to all the group's members all the time. This doesn't mean that the supervisor denies reality to support the employees. If someone's not performing and coaching, training, individual development, and so on, aren't doing the job, then it's time to look for someone else. But give the employees under your command the benefit of every doubt on the few occasions when they need it and they'll do the same for you every minute.

The hands-on techniques are few and simple:

1. Never accuse an employee of something, even if you're sure it's true. First, explain what you've been told or what you believe, and then ask for their story. In half of the cases at least, the employee will be right. Many supervisors throw the tantrum and then have to back off. Nobody forgives the accusation that was made, and everybody in the group hears about it within a day or so, in the worst possible light.

2. The supervisor must fight for every employee on every issue that's brought up. If an employee needs a vacation day or some special training and there's no other extenuating circumstances, the supervisor must be prepared to cinch it up and go to the mat for the employee. It's not the issue that's important; it's the message such a stance sends to the entire group: "Our group leader cares about us and will fight for us." This builds strong emotional bonds which will cause the employees to look out for the supervisor.

3. The supervisor must never be more restrictive or controlling than is absolutely necessary. Many supervisors, even though they're somewhat participatory, still view their main job as that of jail warden and watchdog, on patrol against employee screwups. This type of behavior is a loud and blatant message that screams, "I don't believe you're working hard, and I don't trust you." That's not support. If you send the message that you don't trust your employees, they'll show you why you're right (because they'll have plenty of time as they only go through the motions instead of working hard). Lighten up on them as much as the organization will allow. If there are problems, deal with them through coaching, not through demonstrating that you don't trust the entire group.

Final Words

There's no denying that the typical supervisor would have to make monumental changes in his or her behaviors and attitudes to implement the techniques discussed in this chapter. Big changes are always difficult to implement, especially when they're related to personal issues of authority, prior roles, current organizational norms, and initial suspicion from the employees ("Why is Fred being so nice all of a sudden?") and even from upper levels of management who may not be practicing the techniques themselves. Don't expect it to be easy, even if you're 100 percent in agreement with every technique which was presented. It's hard to change habits, and 95 percent of the ways we react at work are habits. It will be tough, but you won't have to wait long for positive results. As you were no doubt thinking when you read about each supervisory function, you'd like to be supervised that way yourself. We all would. As soon as your employees begin to believe that you're committed to your new supervisory role, they'll begin to respond.

CHAPTER 6

The Mechanics of Millennium Management Planning

The goal-setting supervisory function outlined in chapter 5 described the *Millennium Management* approach to planning which should be used by a supervisor to establish the goals, objectives, and operational details of each of his or her subordinates. If each level of supervision conducted its work-group planning according to the dictates of chapter 5, there would be little need for this chapter. Unfortunately, not more than one in fifty supervisors practices that type of goal setting. A formal planning procedure and structure is therefore essential so that all levels of management are required by policy to conduct planning activities with the participation of their subordinates. A comprehensive system of *Millennium Management* planning isn't going to happen on its own without a push. That's why it's important for an organization to implement a *Millennium Management* planning strategy as *the* planning policy and format.

If the employees are not brought into the planning process in a meaningful manner, two very bad things always happen. First, the employees don't buy into the plans and the objectives because they have no stake in them. They don't have any ownership and aren't encouraged to develop a sense of commitment to them. Typically, goals and objectives for the coming year are determined by upper management and announced to the troops without discussion. You don't have to go far down the ladder in any company to find middle managers who never even get to see a copy of the plan that supposedly dictates their every move and reward for the next year.

Second, there's a good chance that many vital pieces of information won't be considered. Nobody knows the jobs like the employees. Setting any kind of objectives and plans without soliciting their detailed input is worse than stupid; it's an invitation to disaster. The competitive condition of many American industries is an indication that there's been no shortage of companies willing to send out such invitations on a regular basis.

Look around your own organization. Is the participation in planning by different levels of employees real, or is it an illusion? In many larger organizations there's typically an attempt made to appear participatory. Division or facility leaders attend executive-level planning sessions at headquarters, but the end result is always the same; predetermined plans are announced. If the sessions are actually participatory planning sessions, why is it that the slides showing the goals are always prepared in advance of the meeting? And this is the nonparticipation of division presidents and corporate executive vice-presidents who are making $100K to $300K per year! For the majority of employees, including middle managers, annual goals and plans arrive in the overnight pouch; the only participation is the opportunity to listen in a hushed auditorium to your marching orders (if employees are told anything). Believe me, nobody feels any sense of commitment to those types of plans.

In most cases it doesn't even matter how good such plans might be. Few organizations use them for anything more than a framework within which to explain the year's results. If the year was good, the plan was good. If the goals weren't reached, it was because it was a rebuilding year, government regulations caused it, or market trends shifted. Down in the bowels of the company, where the work is going on, such plans have almost no effect. For the most part, the employees (including many senior managers and executives) in any company simply continue to show up and do what they've always done from day to day: try to stay out of trouble. Most of them don't even know what the plans really mean, much less what they have to do specifically to attain the plan goals. If they're told to do something, they do it. If nobody tells them what to do, they just do what they think they should do. Their noninvolvement in the planning process completely eliminates all but coincidental correlation between the organization's goals and the employees' day-to-day activities. Any potential contributions or improvements they could make are lost forever. Everyone keeps an eye out for the remote possibility that they'll be called on to explain a variance from the plan, but even that's not much of a threat. Any manager worth his or her salt can explain or excuse any deviation from any plan in a manner that makes it sound as if the apparent defeat is a victory that's soon to be announced.

Consider the case of a marketing manager in a division of an international conglomerate. In the beginning of the year she was told by corporate what her division's sales for the coming year must be in each product line. A grandiose marketing plan was written according to the corporate style guide (letter heights, types of graphs, etc.) Sound like a tough nut to crack? Not very. Twice a week she would have status meetings in which her people would review plan versus actual. If they made it, they took all the credit ("What a marketing department!"); if not, they made an excuse and moved the lost sales two months to three years down the line, explaining that the schedule had slipped because of customer funding problems or permit delays (these were big-ticket weapons systems). All the while, everyone in the place continued to work only as hard as they normally did at the duties they had always done. Any corresponding difference in their work actions compared to previous years and the requirements of the plan was incidental. They all did what they could, but they didn't do anything extraordinary or strikingly different, in style, effort, or execution. None of the employees owned the plan, so they just continued to work hard as they always had, doing the best as they saw it, always ready and capable of explaining how any of their efforts were targeted at plan goals.

Have you ever been three to six months into the business year before someone has asked you for your objectives? It's happened to me and everyone I know many times. One time I was actually asked for a set of objectives in the eleventh month of the year for which the objectives were intended!

If your organization can afford to continue to disenfranchise its employees by not including them in the planning process, more power to it. Few American businesses have the luxury of being able to waste the valuable resource their employees' input and participation could provide. Effective planning demands the participation of all levels of employees. Anything less is a dangerous waste of time.

General Issues

Before we discuss the mechanics of *Millennium Management* planning, there are a few discrete but related issues which must be addressed.

Managing by the Numbers

It's been said a thousand times, but few organizations have listened. Therefore, it must be said again: planning and performance management based solely on quarterly fiscal performance is short-sighted and dangerous. Part of the problem is an overconfidence in the strength and meaning of financial analysis and projections. Because the technologies of finance and planning typically require complex calculations and are usually performed by those with advanced degrees, many executives and managers forget that these techniques are only data manipulation. They're usually no closer to the true picture than nonmathematical assessments by other intelligent employees. The danger is that the computer paper, the regression analysis, the time-series analysis, the portfolio analysis, and so on, all appear to be so scientific and objective that they're beyond question. But they only look objective. Every such analysis is based on as much subjective manipulation of assumptions as the worst bigot's opinion of equal rights.

Another problem with planning by the numbers is the tendency to always want consistent and predictable results. The world and markets aren't consistent. If you're going to try to get your people involved in planning and decision making, don't bother if you're always going to hold them to 3 percent quarterly profit requirements and always insist that profits go up by 1 percent a year. Given half a chance, your employees will swamp you with creative ideas, new directions, and operational improvements, but they're not going to do so under the harsh demands of short-term performance goals. Many of the ideas they develop will deal with more than minor tweaks of the system; they'll have big things in mind which will require investment and development time. You can't have the half you want without letting them have the half they want.

The bigger problem with quarterly planning goals is the type of mentality it creates. Everyone is always looking for another percent here or there. There's a tendency to sacrifice the long-term good for short-term gain in order to stay out of trouble or look good for the next promotion. The difficulty is that the mortgage process never stops. Who has the courage to be the first to call a halt? The result is that perhaps a good person isn't hired for three months to save the salary, or perhaps a marketing or research expense isn't made because it would "look bad right now." Or the staff is cut by 2 percent, which looks great fiscally but ruins shipping time and affects customer satisfaction. These types of decisions aren't made because they're thought to be what's best for the company in the long (or even the short) run; they're often made simply to help someone look good in terms of quarterly goals. By the time the damage becomes apparent, the people who made the decision are usually working in another group or department (or another company), and the new people in the job start squeezing even harder so they too can look good in a situation that's even worse. We've all got to start looking at what's best for our organizations' long-term competitive situations. Involving the employees in the planning will accomplish that objective.

The Head-Shed Mentality

The head-shed mentality is a powerful force which operates to exclude employees and information from the planning process. The development of the head-shed mentality is a natural and expected result of organizational dynamics when they're left to operate without direction. If you put a group of people in a special setting; show them they're special by providing them with better furniture, higher pay, more status, more promotional opportunities, and less hands-on work; and isolate them from the operational employees, you're creating a group that thinks it's better and different. Then you ask them to come up with a business plan. How eager and willing do you think they're going to be to associate intimately with what they consider to be the great unwashed in your organization? Minimally, I can assure you. They're going to assume that they know more, understand more, and, what's worse, have an inside track about what management wants. This means that they understand what the top executives like to hear. Very often, what top management needs to hear isn't what they want to listen to. With the head-shed mentality in full force, not much else besides pleasant listening gets through.

The Mechanics

Millennium Management planning is a variation of top-down, bottom-up planning. Top-down, bottom-up planning is a technique in which the top, upper management, is supposed to specify broad goals and communicate them to the bottom, lower levels. The bottom then puts together operational plans which target the executives' goals. This approach, if actually implemented, wouldn't be all that bad. Of course, in reality the process is usually bastardized (management by the numbers, the head-shed mentality, etc.) to the point where the lowest bottom that's allowed to participate is located high above the middle-management ranks.

The *Millennium Management* approach to planning is to provide all employees with the opportunity to participate in the planning process. Even if their specific ideas and suggestions don't make it into the final plan, they'll know they had a chance to contribute. This means they'll have some sense of ownership in and commitment to the plan. For most organizations, this would be immeasurably more than they're getting now, since most develop plans that the majority of employees never see. At the same time, the planning exercise itself can be used as a catalyst to induce supervisors at all levels to apply many of the supervisory functions discussed in chapter 5.

In essence, the *Millennium Management* planning process is a top-down, bottom-up, top-down process. This ensures that everyone gets to participate, upper management gets all the information it needs to make wise decisions, upper management controls the strategic thrust for which it's responsible, and all employees (every single one of them) understand exactly what the company will be doing over the period of the plan.

There are three phases of the top-down, bottom-up, top-down planning process. The initial phase is the top-down step, similar in concept to generic top-down, bottom-up planning. The *Millennium Management* approach makes sure that it's done correctly. The second phase, bottom-up, is the step in which the proposals of all personnel for attaining organizational goals are developed and submitted. The third phase is the final top-down step with which top management communicates the final detailed plan to all employees. Let's review each of these three phases in detail. You'll see, as we discuss the activities which occur in each stage, that the *Millennium Management* planning process demands the same types of interactions between supervisors at all levels and their employees as would the practice of the ten supervisory functions described in chapter 5. There's only one proper way to obtain maximum productivity from employees, and it looks the same no matter how you approach it or where you start. The planning methodology being presented in this chapter results in the very same activities which would occur if all supervisors in the organization were actively committed to practicing the *Millennium Management* supervisory functions outlined in chapter 5.

Phase 1. Top-Down

The purpose of the first top-down phase is to solicit the input of each successively lower level of management, all the way to the lowest, by providing them with a description of each proposed organizational goal and the supporting actions which management is thinking about. In essence, the top executives ask everyone, "Here's where we think we want to go. What do you think we need to do to get there?" Properly implemented, this first top-down phase enables every person in the organization to follow the evolution of an objective from the very top of the organization right down to his or her level. Each employee can analyze the types of supporting actions which every higher level has suggested to support each objective. The individual then specifies his or her actions or strategies for each objective with a clear understanding of how his or her objectives and daily work support the overall company plan.

The top-down phase starts with the generation of preliminary organizational objectives by the top executives. Whether it's one person or a committee is immaterial as long as the objectives are supported by the entire top echelon. If the leader of that group is practicing the goal-setting supervisory function, he or she will probably be supported by the consensus of the group, if not its wholehearted agreement. As the organization gets larger, the objectives should be broader, as there are more functional levels to attend to the tactics. If, on the other hand, there are only fifty people in the organization, the top managers probably do double duty as operations people part of the time, so it's appropriate for them to make operational suggestions and decisions. At all times, the goal must be to permit subordinates to make as many of the operational (how to do it) decisions as appropriate to their skills and knowledge. (What they're qualified to do is usually a lot more than what they're permitted to do.)

The mechanism for the top-down phase is the planning objectives response sheet (PORS). Figure 6.1 presents a sample of one PORS which might be completed in a manufacturing organization. The chief executive or committee prepares a PORS for each objective and then sends a set to each person who reports to them. Each recipient reviews each PORS, completes the next section by adding actions or strategies which support the actions of his or her boss, and then sends one copy of each PORS to each of his or her own subordinates. This process continues until all of the PORSs reach the first-line supervisors, who then present and/or discuss the PORSs with their employees.

Note that in Figure 6.1 the CEO specifies that her objective is to increase profits by 3 percent (not the most imaginative or creative goal, but it will serve as an example). Her first objective is labeled I. After generating her objectives, she would send one copy of each PORS to each person who reports to her. The president who reports to her might get a stack of five PORSs, one for each of the CEO's objectives, I through V. As shown in the example, the president's first action/strategy for achieving the CEO's objective I is I.A., which will attempt to attain the profitability objective in part by cutting manufacturing costs by 4 percent. Jack Penny might have four other action/strategy suggestions in response to the CEO's objective I, which would be labeled I.B. through I.E. Five new PORSs would be made by Penny, each showing the CEO's objective I with one for each of objectives I.B through I.E.

After each person fills in all of the PORSs he or she receives and then creates any new PORSs for additional action/strategy suggestions, all of the

---

1. *Name/title*: Frieda Dorfendurfer, CEO
   Objective: I.
   Increase profits 3 percent over 1986 levels.

2. *Name/title*: Jack Penny, President
   Action/strategy: I.A.
   Cut manufacturing costs by 4 percent.

3. *Name/title*: Lorena Jones, VP of Manufacturing
   Action/strategy: I.A.1.
   Reduce scrap 20 percent.

4. *Name/title*: Jorge Garcia, Line 1 Superintendent
   Action/strategy: I.A.1.a.
   Install parts stackers in areas with more than 2 percent scrap.

5. *Name/title*: Molly White, Supervisor
   Action/strategy: I.A.1.a.i.
   Analyze scrap patterns, and determine whether problem is operator error or system damage.

Figure 6.1   A Sample Phase 1 Planning Objectives Response Sheet (PORS)

forms are forwarded to the next level of subordinates, who repeat the process. Only the sheets that are appropriate to the next level of subordinates are passed along. For example, Lorena Jones, the VP of manufacturing, would send her action/strategy I.A.1. about reducing scrap to Jorge Garcia, the superintendent of Line 1. At the same time, Jones might have a second action/strategy for reducing manufacturing costs through automation of some aspect of storage retrieval. That action/strategy, called I.A.2., would be sent only to the superintendent of material handling.

When all of the PORSs finally reach the entry-level personnel, there will be instances in which the employees are not interested or capable of responding in detail in writing to an actual PORS. In these cases, the supervisor should call a meeting and discuss the action/strategy items his or her boss has passed along. The supervisor should solicit input and perhaps form a few small, short-term teams to propose ways of attaining each action/strategy item for the supervisor to use to respond to his or her boss's action/strategy items.

Phase 2. Bottom-Up

The purpose of phase 2 is to collect and synthesize all of the employees' input into a recommended series of actions and strategies which will support the organization's goals and can be reviewed in appropriate detail by successive levels of management.

When the PORSs arrive at the bottom of the organization, they begin their return trip up the organizational ladder. This is where phase 2 begins. In some cases, this may occur at very high staff positions. Many PORSs, in large organizations, will travel through ten or more levels between the entry-level employees and the CEO (which is about five levels too many, but that's another problem).

Clearly, the entire stack of paper can't be passed all the way up the ladder. For each PORS received from his or her boss on the downward trip through the organization, each supervisor fills out a new one for the return trip. The new one displays the same entries as the top-down PORSs for the people up the line (all of the supervisor's bosses). The supervisor's action/strategy section is rewritten to show the action/strategy items he or she believes are most appropriate for the particular objective in question. In other words, the new PORS summarizes and synthesizes all of the suggestions which have been made by all levels of subordinates who report to the supervisor. Each supervisor, at every level, must review all of the suggested action/strategies his or her direct subordinates submit and must select those which are the most promising and appropriate. This is the critical link that will make or break the entire process. Supervisors must be willing to accept new ideas, take a few risks, and shoot a few daring suggestions up the line, both their own and those of their subordinates.

108

Figure 6.2 presents an example of the phase 2 PORS. This one would be prepared by Lorena Jones, VP of manufacturing. Note that the content of the PORS in the sections prepared by Jones's bosses are the same as those in Figure 6.1. Jones has modified the action/strategy section she used in Figure 6.1 to include the best of the recommendations she received from all of her subordinates (the superintendents) relevant to her I.A.1. action/strategy item. Note that one of the items (I.A.1.a.) is the action/strategy item suggested by Jorge Garcia (as shown in Figure 6.1). The other action/strategy items shown (I.A.1.b. and I.A.1.c.) were submitted by other superintendents who report to Jones. Penny, after receiving all of Jones's PORSs and those of her colleagues, would review them all and decide on a set of action/strategy items to put on each of his PORSs to support each of the CEO's objectives.

This specification of subordinate input is tremendously important. The next level of authority has something to go on in deciding on the types of strategies to be used (given approval) to attain each goal. In Figure 6.2, Jones's boss, Penny, knows exactly how she plans to implement her 20 percent scrap reduction so that he can get part of his 4 percent cut in manufacturing costs. Given the input on Jones's phase 2 PORS, Penny has some basis for deciding where limited resources should be routed. After reviewing all of the PORSs from the personnel on Jones's level relevant to his manufacturing cost-reduction action/strategy item, he has a secure basis on which to approve specific actions. When Penny prepares his phase 2 PORS, he combines all of the best input he has received under his manufacturing cost-reduction action/strategy item (I.A.). Each supervisor will do this for every PORS sheet he or she receives.

When all of the rewritten PORSs eventually reach the top of the organization, it's decision time for the executives. They must decide which action/

---

1. *Name/title*: Frieda Dorfendurfer, CEO
   Objective: I
   Increase profits 3 percent over 1986 levels.

2. *Name/title*: Jack Penny, President
   Action/strategy: I.A.
   Cut manufacturing costs by 4 percent.

3. *Name/title*: Lorena Jones, VP of Manufacturing
   Action/strategy: I.A.1.
   Reduce scrap 20 percent.
   a. Install parts stackers in areas with more than 2 percent scrap.
   b. Implement operator tool use training in areas with high-error scrap rates.
   c. Outsource more welding assemblies so that vendors incur scrap losses.

Figure 6.2   A Sample Phase 2 Planning Objectives Response Sheet (PORS)

strategy items from their immediate subordinates to approve. Once that decision process is made, it's time for phase 3.

Phase 3. Top-Down for the Second Time

The purpose of this phase is to communicate to all employees exactly what the goals of the organization are, and exactly how they'll be implemented.

As the executives at the top approve and finalize each phase 2 PORS (perhaps with recommendations or suggestions of their own), they pass them back to the subordinates for implementation. The beauty of this approach is that when an objective is approved, everyone down the command chain knows exactly what that item means to them; they already submitted their suggestions. Nobody is surprised, nobody is shocked, and nobody is wondering what they're supposed to do.

The announcement of the finally approved goals and operational objectives should be communicated through as many channels as possible. Departmental meetings, the company newspaper, and a variety of techniques which will be described in the next chapter should be used to tell every employee loudly and specifically as much about the plan as possible. Ideally (and required for maximum productivity), the objectives of each supervisor should be used to develop each subordinate's performance objectives for the year, using the type of goal-setting and performance review process described in chapter 8.

Important Considerations in Implementing Millennium Management Planning

The Importance of Supervisory Functions

The planning process described above can't operate effectively in isolation. The driving force must be supervisors at all levels who are dedicated to using the full potential of their employees. This means that coaching, joint goal setting, and providing feedback must be an integral part of each supervisor's efforts to put together the most effective set of action/strategy items for each PORS. Many supervisors, without proper guidance and direction, would respond to a PORS by simply putting down their best personal choices about what would work. That's not the purpose of *Millennium Management* planning. *Millennium Management* planning is intended to develop plans which everyone can support and identify with. Any other type of plan, which is most business plans, will simply be viewed as another order from management. Orders are complied with in order to stay out of trouble. That type of grudging support isn't going to motivate the type of creativity and involvement your organization needs. If the supervisors don't make this approach work through their day-to-day performance of the supervisory f doesn't have a chance.

The Filler Factor

While it sometimes seems difficult to find a creative employee when you need one (because you don't ask often enough), there are a lot of them in every organization. When planning time arrives, many who would otherwise not stir from their withdrawn noninvolvement awaken to fill their department's portions of the annual plan with sparkling verbiage. They're not doing it maliciously; they're only attempting to have an impact. Every department generally has at least one of these creative writers, who can make a new way to format memos appear critical to the company's success. Most often, they're pressed into service by supervisors who don't have any ideas, haven't tried to get the employees involved, and are afraid of the visibility they'll get if they don't generate a lot of action items and strategies. So they prod the creative writers into a once-a-year flurry of activity. The result is a lot of flotsam which confounds the plans, lengthens them, and casts an unhealthy pallor on the few good ideas they accompany. It's critically important to the success of the *Millennium Management* planning process that such filler material be excluded from the plan. Supervisors at every level must not be reluctant to ask for operational details of specific action/strategy items in order to determine whether they are valid. Attempt to follow the stream of logic and determine how any objective supports higher-level objectives. Much filler material looks great by itself but doesn't fit easily into a consistent framework. If the supervisor won't be candid, ask to see the subordinates' supporting PORS. *Millennium Management* is participative, employee-involvement-driven management, to be sure, but it is also no-nonsense, everybody-does-their-work-as-expected management. Never be afraid to ask (not accuse) for details and supporting data. If they're not there, it's time for some coaching and feedback.

Summary

This chapter could only outline the basic approach to *Millennium Management* planning. The key is to involve each employee in the process in as specific a manner as possible and then communicate the finally developed plan in just as much detail. There must be no doubt in anyone's mind that they're required to participate, that their input will be taken seriously, and that they'll be completely informed of all pertinent plans. That type of attitude, supported by *Millennium Management* supervisory techniques and norm inoculation procedures, will resu in an informed and committed group of employees, which not one in 10,00 organizations possesses.

CHAPTER 7

Effective Millennium Management of Formal Communication Channels, Rituals, and Ceremonies

How effectively is your organization using its formal communication channels, rituals, and ceremonies (CRCs) to communicate clear signals to all employees and thereby inoculate consistent norms into all parts of the organization? Do the written communications the employees see support what the organization must have to survive? Are the tone, content, and style of your organization's rituals and ceremonies specifically engineered to reward behaviors which are appropriate to productivity? If your organization is typical in its use of CRCs, the best it's doing is wasting a valuable resource. More likely, the CRCs are being used to send messages which are diametrically opposed to increased productivity. This chapter will briefly explore the purpose and function of a variety of CRCs and then provide a clear blueprint for using them effectively to inoculate norms for productivity into the organization. Before reading any further, evaluate the current effectiveness of your organization's CRCs by taking the quiz in Figure 7.1. (You'll find the answers at the end of the chapter.)

Now let's see where your organization stands in regard to its effective use of CRCs. If only one or two of your answers matched those at the end of the chapter, yours is a rare organization, effectively managing its CRCs. If only three or four answers matched, your organization is doing a fair job of utilizing some *Millennium Management* CRC techniques. Unfortunately, the overall effect isn't appreciably helping with the norm inoculation process; too many negative messages are also being sent. If five to seven of the answers matched, your organization is cutting its own throat by sending out all sorts of damaging signals to employees. The few good things that might be happening are being washed out by the noise of bad signals. If you matched more than eight of the answers, the CRCs of your organization are working actively and aggressively

---

1. Is your company newspaper pretty much a collection of smiling pictures of executives shaking hands with retirees, hobby-club news, cutesy articles where the emphasis is on fun, and rah-rah hype about how great the company is doing on this month's hot topic?

2. Does the company newspaper ever contain articles by lower-level employees about their views and/or criticisms of the company?

3. Are your organization's bulletin boards pretty much a collection of yellowing safety posters, the required wage and salary disclosure sheets, and used sofa ads?

4. Do senior executives periodically and regularly have luncheons and/or meetings with small groups of lower-level employees for the purpose of soliciting information about problems, ideas, and progress?

5. Does your organization regularly let everyone know about sales, productivity, turnover, profitability, and problems by means of special announcements, the company paper, and honest face-to-face discussions?

6. Has someone who's generally regarded as a laughingstock received a special service award?

7. Does your organization require all departments to give short periodic briefings to other departments in which they talk about what they do and how they need cooperation and solicit ideas and suggestions about things they should be doing?

8. Do the employees in your organization know (or care) about what goes on in high-level meetings?

9. Is it common to see senior managers or executives walking around in operational departments of the company when they're not on tour with a visiting group?

10. Are the employees who put together your company newspaper pretty much journalist types who have little operational experience in your business, with low status and authority, and who must get approvals for everything they print from ten different people?

Figure 7.1   CRC Quiz

to send out the worst possible signals: productivity isn't important; just put in your time, relax, and stay out of trouble.

Before reading this book, you can't have been expected to recognize the importance of CRCs as part of the norm inoculation process. There are few organizations where anyone could observe them being properly designed and applied. When examined in the watered-down, pale formats most organizations practice, CRCs don't appear to be anything but meaningless peripheral concerns tolerated because "it's expected that we have them, but we all know they're formalities."

Unfortunately, when CRCs aren't used properly, the effect isn't simply a benign waste of effort; improper use of CRCs sends all sorts of negative and contrary signals which reinforce employees' unfavorable views about the organization, its executives, and its goals. For example, your organization no doubt has all sorts of serious problems which it must solve in order to survive, prosper, and remain profitable. Yet what types of suggestions are shown winning the prizes in the company paper? Most often, they're minor paper-flow or forms changes which, while nice, are not of earth-shaking impact. What effect do you think this has on the employees in the company who are struggling with desperate manufacturing, marketing, sales, and engineering problems, who are coming up with great stuff all the time as part of their regular work and never hear any praise? What they're thinking is, "What's going on around here? Here we are, with market share going down the toilet, and the company gives someone $25 and a write-up in the company paper for making a change on the personnel form for requesting discount tickets to theme parks? Doesn't the brass know or care what's going on?" That's the sort of reaction the typical suggestion/award program generates. The result is that the group barriers go up and the organization's norms are resisted because the employees can clearly see that their own norms are much different. They see themselves as struggling to get meaningful work done, and then they see the organization rewarding a bit of fluff instead of dealing with the real problems. This type of reaction is typical when CRCs are viewed as unimportant necessities. ("Well, everyone has a company paper, so we should too, but let's keep it happy and positive." Happy and positive generally means bland, misleading, and condescending to anyone with a brain.)

Some of the recommendations in this chapter can be implemented only by those in higher levels of authority. A first-line supervisor isn't going to be able to walk into the office tomorrow and reorganize the company newsletter. Other types of CRCs are appropriate for all levels of management. Yet, regardless of the CRC techniques appropriate for a specific level of responsibility, there's a common thread of attempting to communicate candor, sincerity, and serious business that pervades them all. If you stick to the spirit of effective CRCs, you'll generate good signals regardless of the actual number of CRCs that you're able to initiate or support.

If you're a higher-level executive, you're going to get a lot of flak from your senior colleagues when you first start to implement the recommendations which follow. In fact, you'll get more overt pressure to go back to the old ways than you'll encounter on any other *Millennium Management* issue. The primary reason is that the open discussions, candor about problems, and honest solicitation of suggestions and participation from the employees will be seen as signs of executive/management weakness and viewed as weak.

Millennium Management is tough, hard-nosed management whose implementation will test the courage and dedication of any executive. But it's a different kind of toughness, which eschews acting tough in favor of being tough and smart enough to do what's best for the organization. That's a toughness most managers aren't used to demonstrating. Many managers have been taught that management doesn't admit problems to anyone; it just fixes them the best it can on its own. In the case of obtaining dramatically increased productivity, the only feasible solution is to get the employees actively and enthusiastically involved. As we've seen, there's no way to do that without giving them information, asking them for information, and sincerely working with them. And there's no way to do that without using your organization's CRCs in an effective manner. Hiding problems from the employees and attempting to be secretive about things they already know about never fixes anything. Most of your managers will quickly fall into line with your new CRC strategy if you're pushing on other *Millennium Management* fronts as well. If they're unable to shape up and get on board after a decent interval and plenty of coaching, get rid of them.

Each of the following sections presents a technique for managing one particular aspect of your organization's CRCs. Don't let the individual presentations mislead you into thinking that one or two of them can stand alone. The entire concept of *Millennium Management* depends on a comprehensive application of techniques across as many of an organization's systems as possible. If you prefer, you can omit one or two of the following techniques from your *Millennium Management* implementation without doing any great harm (as long as you don't allow poorly conceived current programs to remain in place and send contrary signals). On the other hand, you can't implement only one or two of the techniques and expect to do anything but stir up a lot of confusion.

Departmental/Sectional Meetings

Department, section, and work-group meetings are regularly scheduled, agenda-driven functions in which a supervisor meets with his or her subordinates and perhaps their subordinates. In its simplest form, a supervisor gets together with subordinates. Even if the supervisor has only two subordinates and they work together all the time, it's important to have regular meetings so that general issues can be succinctly discussed without possibility of distortion. Regular department meetings are essential as direct norm inoculation devices. All sorts of good news, team play, and employee participation messages can be sent in these meetings.

A supervisor should have a group meeting with his or her subordinates at least once a week. A department head should hold a meeting with the entire department at least once every six weeks, probably not more often than once a month unless there's a major project underway. If there are too many people, several smaller meetings should be held. The meetings should never be made to run for a specified length of time. If it's over in five minutes, fine; don't drag it out just to fill in a time slot. They shouldn't be used exclusively to deal with problems, although problems must be discussed candidly. The supervisor running the meeting should give a brief summary of the organization's current events, any news relevant to the section or department, and a report on the progress of programs or projects the department is operating. Departmental road shows (see below) from other departments would be presented in these meetings. These meetings are the forum for employee groups to present their findings on special assigned projects, for soliciting volunteers to work on special projects, and for passing out congratulations to employees who have done superior special work for the department.

Departmental/Divisional Road Shows

Road shows are an extremely effective way of breaking down the barriers which hinder intergroup cooperation. They can be especially effective when operations are spread out geographically and/or when there's been an absence of cooperation in solving problems which affect many groups or departments in a facility or location. Road shows are presentations in which one group makes a brief (ten minutes to one hour, depending upon the complexity and criticality of the information) presentation to another group. The presenting group describes their staffing, organization, operating characteristics, interface with other groups, resources available, and most pressing problems. They then solicit input about areas of mutual concern and suggestions for improving their services, and they answer questions.

The presentations should take place at the listening group's department meetings. Every department should be required to give one road show each month and to listen to one each month.

The presentations should be designed and presented by a different team from within each group each month. This ensures that the information, perspective, and interest of the presenters remain fresh and enthusiastic. The presenters must not always be senior types; presentations by lower-level employees will be received with less suspicion, and this will help at first to break down intergroup barriers. It also increases the sense of participation by the lower-level employees. The company paper and product/process and information boards should be used to announce schedules of upcoming presentations. The announcements will heighten the "we're all in this together" feeling.

Product/Process and Information Boards

Product/process and information boards are the *Millennium Management* counterparts of the faded, yellowing, and totally ignored bulletin boards which now serve as two-dimensional vertical trashcans in your organization. Each product/process board presents a detailed explanation of the development, design, production, and/or delivery of one of your organization's products (such as plastic widgets) or processes (such as how customer billings are generated). The design of each product/process board incorporates flowcharts and brief (depending on the size of the board) written descriptions of specific aspects of the product/process. Interfaces with other departments are emphasized in terms of input and output. The names and phone numbers of key personnel (not just the managers) are included. Viewers are exhorted to call someone to ask questions or make suggestions.

Information boards are presentations of more generic and topical information, much of which would already be available in the company paper but some of which will be specific to the location in which the board is located. Refer to the section below on company papers for suggested information board content.

The boards should be conspicuously placed and large enough to be read easily. Don't restrict the placement of a particular board to the area with which it's concerned; you'll be surprised at the amount of interest which the employees in, for example, accounting will have in the plastic widget manufacturing process. Rotate each board through different locations on a monthly or bimonthly basis. After six months, recycle the boards or take them out of service. Put them in conspicuous areas in production areas, cafeterias, personnel waiting rooms, lobbies, near tool cribs, near elevators, and near time clocks.

You've got to make the boards attractive and professional in appearance. Assign each department or product area to design a board. Review each board in your areas to make sure they're not fluff, but don't decide the design and content; that's the job of the supervisor and the employees in the area. Make sure that names and phone numbers (a few employee pictures are a good touch on bigger boards) are on them. If there's an area where there's a problem (such as too many B-24 widget rejects), use a few boards which highlight that problem. Make sure the boards are positive but realistic in tone, content, and orientation. Don't use them to blame or accuse.

The Company Paper

The company paper is supposed to be one of the most visible expressions of what's going on in the organization. If that's true, it appears that the employees in most organizations aren't doing much more than having babies, holding retirement and awards dinners, going bowling, and generally having fun. A lot of company papers are so jammed with fluff that it's hard to tell what product the companies make. In contrast, the *Millennium Management* company paper is a carefully designed tool used primarily to inoculate the organization's norms and goals into its many groups. The *Millennium Management* company paper also serves a critical informational purpose. In the typical organization, the employees already know the problems and bad news, but they don't usually have enough information to help solve them. The *Millennium Management* company paper provides them with the data they need to help find the answers.

A company paper designed to serve as an effective communication and inoculation device must contain hard-hitting, interesting, factual, and important information. Among the types of information, sections, and features which meet this requirement are the following:

1. A candid column written by the chief executive in which an important topic about the organization is honestly discussed.
2. An update on how the company is doing against plan in terms of sales, profits, costs, and so on, using numbers, not platitudes.
3. Significant information about competitors' activities which may create problems or opportunities.
4. Unedited (except for grammar) and uncensored (except for vulgarity) articles written by employees in which suggestions, ideas, and complaints are detailed.
5. An "ask the executive" section in which employees ask questions and get answers from the brass and which is not seeded with questions management wants asked so they can give the answers they want to hear.
6. A calendar of executive and committee meetings with lists of randomly selected employees who have been invited to attend (see section on meetings below).
7. A calendar of executive luncheons and the lists of employees who have been randomly selected to attend (see the section on luncheons below).
8. A schedule of executive press conferences (see section on press conferences below).
9. A transcription of the last executive—employee press conference.
10. Letters to the editor.

11. A schedule of departmental road shows.

12. Features about employees who have excelled in attempts to do something significant for the organization's productivity. We're not talking about people who suggest a new line on a form but the rare employee who battles through a good idea, dramatically cuts costs, makes a monster sale, and/or comes up with a real innovation. Forget the "Martha won the knitting contest stuff;" nobody cares except Martha and you don't need to be sending the message that Martha's knitting is more critical than all of the disasters happening all over your organization every day.

13. When applicable, up-to-date information about what the company is planning for the future. Don't argue that you have to keep this type of data under wraps. If it's top secret, that's fine, but don't withhold data that are widely known anyway. Solicit input for new products or processes before all the decisions are made.

14. "I was there reports" in which employees give brief first-person accounts of their attendance at high-level executive meetings. This feature provides readers with a sense that they're all there at the meetings and helps break down intergroup barriers.

15. Information about the achievements of "strike forces" (see below) and the names of the participants.

The above are the essential news and inoculation mechanisms which will very quickly enable the employees to identify what you want (norms), where you want to go (goals), and what the limits are in getting there (expected behaviors). They're all you need for a great company paper. If you've got the resources, a few additional items can be added in order to increase the paper's initial readability and popular appeal. These additional sections will help get the paper picked up and read by more employees, thereby increasing the maximum inoculation effect:

1. Classified ads. Just look at the bulletin boards around your organization—everybody is selling something. If they do it in the paper, more people will read it.

2. The usual contests (photos, baby pictures, etc.). It's OK to have these items in the paper as long as it's clear to anyone with a brain that this type of fluff is just filler, like comics in a daily newspaper. The danger of this type of content is that if there's any controversy with the real news items, gutless managers will want to cut them back and increase the photo contests.

3. Company sports news.

4. Recent promotions (with reasons why), new hires, and departures (no need to give a reason if it's not a retirement or voluntary termina-

tion). Don't worry about the effect of telling the employees that someone's not with the company. Everybody knows who's going and why. It's a bigger shock and causes more talk when someone leaves and management tries to pretend it didn't happen and hopes no one will notice.

You can see from the above that the new company paper isn't going to be the same old sheet of fun and trivia. If you want *Millennium Management* productivity, you don't have any choice. Find someone in the company who's sharp, enthusiastic, outspoken, but responsible and a doer. Put that person in charge as editor (in addition to their regular job—the last thing anyone needs is a full-time paper editor, a real waste of money and sure to put them out of touch with what's going on). Tell the editor that he or she has complete and final editorial control after the top executive has given his or her approval. Don't let anyone else get onto a signoff approval sheet; if they do, you'll end up with the typical wimpy and useless company paper in two months. Have the top executive work closely on the first issue with the editor and the other people (if any) who will be doing the compilation, typing, and coordination, and then let it roll.

Change the editor every six months to keep it fresh. Give a variety of employees a shot at it, and make sure that the top executive provides detailed feedback about what he or she wants. The paper should come out every month if you've got the resources. It doesn't have to be a three-color job with professional artwork; it's the content, not the appearance, that gets the message inoculated. Less than once every two months is a mistake, because the paper won't maintain its visibility and impact at that interval. It's got to arrive on the scene often enough to become an expected and eagerly awaited part of the organization's communication network.

Press Conferences

Press conferences are formal, scheduled gatherings in which the chief executive or very senior management takes questions from the assembled employees and answers them on the spot. This procedure is remarkably effective for showing the employees exactly what you want them to see: an executive who's not afraid to deal with them openly, honestly, and directly. The intergroup barriers come down fast if the executive handles the situation honestly. Employees will no longer view senior managers as part of another elite group that never gives them a straight story. If you deal openly and reasonably with them, they'll respect you for it and work a lot harder for you.

A press conference should be scheduled once every four to six weeks. Pattern it more or less like presidential press conferences. The similarity will provide the event with added impact and prestige. Announce the event in the company paper, on information boards, and in department meetings. Hold the conference in a large room, auditorium, or open outdoor area.

The executive hosting the affair should be the unit, division, or facility manager of the employees who are attending. Executives from other locations and units or those from corporate are not going to be very effective as norm and goal inoculators for employees who don't know them well. The executives who lead each large division or location or corporate areas should hold their own press conferences for their own employees, because they're the ones who have to be perceived as the leaders of the division or location by the employees who work there.

Be sure to provide a microphone for the executive and the employees if it's a large group or the acoustics are poor. Have the individual questioners, when pointed out by the executive or an aide, come forward to a fixed microphone to ask their question.

If executives don't handle these types of situations with ease, they had better get some professional help in speaking and thinking on their feet. The critical thing is to be straightforward at all times. If they don't know an answer, they should admit it and tell the questioner that they'll find out and print the answer in the company paper (you can now see how all of these *Millennium Management* techniques fit together). If a question is insulting or out of order (in terms of propriety), the executive shouldn't be reluctant to say so; if he or she is dealing honestly with the employees, they'll exert a lot of pressure on any malcontents to keep things polite and fair. Nobody is going to get too pushy, because they know they'll pay for any bad moves later. Conversely, it's imperative to spread the word that nobody will be reprimanded for asking direct, tough questions. Don't worry about things getting really tense. The employees never forget who the boss is.

After doing a few press conferences, the executive will find that he or she is at ease. After each press conference, the questions and answers should be printed in the company paper as a feature story. The open communication will generate twice as much good feeling when mentioned again.

Open Management/Executive Meetings

Executive committee meetings, management committee meetings, planning sessions, budget reviews, and their counterparts can be an extremely effective means of norm inoculation. All you've got to do is permit randomly selected employees to sit in as observers at various management meetings. If you've got security or legal problems with this type of participation in some of your meetings because of the nature of the material covered, no problem. However, if you're honest with yourself, you'll admit there are few management meetings which require those types of restrictions. I've worked on top-secret military projects, and most project reviews could have been attended by anyone in the company without a problem. Most of the initial reluctance to accept this idea derives from the fact that many managers would either be embarrassed that "the employees will see how we act" or would believe that "they don't have any right to see what we do."

In the case of embarrassment, most organizations' managers have a lot to worry about. The amount of silly nonsense, sexual double entendres, fooling around, childish behavior, and acting out that goes on in so-called high-level meetings is disgusting. If I were conducting myself in that manner, I wouldn't want anyone who wasn't in on it to see it either. That's one very strong reason to include employees, aside from the more important purpose of permitting the invited employees to feel involved and to understand the decision processes which influence their work. You'll find that the meetings will proceed in a more orderly, more professional manner and with less horseplay if there are occasionally one or two lower-level employees present.

Announce the new policy in the next company paper. Publish a schedule of the next month's or the next quarter's meetings and, for each meeting, the names of one or two employees who have been randomly selected to attend. Make it clear that the attendance is voluntary (some won't want to go; they'll feel uncomfortable) but that supervisors must permit selected employees to attend if they wish. Select the employees from all levels of the organization, the only restriction being that selected employees must not be employees who are already eligible to attend. Announce that the attendees may, if they wish, write a brief description of what they thought of the meeting for submission to the company paper. Have the editor select two or three of the attendees' articles for the next paper. Make sure there's not a whitewash going on; if employees sense a coverup of negative reviews, you'll lose credibility. If you're not sure or too scared to jump in with this technique all at once, run a little experiment and have a lower-level employee or two sit in on a meeting and tell you what they think (if you can find any who will be honest with you before the implementation of *Millennium Management*). You'll generally find that the feedback will be remarkably positive, regardless of the way your meetings are running now. This will be a result of the attendees' pride at being picked and their feelings of being a part, if only for a few minutes, of the decision-making process. This is just the type of norm you want to propagate.

Walking Around

The concept of management by walking around (MBWA) has received a lot of attention since it was popularized by *In Pursuit of Excellence*. As originally conceived, MBWA was a device whereby members of management would spend a great deal of time wandering around operational departments, poking through work in progress, asking questions, and generally finding out about problems and opportunities through first-hand contact. The Hewlett-Packard company is most often mentioned as an example of successful use of MBWA. Several stories make the rounds in which executives at Hewlett-Packard are supposed to have stumbled across great ideas as they wandered around. This type of MBWA may be appropriate for an engineering company which always practiced it, but it's not appropriate for most organizations. MBWA sounds nice as a way for executives to learn about the work in progress, but in most environments they don't know enough about the technical, hands-on details to interpret the actual work correctly. The more meaningful technique to learn about these items is the *Millennium Management* planning process described in chapter 6. The proper way for a supervisor to learn about such things is through consistent practice of the ten supervisory functions outlined in chapter 5.

Yet MBWA does serve a critical function. In most organizations, the executives are distant from most of the employees in terms of both their office locations and psychological distance. The employees don't know and perceive them as people; the executives are figureheads. This helps perpetuate counterproductive informal norms about management ("It's us and them," "They don't care about us," "They think they're better, that's why they don't come around," and so on). Periodic informal walkthroughs in operational areas (it doesn't do any good to perform these only within ten feet of executive row) by individual executives are an extremely effective way to show employees that the executives are real people. These walkthroughs also make the employees feel special and important, giving a critical boost to the local supervisor's efforts to provide individual recognition. If an executive routinely practices such walkthroughs, the employees will quickly come to perceive him or her as more than just a figurehead. The executive will begin to be perceived as the leader who originates the norms and goals for the entire group of employees. This will result in less conflict between informal group norms and those of the employees. Although many of the other CRCs also support this process, walking around is a very powerful way to influence many employees at one time with a minimum investment of time.

It's very simple in concept. An executive simply takes a walk through an operational area, perhaps with the local supervisor as an introducer. They take time to stop and talk to a few employees, shake everyone's hand, introduce themselves (you'd be surprised at the number of people who won't know the top executive in person), and generally visit for a few minutes with no ulterior motive. The executive must not use the walkthroughs to look for problems, talk down to anyone, or lecture about keeping work areas clean, desks organized, and so on. If the walkthroughs are used to find problems, they'll only be reinforcing every bad perception of executives that the employees already have.

If the executive does see something that needs attention, he or she should mention it privately to the supervisor. They shouldn't rush through the visits as if they're pressed for time; the whole purpose is to show that they care enough about meeting a few employees that they're willing to take some time to do it. One great way to incorporate walking around into an executive's daily routine is for him or her to walk to subordinates' offices for meetings once or twice a day instead of summoning them up to the royal enclave. On the way through, they should introduce themselves to a few people, say hi, mention that they were just passing through. The employees will love it as soon as they realize the sky isn't about to fall.

It's best for an executive to initiate walking around by example. If the top executive does it, talks it up, perhaps relates an interesting incident in the company paper, some of the other executives will follow suit. If a mandate is issued that all the brass should start walking around, there will be a flurry of walkthroughs for a day or two that will look mighty strange to the employees; they'll know it's a mandated policy and be suspicious. And if it's mandated, it will stop in a week or so as everyone comes up with excuses about why they couldn't do it. The top executives should introduce this technique by example and then privately encourage a few of their colleagues to try it every now and then. Executives must be sure to write down any questions they're asked by employees if they can't answer them on the spot. The response can be made in person on the next walkthrough, by phone, or in the company paper.

Luncheons with Executives

Unless your organization has an atypical group of executives, there will be a lot of resistance when the concept of walking around is introduced. All sorts of mental gymnastics will be used to justify a lack of visibility or interaction behaviors ("I'm too busy," "Wanted to but something came up," etc.). The top-level executives may need a little help and encouragement. Luncheons can provide this. They can be incredibly powerful tools for opening up honest communication between the executives and employees. Once luncheons are an ongoing event, the employees will volunteer all sorts of information and suggestions to all supervisors and managers, because they'll know it's OK to be frank with management; they'll know them as individuals and won't feel threatened or believe that their input will just be ignored (which is how they perceive the situation now).

Every month, each top executive should take a small group of employees (less than ten) to lunch or breakfast. If your organization is particularly tight with the bucks, set aside some tables in the cafeteria and use them for this purpose. An alternative is to cater in a deli spread or the like and hold the luncheon in a conference room. The executive should use the luncheons to communicate their views of what's happening to the organization, to honestly probe into how things are going, to solicit input about problems, and so on. If the organization is implementing the other *Millennium Management* techniques, the executives will soon get a sense of how to handle these meetings if they aren't comfortable at first.

The employees at a specific lunch should be more or less from the same level (but not necessarily the same department) so that a higher-ranking employee doesn't intimidate everyone. Announce the schedule of lunches on information boards and in the company paper with the names of randomly selected (within job levels) attendees. Tell each group where and when to meet.

Each executive must understand that it's critical to follow up on any questions or suggestions which can't be answered right at the luncheon. Only top-level executives should host the luncheons; they're the ones who will make the biggest impact on employees. If any executives are too arrogant or rub employees the wrong way, they shouldn't participate in this program.

These luncheons have powerful impact, but they can reinforce bad feelings about executives and the company if misused. Above all, don't permit anyone to use these luncheons to dig for trouble or to come down hard if problems are uncovered.

Feedback Charts on Highly Visible Issues

At any one time, there are probably two or three key issues, projects, or problems whose successful resolution is crucial to a section, department, or organization's success. A supervisor or manager can use these high-visibility items to facilitate norm inoculation efforts and to channel additional group and individual effort toward solution of the problems. This is done by placing large feedback charts in key areas. These feedback charts are information boards which deal with a specific topic, are generally very large, and display ongoing results toward a goal. The charity-drive charts, most often shaped like a thermometer, used to show progress in contributions by successively shading in the middle of the thermometer, are a common form of feedback chart.

The availability of constant feedback on key issues does several important things you can't afford to pass up. First of all, the obvious presence of a large, continually updated display makes it crystal clear that the issue is important. Secondly, the mere presence of the information orients a work group to view the topic as something that affects their group's status. This is a natural consequence of group dynamics if the organization has been practicing other *Millennium Management* techniques and the employees have confidence in their leadership. Thirdly, and most importantly, the feedback chart will cause individuals and the group to improve their performance simply because they'll want to have an effect on the displayed data. As they work, they'll be a little more careful of errors, a little more intense, and they'll support others who do the same. A lot of this effect won't even be conscious, but it will happen. I've worked with organizations that had atrocious quality problems which significantly improved simply because of the presence of large feedback charts showing number of parts rejected. When the feedback charts are paired with any necessary training, coaching, information, and a *Millennium Management* atmosphere, the results will be outstanding.

The charts must be large, visible, and straightforward. They must show, by means of a graph or table, quantitative results toward a reasonable goal. The results must be updated daily, weekly, or monthly as appropriate. Once they're left unattended, everyone will know the issue's not important anymore. The employees must be told exactly what the charts mean, why they're important, and how progress is to be measured. Use the company paper, luncheons with executives, and information boards to spread the word. The construction of each board should be assigned to the supervisor (who must involve his or her employees) of the area involved with the subject. Don't use feedback charts to track things over which individual work groups have little direct control, as in yearly revenue. That sort of information is more appropriate for the company paper. Don't dilute the effectiveness of feedback charts by using them as bulletin boards. Use them only for items that are topical, changing, and directly related to the efforts of a particular work group or groups.

For example, a chart which tracks sales would be ideal for the sales or marketing department but wouldn't be of more than informational interest to the crew in production. (Put such general data in the paper for everyone to see.) On the other hand, the number of defect-free parts would profit from display and tracking in production areas on a feedback chart but wouldn't help much in the marketing department. Don't fall prey to the temptation to make every issue a feedback chart issue; use them only for urgent topics that need a little extra push. Be sure to use the other channels to push them as well.

Ceremonial Functions

Ceremonial functions are the ubiquitous award dinners, annual management dinners, holiday parties, picnics, building dedications, open houses, and ribbon cuttings. A quick glance at the social calendar of any organization will demonstrate that such events are a frequent and highly visible part of the organization's social environment. As such, ceremonial events can play a very effective role in inoculating your norms into the organization. As they're commonly staged, however, they're inadvertently used to send damaging and counterproductive messages deep into every corner of the organization. The typical company awards dinner, for example, reinforces almost every negative perception and association about management which any group of workers could possibly harbor.

Think back to your last one. Several executives got up and gave long-winded, rah-rah speeches which completely avoided an honest look at the organization's situation. Then the awards were given out. Who got them? The longevity awards went to a number of folks who hadn't done anything much besides show up for five, ten, fifteen, twenty, or twenty-five years. (That's why they could tough it out and stay; they weren't frustrated to death trying to get things done.) After the longevity awards, the special achievement awards were distributed. They're typically presented to the process-protecting bureaucrats who interfere with the real workers. As these awards are announced, the people at the head table always think the buzz from the crowd is approval. But it's actually muffled jokes, irritation, and outrage over the fact that the frumps of the organization got the awards while the ones who are fighting to save the company are ignored. Witnessing such travesties, the creative and hard-working people feel betrayed. They begin to give up or throttle back. Some of them keep trying, but they accompany their work with bitter complaints which serve to further degrade the norms of their groups. When they see executives get up and make a lot of pompous remarks, it reinforces their perceptions that the brass is working to a different set of norms: those of executives who not only don't respect them, but don't even know what's going on.

The typical slate of awards ceremonies must be completely overhauled. Forget the company sponsored retirement dinners and the service awards. The retirees are rewarded by their pensions, and the reward for the people who have been there for twenty years is still having a job. Service awards send all the wrong messages about all the wrong things. Are you rewarding folks who stick around because they couldn't get work elsewhere? Are you particularly interested in encouraging employees to settle in and not make waves when they see something wrong? Do you want to give the impression that time in service and not results is the key to recognition? If not, drop the service awards. Nobody should receive extra praise or reward simply because they've been around or because they're still showing up every day. Focus instead on rewarding bold new solutions, incredible feats of productivity, and people who don't give up on a problem until it's solved. Start rewarding attempts to do things better. Start giving awards to the front-line employees who deal valiantly with the day-to-day struggles on the production line and with the customers. Start recognizing achievement, whether it's done by someone who's only been on the job a month or someone who's been there twenty years. You can give just as many rewards just as often. Just make sure that everyone knows your organization rewards performance, not longevity. Then it won't matter if someone gets passed over in favor of someone else a little less deserving. The important thing will be that everyone will recognize that achievement, hard work, creativity, and not taking no for an answer are the norms of your organization. Everyone will know this, work for it, and reinforce it when they see it.

Strike Forces

Strike forces are groups of employees temporarily taken off their regular jobs and assigned to special projects, most typically problem-solving teams. These efforts provide a lot of good press for the company paper, send very good signals about working together, enable people from different parts of the organization to get to know each other and each other's departments a little better, and solve a lot of problems. The amount of solid problem solving that such groups can accomplish, freed of their regular duties, is incredible. After a preset time period or after the project is completed, the employees return to their usual assignments.

The number of strike forces your organization forms, the sizes of the teams, and the length of time they're assigned to their projects will depend on the number of employees and the type of work processes you have. The teams themselves should never be made up of less than three people or more than five. If you've got only fifty people in your organization, department, or work area, you might want to form a team of three only once every six months. If you've got 2,000 employees, it's not unreasonable (and it's usually a great investment) to have one team of three to five people working each week, year round. The group members should be selected from various departments and functions in the organization. The more diverse the mix, the better for problem solving and for the messages it sends to everyone.

One program I established in a large industrial facility represents how strike forces can be organized. Each month, twenty employees were selected at random (stratified random sampling among departments and functions to ensure a mix of skills) and assigned to one of four teams. At the start of each week, each team was given several hours of instruction in a general problem-solving approach and was introduced to the format of the proposal they would have to submit at the end of the week. The proposal was a six-page form which outlined the problem they worked on, its causes, their proposed solution, impacts, and so on, including a cost-benefit analysis. After the few hours of training, they were assigned a problem to work on. The problem was selected from a list of problems approved and ranked in importance by the executive committee. The ranked list was selected from all of the problems submitted by employees. Anyone could submit a problem by means of a one-page problem suggestion sheet. At the end of the month, after each team had completed its week of problem solving, all four groups would get together to formally present their findings to the executive committee. Actions and decisions regarding the problems and the proposed solutions were printed in the company paper. There was also an awards dinner at the end of the month for all the participants at which caps, tee-shirts, and award certificates were given out. This facility even went so far as to set up a special task-force headquarters room for each group to use during its week of problem solving. Occasionally, groups were formed from within individual departments to attack specific problems in those departments. On some occasions, groups were allowed to run for several weeks or to reconvene for an additional week at a later date in order to continue on a problem after more data had been collected. There are many effective variations of this program. The most important thing is to make sure that the task forces and their results get plenty of publicity around the organization. You can't lose with this type of program.

Interdepartmental Sabbaticals

Interdepartmental sabbaticals are employee exchanges between departments in which traded employees do each other's jobs for a period of three to four months and then return to their own departments. This type of program serves many important purposes:

1. It enables employees to gain an understanding of the problems and accomplishments of other areas.

2. It provides bored employees with a challenge they may require to maintain their interest if they're stuck in a dead-end job or waiting for a promotion.

3. It brings an entirely new perspective to the job. Every specialty has unique ways of organizing and performing a task. Frequently, a fresh look from someone in a totally different field can result in startling and productive changes.

4. It breaks down the barriers between the departments.

5. It sends good signals about the organization's commitment to developing its people which reinforces the individual development supervisory function.

The program must be voluntary. Explain the nature of the program, why you're doing it (the above purposes), and how it will work in the company paper, on information boards, and in small talks at luncheons, press conferences, and so on. Once the list of volunteers is ready, develop a list of jobs by conferring with the appropriate department heads. Especially good jobs to consider for the switch are positions in which the turnover is high, where there have been a lot of problems, or where there are some contemplated changes on the horizon. Of course, almost any position is useful, unless it's perceived as a punishment tour. Set a definite limit on the time period for which the switch will remain in effect. (This eliminates any misunderstandings if employees discover they don't want to leave the new job or they want the old one back in a week.) The supervisors must have final say about whether a candidate is acceptable. Before the actual switch, assign each of the switchees to spend two hours a day for two weeks training on the new job under the supervision of the current position holder. This serves to make the transition easier and provides an opportunity to withdraw if the job turns out to be something they can't do or don't like. Once the people have completed their tour of duty in the new job, it's a good idea to write up their story in the company paper and perhaps have a special luncheon or dinner every six months or so for the employees who have completed the program. Don't use these people to fill in on the old job if somebody calls in sick or goes on vacation unless the newly-trained employee requests that he or she be permitted to substitute on such occasions. This program isn't designed as a cross-training effort to help with staffing problems. If it's perceived that way, much of the effect is lost; it must function as a personal development effort.

Summary

The techniques presented in this chapter aren't technically complex and don't require in-depth training and coaching. Yet how many of you have worked in an organization which used even two of these techniques? Most organizations don't have an appreciation of the powerful influence CRCs can have on all employees. To the unknowledgeable, the company paper, information boards, luncheons, press conferences, and so on, appear to be nothing but bothersome programs which, if they're performed at all, are typically assigned to lower-level employees. I hope you've now come to a different conclusion. The simultaneous application of four or five (or, better yet, all) of these techniques will bathe your entire organization in a steady stream of norms for productivity and hard work. If they're not used, or if their typical pale, watered-down counterparts (such as a "happy" company paper) are in place, the organization gets only a confused blend of bad messages about productivity. The proper design, management, and direction of an organization's CRCs should be a top-priority concern of its highest-level executives.

Answers to the quiz

1. Yes	6. Yes
2. No	7. No
3. Yes	8. No
4. No	9. No
5. No	10. Yes

CHAPTER 8

Compensating and Rewarding Productivity

The recent emphasis on increasing productivity has given rise to all manner of compensation and reward systems designed to spur employees on to greater efforts. Many organizations have instituted so-called pay-for-performance systems under which the employees' compensation is supposed to be closely linked to real performance. If anyone thinks that simply installing a new compensation system is going to do anything to help get more productivity from employees, they can forget it.

The recent emphasis on pay for performance is a partial step in the right direction. Compensation should be tied to performance. When the people who do the best and the most work get the biggest rewards, the organization is suffused with the norm that it pays to be productive. That sort of message motivates everyone to work a little harder to pursue the organization's goals (assuming proper supervisory practices and norm inoculation techniques are in use). Yet most pay-for-performance systems don't do the job. They fail for two reasons:

1. The pay-for-performance system is built on the shaky foundation of poor supervision. Employees aren't coached, and they're not involved in goal setting and planning. While the pay-for-performance system

may look and sound different when it's discussed, the goals toward which employees are working and the evaluation methods for determining success or failure in the pursuit of those goals are just as vague as in the past.

2. Despite the presence of pay-for-performance guidelines in determining merit increases, the bulk of the typical organization's compensation practices are not based on pay for performance. Mixed signals are sent and perceived, and the entire pay-for-performance program generally functions as simply one more corporate program which doesn't do much of anything except change the jargon used to describe the same old compensation practices.

This chapter will review the elements which comprise compensation systems and evaluate them in terms of how they operate or don't operate to reward productivity. The basic ingredients and mechanics of a true pay-for-performance system will be presented.

Basic Facts About Compensation as a Reward

It's important to face the truth about the limitations and nature of compensation as a behavior reinforcer and motivator. The following four principles provide the foundation on which this chapter's analyses and evaluations rest.

Money Doesn't Make an Employee Work Harder for More Than Two Weeks

Employees don't work day to day for money (we examined the real motivators in chapter 2). While it's true that most employees wouldn't show up if they weren't paid, once someone's employed a paycheck doesn't motivate the more productive hour-to-hour and day-to-day performance you've got to have. Once an employee lands a job and settles into it, the paycheck turns into a dissatisfier (it's only a problem if it's not adequate; more of it doesn't help much). Let's face it, most of us don't perceive our paycheck as a special reward. It's sort of an expected constant; it goes from the company's account to ours to our creditors'. Paychecks don't serve as rewards for adults as effectively as nickels (or is it now dollars?) work with two-year-olds. And even if they did, the types of pay increases handed out in so-called pay-for-performance systems are too low (2 to 8 percent) to work for even two weeks. In fact, given the inequities in almost all compensation systems, those types of increases do more harm than good.

Given The Nature of Organizations and Federal and State Laws, It's Impossible to Design a Compensation System Which Actually Bases Pay on Performance According to the Principles of Behavior Modification

Can you imagine the outcry in your organization if two or three employees didn't get paychecks one week because they hadn't done enough work? Yet that would be only one consequence of a true pay-for-performance system. It's easy to conceptually design a compensation system which operates according to the well-understood principles of behavior modification. Compensation could theoretically be turned into a true performance reinforcer, unlike the dissatisfier it's become under present systems. But it could never work in practice. First of all, it would appear to violate all sorts of laws about fair pay. Your legal fees would make the national debt look like a ten-year-old's allowance, and you'd have branch offices of federal and state regulatory commissions set up in your personnel department. Face it, we've set up a system in this country in which employees are pretty much paid to show up. Once they do that, and if they don't steal too much or attack someone, you're almost presumed guilty if you take aggressive action to punish them for not performing.

Secondly, it would be extremely difficult to ensure that a true pay-for-performance system would be equitably administered. Given the quality of supervision in most organizations, there would be many abuses in performance evaluations and rewards. Thus, even a true performance-for-pay system, based on behavior modification, won't work.

Of course, the most damning indictment of compensation as a behavior reinforcer was discussed in chapter 2: money just doesn't satisfy employees as much as the top-ranked job satisfaction factors. Even the best compensation-based behavioral reinforcement system can't induce productivity as effectively as personal recognition, feeling of accomplishment, feeling involved, and so on.

Compensation Systems Can't Help a Lot with Productivity; At Best, All They Can Do Is Not Hurt You

The above two principles make it clear that compensation systems can't do much to positively influence performance. Unfortunately, compensation systems have almost unlimited power to damage norm inoculation efforts and to compromise the efforts of supervisors to provide employees with opportunities to earn job satisfaction. All of the techniques discussed in chapter 7 are designed to send positive signals about the organization's goals and norms to all employees. A compensation system operates much like a completely separate communication system which sends out strong signals to every employee. In the typical organization, the signals are diametrically opposed to the positive signals you're trying to send by using chapter 7 techniques. If you doubt it, consider the mood around your organization at annual review time. Is everyone happy? Does everyone think they're being treated fairly? The air around the coffee machines is filled with back-biting gossip and insinuation about who got what and how outrageous it is. There's not much an organization can do to eliminate all such grousing (or the basis for it), but it is possible to initiate compensation practices which send many positive signals.

Traditional Systems of Benefits, Perks, and Compensation-Related Items Send Powerful and Damaging Signals to Everyone in the Organization

Many organizations have taken to providing employees with yearly brochures which state something to the effect that, "Your compensation is more than a paycheck." The brochure goes on to describe the cost of medical coverage, insurance, vacation time, and so on. This is a clever public relations gambit which attempts to realize some return from the soaring costs of company-paid benefits (although such brochures have no effect on motivating employees). Yet there's a serious problem even in these aspects of compensation systems. The sad truth is that most organizations' systems of benefits actually operate to kill the very productivity they're designed to motivate and reward. They send a damaging combination of signals that simultaneously attack incentive on several fronts. The messages sent by the typical system of benefits and perks range from "It's OK to settle in for the duration," to "Sit back and let the company take care of you," to "Management thinks we're just a bunch of pigs," and "The longer you're here, the less you have to do." It's possible to put together a system of perks, fringes, and benefits that sends a minimum number of these horrendous signals. That's what the remainder of this chapter is designed to do.

The Purpose of a Compensation System

As mentioned above, compensation systems are notoriously bad motivators because money generally functions only as a dissatisfier. Yet the system by which an organization rewards productivity with money and other perks sends extremely powerful and consistent messages to every employee; the money itself isn't as important as the perceived logic and fairness which operates to compensate employees. The effect of a pay increase or a vacation on an individual employee is insignificant compared to the overall perceptions of the employees about the equity of the system. If a compensation system is to be perceived as effective and equitable by the employees, it must serve several concurrent purposes:

1. *Signal that performance is valued.* It must send a strong and consistent signal to all employees that the organization values meaningful performance above all else. Every time there's a performance review, a promotion, a pay increase, or an increase in status, the message "We are paying for productivity" must be loud and clear.

2. *Signal that rewards are proportionate to contributions.* It must distribute rewards in direct proportion to the contributions that earned them. Small, routine contributions deserve no increase in any type of compensation. Extensive, comprehensive contributions deserve extensive increases in overall compensation.

3. *Break down barriers.* It must support the norm inoculation efforts of the organization by acting to counter the formation of unfavorable informal group norms. The compensation system must not contribute, as so many do, to the establishment of group divisions.

Let's look at a variety of compensation practices and evaluate where each of them stands in terms of the above three purposes.

Merit Increases

Merit increases are periodic increases in pay which are supposed to be tied to performance. If that were the case in actual practice, merit increases would be sending positive signals to everyone in the organization. As typically practiced, the awarding of merit increases does a great deal of damage.

Signal That Performance Is Valued

When it's time for merit increases, it's the rare employee who doesn't get something. Yet employees who don't do anything aren't so rare. The plain fact is that organizations are generally unwilling *not* to give merit increases to people who don't deserve them; the so-called tough captains of industry can't handle complaints and whining from the nonperformers who don't get anything. Or, worse yet, it's often assumed that everyone deserves something because the organization is doing well. This is dangerous and erroneous thinking. Everyone knows there are all sorts of employees around who aren't doing anything to help. And everyone knows that the good performers are getting the job done in spite of these losers. When the losers get any increase at all, the organization (and the supervisor who approves the increase) is sending signals which demonstrate that what's valued is not rocking the boat, not being candid, and not worrying about performance.

Signal That Rewards Are Proportionate to Contributions

It's routine practice to give "a little something" to everyone when it's time to parcel out the merit increase money. The first thing most organizations do is determine how much money is needed or available in order to give an average increase of a certain amount to each employee. Then guidelines are issued. All of this is superimposed on a rigid pay scale and grade structure which restricts how much an employee can receive before hitting the maximum. A common merit increase schedule is that adequate performers get 2 to 3 percent and good performers get 4 to 6 percent. If the scale doesn't top out at 6 percent (meaning that the organization is doing pretty well), outstanding performers might get 7 to 8 percent. All of these guidelines and averages plant the seed in everyone's mind that what's important is to evenly distribute the goodies, with only minor variations from the mean of about 4 to 6 percent. No other approach, except perhaps actively rewarding only poor performers, could send such bad signals. An employee who breaks his or her back gets at best 8 percent, and a loser who does nothing except cause trouble gets 2, perhaps 3 percent so he or she won't feel bad. On a $25,000-per-year salary, the 6 percent difference between the two merit increases amounts to $28.85 per week before taxes. Big deal! While the increased pay itself isn't going to do much in any case, even if it were five times as much, the message such a system sends is that it's not worth it to break your back because nobody knows the difference.

Break Down Barriers

Merit increases in and of themselves don't do anything to perpetuate unfavorable group barriers. However, if there are different rates of merit increases for different salary grades of job types (meaning that executives get bigger-percentage increases), then merit increases intensify management-employee suspicion and distrust. It's fairly common for the executives and higher management levels to get 1 to 3 percent greater increases straight across the board. Where an employee rated good might get 4 to 6 percent, an executive rated good is frequently eligible for 6 to 8 percent. This is a morally outrageous and unethical practice in and of itself, regardless of the bad signals it sends. If a 4 percent increase is appropriate for someone only making $25,000 per year, what justifies a larger-percentage increase for someone making $60,000 who has a much larger disposable income? For example, 4 percent increases on salaries of $25,000 and $60,000 are $1,000 and $2,400, respectively. The executive is already getting a $1,400 bigger increase than the other employee for the same type of performance. If the executive were to get a 6 percent increase rather than 4, the total increase would be $3,600, or $2,200 more than the lower-level employee. Where's the proportionality there? Why do executives qualify for fatter percentage increases than lower level employees? The answer is simple and disgusting: they set the rates, and they take what they want. This type of practice only serves to reinforce employees' perceptions that management is first and foremost concerned with its comfort and only secondarily with productivity.

136

The Millennium Management Recommendation

Adequate, run-of-the-mill employees should get no increase at any time; their reward is having a job. The choice is theirs. If they want to do some hard work and make some significant contributions, they can earn an increase. If they won't work harder and they're not happy to get regular pay increases, it's an excellent opportunity for them to test the waters of the employment market. Substandard employees should be initiated into the first phase of the termination process if coaching and feedback have failed. Exceptional employees should get exceptional increases, not because the money will spur them to even greater performances (you'll get that from these types anyway) but because it sends a clear signal to everyone that performance means recognition and status. Merit increases of 15 to 20 percent are not out of line for superior performers. The restrictions of any existing pay-grade structures must be modified to remove upper limits for superior performers who are already at or near the top of their range. Again, it's not the additional raises they might earn but the signals such a practice sends: this organization never stops rewarding productivity.

Bonuses

The word *bonus* seems to be part and parcel of reward for productivity. Once again, the reality is not quite as straightforward as the theory. A bonus is a nonrecurrent compensation award for a specific performance or period of performance. Usually it's a one-time cash award. Many organizations have across-the-board bonuses which are awarded if the organization makes its overall goals. These aren't really bonuses but function more as cost-of-living increases. Of course, the executives always get bigger percentages of bigger salaries, which is why this type of bonus is put in place.

From an organization's standpoint, a bonus system makes a lot more sense than merit increases. Once an employee receives a merit increase, he or she is entitled to that additional income from then on, year after year, more or less independent of future performance. For example, consider an employee who makes $20,000 per year and who receives a 5 percent merit increase. That's an increase of $1,000 per year. Over ten years, that one-time increase of 5 percent has hard-wired $10,000 more into the employee's paycheck, all because someone once gave him or her a 5 percent increase. What's worse, that 5 percent compounds with any other merit increases and cost-of-living increases. Yet even a one-time bonus of $2,000 would cost nothing after the first year, and the employee would be forced to maintain peak performance in order to earn additional bonuses. If it weren't for the reality of the typical business environment, bonus systems would be used to replace all merit increases.

The difficulties revolve around the criterion used for awarding bonuses. Even one little hint of unfair awards, favoritism, or perceived failure to recognize performance would wreak havoc with the workforce. As things typically stand now, there are so many nonperformance compensation awards and so many unearned merit increases that most employees don't get too upset if they get short changed by a few percent once in a while. They figure they got some last year, they'll probably get a few percent more next year, so it's no big deal. Once the dole is cut off, the bonuses would be their only means of increasing compensation over base salary. In that case, there would be a hue and outcry few organizations would be strong enough to face down. Of course, it's not the reaction of nonperformers that's the cause for concern. The larger problem is that many of these nonperformers would be the very supervisors doing the evaluations. Many productive employees wouldn't get what they deserve. Since the bonus system would be so critical to total compensation, the good people would begin to leave.

Signal That Performance Is Valued

If properly administered, very good signals are sent. As typically used, the signals are not so good; the criterion of success is not always clear in advance. In its purest form, when employees such as salespeople are awarded bonuses for reaching their goals, a bonus system will do as much as any money award to spur productivity.

Signal That Rewards Are Proportionate to Contributions

If bonus amounts are tied to specific goals and the percentages of the awards aren't adjusted to favor certain groups, very good signals are sent.

Break Down Barriers

There's no particular impact here unless the bonus system is an across-the-board award with lower-level employees getting $100 to $200 and executives getting $10,000 to $50,000.

The Millennium Management Recommendation

If your organization could implement true *Millennium Management* supervisory practices and a performance review system such as the one recommended later in this chapter, a base salary and bonus system with no merit increases is the ideal. Otherwise, use bonus systems only for employee groups such as sales where performance can be objectively tracked. Even there, difficulties arise such as with salespeople who give the best customer service but don't qualify for the volume sales bonus. Across-the-board bonuses are a waste of money and should be eliminated completely, without exception.

138

Cost-of-Living Increases

Cost-of-living increases are periodic increases given across the board to all employees. They're generally tied to some economic index such as the Consumer Price Index.

Signal That Performance Is Valued

Cost-of-living increases are a serious mistake in any situation (except perhaps runaway inflation in the 15 to 20 percent range). Automatically giving away more money for no performance-based reason at all is always bad business because it signals that what's being rewarded is simply being there. You don't want anyone thinking they get paid for occupying space. All pay increases must be the result of performance received by the organization. An organization is wasting its money and compromising its norms for productivity when money is indiscriminately distributed across the board.

Signal That Rewards Are Proportionate to Contributions

If everyone gets the same percentage amount, this purpose is violated and bad messages are sent.

Break Down Barriers

This is not an issue here.

The Millennium Management Recommendation

Award absolutely no across the board increases unless mandated by economic necessity (runaway inflation or to match industry practices in a tight labor market). Even then, you get more bang for your buck by putting all of the available increase money into a merit increase or bonus pool. Bigger increases for performance leaves no doubt about what the organization wants.

Vacations, Sick Time, Personal Leave

Signal That Performance Is Valued

The customary policy for vacation time is to allow more time off as years of service with the company increase. This is a serious mistake. What's shown is that longevity, simply being there, is sufficient to earn increased rewards. Do you want your new people believing they should work less strenuously than someone who's been there ten years? Actually, given the manner in which employees settle into jobs and adapt to informal norms and given the enthusiasm of new hires, you're probably getting more work from your new employees than from those who've been around for years. What you're saying to everyone with increased vacation for years of service is, "If you have the endurance to hang around, we'll reward you by cutting the amount of time you have to spend here." That's not a very healthy message.

Sick time is a necessary and humane practice which says good things about an organization. The policy of paying employees for sick time that's not used sends positive messages that it's possible to earn a small reward by showing up for work. Personal leave time, defined as a day or two which can be taken with pay for any purpose, is actually increased vacation time and should be considered in the same light.

Signal That Rewards Are Proportionate to Contributions

In the typical system, the worst signal possible is sent: the increased reward of more time off with increasing years of seniority has nothing to do with performance.

Break Down Barriers

It's common practice for an organization to permit various categories of employees to take more vacation time or days off without counting it as vacation. Executives and higher-level managers in many organizations are routinely permitted to come in a little late or leave a little early whenever they want, without having it count against vacation time. Yet the same organizations will typically reprimand clerical, blue-collar workers, and lower levels of white-collar workers for arriving five minutes late. That's an us-versus-them message of the most damaging type. Equally powerful in throwing up barriers and differential sets of informal norms between groups is the practice of permitting executives and managers to take "working vacations." Many companies make it a practice to pack off the top 50 to 500 (depending on their size) executives to some exotic spot for a week of "seminars." These are bald-faced perks for the executives which are no more work than half-days spent on the golf course.

The Millennium Management Recommendation

Two weeks of vacation isn't enough time for employees who are working hard. Those who aren't working hard shouldn't be there. Three weeks of vacation for all employees regardless of time on the job is reasonable. Everybody should be required to take their vacation every year. All employees should be given the same sick-time allowance, ten days per year, with more serious problems covered by short-term or long-term disability programs. Up to one week would be reimbursed if not used. All half-days for getting in late, leaving a bit early, and visits to doctors should be counted against sick time or vacation time for all employees.

Investment, Stock, Savings Programs

It's been increasingly popular for organizations to offer stock purchase and investment programs in which employees are encouraged to become "part owners of the company." Often the employee's contribution is matched to some degree by a company contribution. The company's contribution generally becomes fully vested (the employee gets the money) after five to ten years of service.

Signal That Performance Is Valued

These programs are a misapplication of funds that would be better spent on merit increases or bonuses. These programs have nothing whatsoever to do with performance. They're plain and simple dissatisfiers that are available to everyone, a throwback to the type of thinking that advocates the increased use of dissatisfiers to motivate productivity. They don't work. The argument is often made that these programs are strong recruiting tools. A much stronger tool would be to point out that it's possible to earn large merit increases or bonuses by doing exceptional work. That sends the message that productivity, not being there, is the important factor.

A tangential argument deserves a comment. Organizational leaders often state that encouraging employees to be stockholders will spur them to greater efforts because they've got a piece of the action and will be part owners. In truth, the stock purchase plans are designed to help the organization by selling a growing number of shares to purchasers who won't be turning them over as often (because they'd lose the company contribution). This keeps stock prices higher and doesn't cost the company too much, as many employees leave before they're vested. The claimed effect of stock ownership on productivity is negligible. If a weekly or monthly paycheck isn't going to do it, how much effect can a dollar or two (if your organization is doing well) per share per year have?

Signal That Rewards Are Proportionate to Contributions

Bad signals are sent here as well. Since everybody is eligible after a certain date, the signal is that the company's contribution and the privilege of participating are totally unrelated to individual productivity.

Break Down Barriers

This is not an issue if all groups are treated equally.

The Millennium Management Recommendation

Forget stock purchase plans unless your organization needs to sell the stock. It doesn't do anything to motivate performance. Any net costs of such a program would be better spent to provide larger merit increases or bonuses.

Health Benefits, Insurance

Given the outrageous costs of health care, it's in the best interests of organizations to cushion employees from the disastrous financial effects of illness and injury. And since such benefits in some form are almost universal, a failure to offer them would be a serious recruiting liability. They don't send productivity messages, but neither does the presence of restrooms; they're both so essential that they must be offered regardless of their cost.

Quality-of-Life Perks

These are benefits such as day care for children, exercise facilities, company-sponsored sports teams, and so on. As shown below, these benefits don't have a lot to recommend them in terms of sending signals about individual productivity. However, benefits such as day care and exercise facilities (if properly and prudently managed) can have considerable impact on employee well-being and health. Given the rising cost of health care, anything an organization can do to improve the health of its personnel will probably pay for itself simply in reductions of sick time, not to mention health-care costs. Programs directed at smoking and weight-loss programs, hypertension control, exercise, and so on, can all be helpful in reducing health-care costs. Day-care centers can have a tremendous impact on recruiting if an organization is targeting younger workers, particularly professionals. Thus, while quality-of-life perks are dissatisfiers, they're often wise investments because they can assist an organization in meeting goals not directly related to productivity such as recruiting and lowering health-care costs.

Signal That Performance Is Valued

These benefits don't send good signals about performance-related rewards. Yet, because they send good signals of other types and may be cost-beneficial, they can be a wise investment if properly managed.

Signal That Rewards Are Proportionate to Contributions

There are no good signals here.

Break Down Barriers

Perks such as exercise programs, sports teams, health programs, and so on, can have a positive effect on norm inoculation because they often bring employees of all levels together where they get to know each other as people rather than positions. This makes communication easier in the future. This effect alone isn't enough to justify these programs, but it's a factor if such programs are being considered for other reasons.

142

The Millennium Management Recommendation

Stay away from these perks unless they appear to be cost-beneficial in and of themselves. For example, if you've got high health-care costs, a lot of sick time, and a lot of smokers, a smoking cessation program will pay for itself. A day-care center can be helpful in recruiting younger professionals, but it's got to be publicized in your classified ads or it's not going to help very much. Don't implement these perks just to be nice. Being nice by supplying dissatisfiers doesn't make anyone happy at work for long, and it has no effect on productivity.

Status and Executive Perks

If an employee is provided with a benefit, consideration, or compensation item that lower-level employees don't get simply because of a difference in status, and if the item isn't essential to the job duties, it's a status or executive perk. This category of compensation includes all of the extras routinely associated with upper management and executives. They range from the corner office with a window to special dining rooms for executives. These perks are insidious, incredibly harmful dangers which sabotage top management's norm inoculation efforts and tear at the very fabric of organizational teamwork.

Signal That Performance Is Valued

These perks send strong negative signals. All of the executive dining rooms, special parking lots, special stock deals, lease cars, better travel reservations and airline seats, larger and nicer offices, more plentiful support services, free coffee, and so on, are not rewards for productivity. They're status symbols which the executives assign to themselves simply because they want them and they can get away with taking them. They aren't awarded for specific or even general accomplishments; they're simply assigned when an employee reaches a certain level. Everybody who reaches that level or grade gets them without concern for whether the employee is doing a comparatively better or worse job than another employee at that grade. And no employees at lower levels can earn them regardless of their contributions. In effect, the organization is giving away the award with absolutely no condition of performance other than to assume that all higher-level executives work harder and better than lower-level employees.

Signal That Rewards Are Proportionate to Contributions

There are bad signals here. Executive perks simply signal that executives get more regardless of what they do.

Break Down Barriers

This is the area where executive perks do the most horrendous and lasting damage. Almost all of the perks involve psychological or geographical territorial distinctions. Executives and high-level managers get special parking in a different location; they may get special dining rooms; their larger, more comfortably furnished offices are usually in a nicer and quieter part of the building with more and better support services and free refreshments. They're often provided with free cars, better lease deals or newer and better company cars. In addition, they may attend "upper level only" social functions, be provided with special club memberships, and take "upper management only" group trips to exotic places for "working holidays."

All of the above demonstrate (and are subconsciously intended to accomplish the fact) that executives and managers are different, special, and generally better people than lower-level employees. This sets up two very strong sets of group values and norms that are diametrically opposed to the types of participation and mutual decision making that are the key to increased worker involvement and productivity. Among the employees, these perks create a strong us-versus-them norm in which the employees assume (correctly) that the executives think they are better and are putting them down as not worthwhile. The result is that the employees develop a norm which sets the concerns and priorities of the executives off to the side. If the employees don't perceive that the executives are on the same team in regard to where they eat, work, park, and even go to the bathroom, do you think the employees will view them as team members when planning and problem solving?

I've worked in two environments where the executives had special dining rooms that middle managers and below could not use. In the executives' dining room, there was always linen, liveried waiters, sterling, china, crystal, and daily entrees such as prime rib or shrimp. Out in the employee cafeteria, the unclean castes were fed on styrofoam plates with plastic forks and were charged more for grease burgers than the executives paid for their fine dining. The executives would comment that they needed the opportunity to talk together without being interrupted. By whom, the employees? If the executives had been eating with the employees, they might have learned about problems, discovered new ways of handling things, started to forge leader-employee bonds, weakened some of the employee feelings of distrust, and perhaps gotten a head start in demonstrating that all of the employees were on one team.

Even more damaging is the effect of such perks on the executives' own effectiveness. After years of dining so fine, officing in paneled and carpeted splendor, and enjoying their other perks, executives and managers begin to feel that they are indeed different, that their insights are better, and that they don't need as much input or help from the troops. The killing blow to productivity is the tendency for these executives to dramatically reduce their contact with lower-level employees and spend more time with one another and their direct support staffs (who begin to act aloof themselves). The result is the almost automatic sequestering of executives and the creation of the head-shed mentality. The signals sent are so strong that the employees withdraw further out of anxiety and resentment. Pretty soon, there's little more than ceremonial contact of the most superficial type between the two groups. This is a cancer that's deep in upper levels of most organizations.

The Millennium Management Recommendation

Many will contend that executives need their perks in order to do their jobs. If that's true, how can the initial success of entrepreneurs be explained? These companies do the most and make the most staggering gains before there are any executives. Face it, executive perks are an out-and-out ripoff of resources which could be more profitably applied. All class distinctions at work must be removed if the employees and management are to perceive each other as being on the same team. This doesn't mean that office workers can't have offices or that carpeting has to come out. What it does mean is that, without exception, the special parking, cafeterias, cars, vacations, club memberships, and so on, must go. If it's necessary to have a special dining room for clients, make it open to everyone, and establish prices that make it self-supporting so that those who care to pay can use it. Management offices should be located closer to the work so that all employees see the executives more often and have an opportunity to interact with them. In most organizations, the executive offices are deliberately located away from the workers so there won't be so much distraction (team work and interaction can create distractions). The distance between management and employees, in all senses of the word, must be reduced in order to facilitate the involvement and commitment of all employees. Removal of management and executive perks will do a lot to force the interactions essential to *Millennium Management*.

Performance Reviews

The effectiveness of an organization's efforts to reward performance rest squarely on the shoulders of the formal performance review system which is used. Unfortunately, these shoulders are most often stooped, narrow, and weak. Annual or semiannual performance reviews are perceived by most supervisors and their subordinates as nothing more than the mechanism by which the almost automatic yearly merit increases are announced. The performance review process and interview itself is regarded as an unpleasant affair by both the supervisor and the employee. The supervisor feels uncomfortable having to evaluate the performance he or she has ignored all year, and the employee doesn't listen to anything except how much of an increase he or she is going to get. While we've seen that money itself can't do much to increase performance for any meaningful period of time, these types of performance reviews destroy what little effect merit increases might have. Worst of all, the entire process sends the monstrously bad signal to all employees that the organization's norms for goal setting, performance evaluation, and productivity are a joke.

Elements and Mechanics of an Effective System

In order to be effective, which means that positive signals about productivity and the organization's norms are broadcast, the performance review process must contain the following elements and procedures:

1. The performance goals of each employee must be established through joint goal-setting efforts between the employee and his or her supervisor (supervisory function 2 in chapter 5).

2. The employee's goals must be couched in behavioral terms. That is, the actual results, products, or behaviors which are expected must be concrete and straightforward to assess. "Working more productively" isn't such a goal, as it might mean anything from making sure that the supervisor gets coffee every morning to processing more claims. The goal of "improving first-run-perfect assemblies to 95 percent" is a behavioral goal, as is "learning the new data management software and creating a customer analysis and mailing system" (assuming that the parameters are jointly understood).

3. The performance review interview must not be a once- or twice-a-year event. The final, "here's how much you're getting" performance review of the year should contain no surprises. If there are surprises, good or bad, the supervisor has been doing a poor job of coaching and joint goal setting. The supervisor should be meeting with each employee on at least a monthly basis to formally review performance in terms of progress toward the goals which were negotiated earlier and may have been revised periodically. All too often, employees are shocked and outraged over the year-end assessments made of them by supervisors; they had no inkling that their supervisor was that unhappy. Those employees should be getting weekly and perhaps daily coaching and feedback. Then, even if they can't turn their performance around, there won't be any surprises; the final performance review of the year will simply be another coaching session to improve performance. In an organization handling performance reviews as an ongoing supervisory tool, there is no uproar when performance review time comes around. The only difference between that final review and the mechanics of day-to-day supervision is the actual announcement of merit increases. If the organization is using the informational and norm inoculation techniques of chapter 7, even the

amount of an individual's merit increase should be no surprise. The employee should know exactly where he or she stands in regard to the general guidelines for merit increases.

In advance of the performance review year (which ideally should coincide with the period in which the business plan for the year is prepared), supervisors must meet with each employee and negotiate goals. Negotiating doesn't mean voting. It means reaching an understanding of what's been determined. The employee doesn't have to agree wholeheartedly with every goal, but it's important that he or she understand the reason for the goal, exactly what it means in terms of observable performances and/or products, and how and when progress toward the goal will be evaluated.

The *Millennium Management* performance review technique for each employee is developed and maintained on two forms. They are the performance review objective form (PROF) and the performance review objective detail (appropriately acronymed PROD) sheet. The PROF is the master control document which lists the various objectives that have been negotiated and assigned to the employee. Figure 8.1 presents a portion of a PROF for a marketing manager. As many of these PROFs as necessary would be prepared, each listing several of the employee's objectives. The example shown in Figure 8.1 presents five objectives which, for purposes of illustration, we'll assume are all of the employee's objectives for the year. Additional PROF sheets would be used to show additional objectives. Figure 8.1 presents the form as it would appear at the start of the year, shortly after the goals were negotiated but before any work on them had been done.

The column labeled "PROD" indicates the specific performance review objective detail sheet in which the objective's parameters are fully explained. We'll discuss the PRODs in a moment. The column labeled "Weight" is extremely important. This factor is the negotiated importance rating of each objective, taking all of the objectives into consideration. Thus, the 20 percent shown for objective 1 ("client data base") demonstrates that attainment of objective 1 will contribute 20 percent toward the overall performance rating of the employee. All other things being equal, objective 1 should get about 20 percent of the employee's attention. The 40 percent weight shown for objective 3 ("develop business to support a branch office") demonstrates that it was considered to be twice as important as any other objective. The sum of weights for all of an employee's objectives should be 100. The weight column is critical for employee use in allocating time and effort. There can no longer be claims of "I didn't know you thought it was so important." It's right there in negotiated-on black and white. For employees who have other employees reporting to them, the weights provide a good approximation of where the employee's subordinates should be directing their attention.

You'll note that the final objective is labeled "Maintenance"and is given a weight of 5 percent. Every job has a number of duties which must occur day in

Performance Review Objective Form

Employee name: Joan Marketeer

Performance year covered: July 1, 1987–June 30, 1988   *Date of review*: 7/1/87

Date	No.	Objective	PROD	Weight (%)	Percent	Progress
6/24/87	1	Develop client data base as per attachment 1.	1	20		
6/24/87	2	Recruit three top-caliber salespeople in first quarter for East Coast.	2	15		
6/24/87	3	Develop sufficient business in West to support a branch office by end of year.	3	40		
6/24/87	4	Increase total sales revenue by 8 percent.	4	20		
6/24/87	5	Maintenance.	6	5		

Figure 8.1 Performance Review Objective Form (PROF) At Start of Year

and day out but aren't necessarily part of any particular project or objective. It would be ludicrous to list these maintenance duties as objectives (which is how the filler effect mentioned in chapter 6 gets started). Therefore, they're lumped into a single category and given a representative weight. The weight for maintenance duties might well be higher. For example, a receptionist might have a maintenance weight of 95 or 100 percent. It's essential to recognize the importance of maintenance activities to an organization and not to discriminate against employees who aren't engaged in highly visible and glamorous tasks (a rude receptionist can sink sales faster than ten blundering salespeople).

The righthand side of each PROF has columns marked "Percent," and "Progress." These are the locations where the employee's progress toward each goal are charted throughout the year as coaching sessions are conducted. A copy of the original, year-beginning PROF would be made for each review session, and the appropriate entries would be made in the percent and progress columns. As the year progressed there would be many successive versions of the original PROF, each (it is hoped) showing more progress.

Figure 8.2 displays the Figure 8.1 PROF as it might look after a performance review halfway through the year. The percent column indicates the percentage of each goal that's been completed up to the point of the review. Joan Marketeer has completed 75 percent of objective 1. We'll discuss how the assessment of 75 percent was made in a moment. The progress column is the percentage of the objective completed multiplied by the initial weight given to the objective. Thus, 75 completed percent multiplied by an initial weight of 20 percent yields 15 percent. This means that the work completed on objective 1 represents 15 percent of Joan Marketeer's work for the year. After the review, it's clear to both the employee and the supervisor exactly what's been done and what remains to be done. In terms of the example, Joan Marketeer has completed 58.5 percent (the sum of the progress column entries multiplied by 100) of the year's planned work. She appears to be ahead of schedule.

A critical aspect of the PROF is the percentage of each task completed at the time of each review. Without accurate assessments of progress, it's not much use to go to the trouble to track each objective so carefully. Each objective on the PROF is supported by a performance review objective detail (PROD) sheet. Each PROD sheet details the criteria of success and performance for one objective. The PROD sheet is, in effect, a one-page (or possibly several-page) project management summary of the critical tasks, milestones, and schedules behind the objective. The PROD sheets are jointly developed by the supervisor and the subordinate after each objective has been approved by management (phase 3 of the planning process described in chapter 6).

Figure 8.3 displays a PROD sheet for Joan Marketeer's objective 3 ("develop a self-supporting branch office"). The example shown in Figure 8.3 is relatively straightforward, presenting only a brief task name, a completion date, and a weight. The "weight" column indicates the relative percentage of

Performance Review Objective Form

Employee name: Joan Marketeer

Performance year covered: July 1, 1987–June 30, 1988

Date of review: 1/7/88

Date	No.	Objective	PROD	Weight (%)	Percent	Progress
6/24/87	1	Develop client data base as per attachment 1.	1	20	75	0.15
6/24/87	2	Recruit three top-caliber salespeople in first quarter for East Coast.	2	15	100	0.15
6/24/87	3	Develop sufficient business in West to support a branch office by end of year.	3	40	40	0.16
6/24/87	4	Increase total sales revenue by 8 percent.	4	20	50	0.10
6/24/87	5	Maintenance.	6	5	50	0.025

Figure 8.2   Performance Review Objective Form (PROF) After Six-Month Performance Review

the entire objective accounted for by the completion of the individual task by the date shown. For example, by 10/1/87, Joan Marketeer must have task 6, "Begin sales campaign," underway in order to be on schedule. As her 1/7/88 review (Figure 8.2) displayed, she was on schedule and earned a total weight of 40 for objective 3. You'll note that 40 is the sum of the first six task weights from Figure 8.3.

It's possible to go to considerably greater lengths in terms of the detail on a PROD sheet. There's no sense in making it an entire project management document (unless there's no other planning document and you need one anyway). For employees who are having problems, who are new to a job, and/or for very critical and complex objectives, more detail on the PROD sheet may be appropriate. In most other cases, more detail than that shown in Figure 8.3 is not necessary or desirable. The PROD sheet is intended primarily to provide a clear and accurate framework which the supervisor and the employee can use to determine the number and value of tasks comprising each objective for the coming period. With a PROD sheet to back up each objective shown on the PROF, there should be no misunderstandings about what has to be done and how important it is to both the supervisor and the employee.

Number: 3

Employee name: Joan Marketeer

Performance year covered: July 1, 1987–June 30, 1988

Objective: 3.   Develop sufficient business in Far West to support a branch office by the end of the year ($350K in adjusted billings).

Task		Target Date	Weight
1.	Analyze market data	7/15/87	5
2.	Develop potential client list	7/30	5
3.	Hire L.A. based field rep	7/30	10
4.	Recruit 10 local manufacturer's reps	9/30	10
5.	Develop sales materials	8/21	5
6.	Begin sales campaign	10/1	5
7.	Reach $100K in billings	1/30/88	20
8.	Reach $200K in billings	3/15	20
9.	Reach $350K in billings	6/15	20

Figure 8.3   Performance Review Objective Detail (PROD) Sheet

Summary

Compensation systems are a lot like termites; you may not see them or hear them, but they don't have to make noise to hurt you badly. As you read this chapter, you no doubt recognized a number of ill-advised compensation practices your organization is practicing. If you're not a very high-level executive, there's not a lot you can do to modify the overall compensation system. You'll just have to live with all of the bad signals and do what you can to balance their effect among your personnel by practicing proper supervision. Fortunately, an effective supervisor can establish a set of group norms which blocks out most of the effects of a poor environment. The best way to do this is to implement a performance review process similar to the one described in this chapter and use it as your basic coaching tool. You don't have to substitute your forms for the one the company uses (the personnel department wouldn't like that at all). Simply use your forms in conjunction with the existing system. Conduct monthly reviews of each employee's progress on PROFs and PROD sheets, and use the results as the input to the existing performance review process.You'll have a firm basis on which to conduct coaching sessions, and your employees will always know where they and you stand on their performance and goals for the year. That's more direction than most of us will ever get.

CHAPTER 9

A No-Nonsense Approach to Training and Organizational Development Programs

As you've no doubt concluded by now, the implementation of *Millennium Management* in the typical business organization would require sweeping changes in attitudes and behaviors. One of your first thoughts about such changes probably involved training: "What kind of training program would do the job?" If you've already had that thought, you could be very close to making some big mistakes.

Training is the most misunderstood and improperly applied technique in business. In the area of organizational and management development (OMD) training and programs, the abuse and misuse are nothing short of criminal. Fantastic sums are flushed down the toilet every year by organizations which apparently have no idea of what different types of training can or can't do. The wasted money isn't even the worst part. Inappropriate training wastes time and abuses employees who are forced to sit through pointless exercises given by poorly trained jargon merchants.

The underlying problem is that managers, supervisors, and many so-called training professionals don't have a clear idea of what it takes to change behaviors, habits, and attitudes. These changes require a lot more than a few hours of sitting in a seminar room. There's a lot more to organizational change than training as it's typically characterized. This chapter will explain how behavior change works and the role of different types of training in such changes. I'll then discuss the only workable approach for implementing *Millennium Management* practices (and any other change) in an organization.

What Does It Take to Change a Behavior in an Organizational Setting?

It's easy to get almost anyone to change a behavior for a short time. An arbitrary, authoritarian supervisor can be a participative manager for a few minutes or hours now and then if he or she just got back from an inspirational management development seminar and is in a good mood, and if the circumstances are correct (no major problems or time pressures). And a substandard employee can be made to produce for a short time if the boss threatens and maintains constant surveillance. Yet these types of temporary changes aren't significant or important to long-term behavior change and productivity in a business setting. Once the supervisor is faced with the usual problems and pressures, once the bad employee is left unattended (and uncoached), more typical behaviors reappear. Long-term, reliable, and self-sustaining behavior change is the only kind that can have any lasting effect on the supervisory practices and management style of an organization. In order to obtain such changes in the real world of a business organization, there are a number of absolutely essential requirements which must be satisfied.

Knowledge

The first essential for behavior change is the easiest to provide: the facts about a particular situation. Knowledge training simply involves telling the employee what you want, what's going to happen, and what the situation is. The most common training of this type is new employee orientation, in which the employee is told about the organization so that he or she has a clearer picture of what's going on. Knowledge training does not lead to lasting behavior change. In fact, that's the problem many business leaders find with the most common knowledge training of all: college education. Students don't learn appropriate business skills and behaviors; they just learn facts. Unfortunately, almost all management development and supervisory training is knowledge training; employees are sent to seminars where they are exposed to a lot of facts about the behaviors they're supposed to practice. It's a laudable first step but worthless to lasting behavior change by itself.

Skill

Knowledge about a supervisory or management technique isn't enough. A student must be taught the skill of using the knowledge in conditions which approximate the actual situation. For example, it's fairly straightforward to tell supervisors the facts about a coaching session. But that's not enough. If you want supervisors to be able to conduct coaching sessions on their own, they must have an opportunity to learn the set of behaviors which make up a coaching session. Without skill training, factors such as fear of failure, the deviation from the expected ideal script, and the complexity of dealing with real situations make supervisors too uncertain and anxious to apply the knowledge confidently. Without skill training, most supervisors won't use what they've been exposed to in knowledge training.

Skill training can be accomplished in several ways. The most common is role playing, in which students take turns acting the parts of supervisors and employees. Role playing can be useful, but it's hardly ever extensive enough or sufficiently controlled to be effective. In most seminars, employees role play with one another for brief periods between lectures. Role playing a coaching session for five to ten minutes doesn't amount to much more than glorified knowledge training.

Simulation techniques are occasionally encountered in skills training. These are more complex and refined versions of role playing in which the actors (trainers) who will be working with the trainees have had extensive preparation and training in playing their roles. This type of training, if intensive enough, can build solid skills. The problem is that intensive simulation skills training is hardly ever followed by conditions which meet the remaining requirements for long-term change.

The best way to build supervisory and management skills is through on-the-job training (OJT). If properly conducted, OJT meets all of the requirements for implementing long-term behavior changes. Not only does OJT teach supervisory and management style skills, but it also provides extensive satisfaction of the remaining requirements for successful organizational change. The difficulty is that few supervisors have the necessary skills or motivation to provide this type of training to their own subordinates.

Practice

Possessing the basic knowledge and skills necessary to be a good supervisor or manager would seem to be enough, but it's not. In order to build a skill repertoire to the point where it can adapt and function in a rapidly changing environment, it's necessary to have the opportunity to practice the skill under realistic conditions. Practice enables a learner to adapt the use of the skill to his or her unique approach, examine areas of weakness and work on them, and develop techniques for dealing with situations which weren't encountered during basic knowledge and skill training. Most management and supervisory skills training doesn't provide any opportunity for practice. Think of the last seminar you attended. You were lucky if there was any skills training at all, much less any opportunity for extensive practice. Supervisory skills are a lot more difficult to learn than developing a skill in a sport. Hour upon hour of practice is involved in sharpening golf, tennis, pool, and softball skills, but hardly any practice is devoted to honing supervisory skills. It's assumed that all you have to do is be exposed to the knowledge and—presto!—you're a good supervisor. After most management development training, if the trainee wishes to practice and develop the learned skills, he or she must do so alone, back on the job. Given that there's hardly ever an organizational policy and program to support, encourage, and reward the practice of such skills after seminars (or anytime), it's unreasonable to expect that many supervisors will stick with the effort. In fact, recognizing the futility of it, hardly any of them try. Without an opportunity to practice, even well-learned basic supervisory skills won't be used effectively, if at all.

Feedback

Here we're talking about objective evaluations of accuracy against a standard rather than rewards for good performance. The reward and reinforcement aspects of feedback are so critical they'll be discussed separately.

If practice is to be successful in developing a useful skill, feedback is essential. Without accurate and consistent feedback about how well the performed behavior matches the standard, the performer has no way of knowing if there's a problem, if adjustments must be made, or if everything is fine. Without accurate feedback, even the most dedicated supervisor will never be sure that he or she is on-target. Worse yet, the supervisor may read the wrong signs and continue to perform behaviors which are harmful to the organization and subordinates. This is why so many supervisors continue not to supervise and, instead, only deal with crises; that's what they believe the organization wants. You can't blame the supervisors. That's what they see and that's what they're taught by example. Feedback is also essential so the supervisor will know that performance of the behavior in question is important to the organization. For example, take the supervisory skill of coaching as discussed in chapter 5. If a supervisor learns how to coach, gets a chance for lots of practice, but never hears anyone talk about it, never gets a comment about how he or she is doing, never receives any coaching from his or her boss, and never gets an indication that coaching of subordinates is valued by the organization (by observing executives who perform the behavior), what's the supervisor going to do if the heat's on and there are more "important" things to do? People at work are extremely crafty about reading the signs about what's important. If there's no news about an issue, behavior, problem, and so on, employees perceive that the organization doesn't care. What they don't care about they don't do (except enough to stay out of trouble). If you're trying to implement organizational change and there isn't lots of constant feedback from all sources about the importance of each of the skills that comprise effective supervision and management style, very few people will take the trouble to modify what they're already doing. That's why it's critical to keep all sorts of information flowing to all employees about the importance of what you're trying to do.

Consistent Reward and Reinforcement

Employees generally attempt to perform behaviors which earn rewards and avoid punishments. In a typical work environment, employees have discovered that they're going to obtain very little satisfaction of the top job factors discussed in chapter 2. In fact, they usually find that attempts at participation are punished ("When I want your ideas, I'll ask," "Why were you having lunch with that guy from finance? We don't want them to know about our problems," and so on). The result is that they stop performing the very participative behaviors the organization needs and may even says it wants (through rah-rah propagandizing efforts). If an organization wants to see any semblance of *Millennium Management* practices effectively implemented, it's got to provide an array of consistent, mutually supporting rewards of all types.

Compensation

As we saw in chapter 8, a compensation system based on performance sends signals about what's important to everyone. It's not the effect of money on an individual's performance that's important. What's important is that everyone perceives that the compensation system appears to reward the target behaviors.

Praise and Recognition From Superiors

As I've said many times, supervisors are the most important influences on employee behavior. The supervisors and other managers who have contact with the employee must aggressively reward the behaviors they want by telling the employee that they like what they see, appreciate it, and consider it to be an indication of the employee's value to the organization. This type of reward, so often missing in the typical organization, provides many of the satisfiers which are more important than money to employees.

Social Approval

There are many types of social approval. It consists of all of the positive messages about their behaviors which employees receive from sources other than their supervisors. This is where the influence of informal group norms is felt. What other people say, the way they may look at someone who performs a behavior that supports the norms, the things the organization says about what it wants, and the way employees react to what the organization says are all elements of the social reward mechanism. When all or most of these types of influences work in concert to reward a set of behaviors, that behavior will be performed again because the employee perceives that it will put him or her more in tune with what the group wants, thereby earning more social approval. As we saw in chapter 3, the effects of group dynamics on behavior are pervasive and powerful. It's not enough to hope that an occasional statement that supervisors should be participative will do the trick. If the social rewards aren't there, even the best employees won't do the job.

An example demonstrates the power of these social rewards. An employee worked as an assembler in a manufacturing plant. When a certain assembly arrived at his station, a particular part was frequently damaged. Unable to get them fixed on a regular basis through normal channels (contacting the supervisor, talking to the quality control department, and so on), the worker decided it was easier to fix it himself. Each day, on his own time at lunch, he would walk about 300 yards from his department to another department and get a handful of replacement parts from the department which was building them wrong. Then, when a unit came through damaged, he would replace the broken part by working a little faster on his regular duties. When he was asked if the company newspaper could write a story about his extra effort he said, "Oh, no. Please don't. If the guys even begin to think that I'm doing this, they'll think I'm a company man and a hot dog. I wouldn't have any friends left back here. I'm just trying to do a good job." Here's an employee in a threatened industry, going out of his way to make the product better, and he's afraid he'll be ostracized if his fellow employees find out he's trying to turn out a better product. In fact, several managers, when they heard this tale, snorted, "Well, he ought to know better than to try that around here." With those types of signals as part of the social reward structure, what hope could any knowledge and skill training program or publicity effort have on rewarding participation and involvement? If any organization change effort is going to be effective, it must be supported by a wide array of activities and programs which generate social rewards from all groups and interests. That's why the programs described in chapters 6, 7, and 8 are such important elements of organizational change.

Training That Doesn't Work and Wastes Money

There are a wide variety of interesting ways in which your organization can waste money. Even if you're not going to do anything significant to implement *Millennium Management* techniques, there's no point in throwing money away on useless organizational change programs.

158

Isolated One- to Five-Day Seminars

These management development and supervisory skills programs won't be followed up by ongoing change efforts. If you've already got a *Millennium Management* work environment (a 75 percent or higher rating on the survey presented in appendix A), seminars on isolated topics such as communication skills, effective listening, coaching, and so on, are OK for orienting new employees and as tune-ups for supervisors. If your organization is more typical, these types of stand alone programs are flat-out wastes of money. The employees attend them and then return to their jobs and do things the old way because they get no skills training, practice, feedback, or ongoing rewards for performing the behaviors. To the naive, these programs appear to be of some value simply because every organization does so many of them. Believe me, they're total and complete, raging and gaping wastes of your profits. If you're not going to do anything substantial about *Millennium Management*, don't compound your problems by throwing good money away on junk.

PR, Rah-Rah Programs

These sixty-day wonder programs most often hatch from a collaboration of outside consultants and the organization's top brass. The executives typically want to do something significant but don't know what it is, except that they personally don't want to have to change any of their own behaviors (which means you can forget any real change). The consultants want to sell something the executives will like, so they propose something that's easy to do (which probably means it won't work; it's not easy to change bad habits and management styles). What usually springs forth is a media blitz announced to the organization with much fanfare. In larger organizations, the program usually consists of a videotape in which top executives announce the new program, a lot of posters, perhaps a memo or workbook explaining the virtues of the program, and handy wallet-sized reference cards summarizing the main points so workers will always be able to refer to the cards in an emergency. These materials are often supplemented by required one-day seminars in which corporate trainers drag groups face down through the notebooks. In other configurations, the training consists of supervisors being ordered to meet with their subordinates to discuss the tapes and workbooks. In smaller organizations, the program may only consist of a memo and an exhortation to work harder with each other. These programs are recognizable by their names. If you see the words "vision," "mission," "management values," "stretch," "credo," "guiding principles," "excellence goals," and so on, you can expect the videotape, laminated wallet cards, and corporate trainers to follow shortly. These programs sell because top executives are led to believe (and want to believe) that a speech and a motto can lead to organizational change.

These programs are laughable wastes of time. If the executives who approve them could ever see the reaction these materials get at the lower management levels, they'd never make another videotape or use their wallets for anything besides money. In one organization, shortly after the laminated wallet cards were distributed, managers, as they passed each other in the hall, would square off and draw their cards from their pockets in gun-slinger fashion. There were constant jokes about the risks of getting caught in a management crisis without the card and wearing the laminated cards next to the skin so the benefits of the corporate credo and operational excellence goals would be greater. One clever (and independently wealthy) manager obtained a large supply of the motto posters and cut them into a large pentagram which he placed on the floor in the middle of the office. Whenever a visitor came by with a problem, he would jump into the pentagram and proclaim that he was protected from the problem by the power of the credo. Within three months, the videotapes and cards were a memory, and management styles hadn't changed an inch.

Offsites

Offsites are one- to five-day rah-rah efforts in which managers (typically only the higher-level managers) of a facility or work group go offsite to a hotel or conference center to discuss organizational change. If the organization is large or wealthy or especially desperate, one of the many gurus of organizational change may be paid to attend and give a few speeches. In the shorter versions, the executives will be told by the authority figure or his or her consultant to "be candid, open, and honest so we can go back to the office with an action plan that works." A day or two is spent in developing company visions, missions, and so on, and various exercises are used in an attempt to prove to the executives that interpersonal skills are important in supervision. If either the ubiquitous Myers-Briggs Type Scale or Kiersey Temperament Sorter appears, you can be sure nobody knows how to spend the time usefully and has had to resort to filler (these two tests have many fine uses, but this is not one of them). One of the gimmicks used to provide a lasting effect from these offsites is to encourage managers to send "attaboy" memos to each other when someone does something laudable. One sure sign that this has occurred at an offsite is the flurry of thank-you memos which will flood the organization for a month or two after the seminar. The longer, three- to five-day versions of offsites are generally more elaborate and usually involve a day of speeches (often via videotape) by a highly paid consultant or organizational change personality. Since these types are usually too expensive to keep around for more than a day or so, the remainder of the week is used to develop lists of the company's good qualities and challenges and devise action plans. A frequent gimmick is to have all of the executives sign an oath that they'll work on some

160

of their challenges. When the week is concluded, everyone heads home, eager to renew their organizations. The problem is that nobody involved the lower-level supervisors and employees; nobody showed or told anyone how to actually supervise more effectively; nobody initiated any changes in the organization's rituals, communications channels, or ceremonies; and nobody did anything to provide for ongoing reinforcement of the behaviors they say they want. The result: there's no change except for short-term variations in the jargon of the executives and their "attaboy" memo volume. I've worked with organizations that have tried these offsites two and three times over a six- to seven-year period and never experienced any lasting change (as evidenced by observations, new product successes, surveys, etc.). Yet the executives were ready to try again and did not take kindly to my recommendation to forget that approach. Offsites are deceptively appealing because they generate a lot of good feelings among managers who may not have the time during the day to get to know their colleagues. When they find out that their colleagues are nice people and are also trying to do a good job, a short lived sense of camaraderie develops. These good feelings are laudable but not enough to lead to any long-term changes. Without mechanisms to sustain them (many of the techniques outlined in chapters 6, 7, and 8), these good feelings dissolve soon after the managers return to work. These programs can't have any effect because they don't satisfy any of the requirements for organizational change. All they do is waste money, create false hopes among top management, and alienate lower-level employees. Forget them unless you're serious about providing the other essential elements of organizational change.

Consultants

Consultants are technical experts who are typically not employees of the organization and are brought in to analyze problems, make recommendations, and/or implement programs. Properly applied, consultants can be a tremendous asset. Unfortunately, many consultants in the fields of organizational change and management development are poorly qualified. There are legions working the business fields, selling programs they don't understand for purposes that have no chance of making an impact on organizational change. Many of these programs are simple supervisory skills workshops and offsites. Others are even more strange. A recently popular program is an incredibly complex series of notebooks for organizing a person's business and personal life around goals and objectives. Many organizations have been sold these expensive kits for every manager and supervisor in the hopes that more efficient use of time will lead to more productivity. Now that you've read this far, you realize that such a one-dimensional program couldn't possible have any effect except to require all users to spend hours a day maintaining their personal recordkeeping systems.

Even if the consultant is properly qualified, there's the very true economic reality of "The customer is always right." Consultants are often faced with clients who don't want to hear about what they should do; they know what they want, and that's what they're going to buy. After having their recommendations rejected, most consultants quickly review their financial situation and almost always come to the conclusion that our free-market system depends on allowing customers to purchase what they want to buy. So they give the clients what they want. The less scrupulous consultants don't even try to sell what's best; they maneuver the client into buying the one product they offer.

In-house Training Departments

An in-house training department can be an integral part of an organizational change effort. If an organization is involved in a comprehensive attempt to implement *Millennium Management* attitudes and behaviors, if the training department is staffed with knowledgeable personnel, and if those personnel are involved in designing the knowledge and skills training portions of the change program, an in-house training department can be extremely useful. However, that's usually not the case. As they more typically function, their programs are a collection of one- to three-day seminars on various topics ranging from time management to interpersonal communications, there's no on-the-job followup, and the department operates totally outside the executive chain of command. The executives aren't using the training function as part of any thrust toward better management. Most such departments evolved to fill a narrow technical training need (such as training tellers in a bank) and then built themselves into large training departments when the interest in management development programs hit the scene in the early 1970s.

Since most organizations don't have a comprehensive change effort underway, the typical training department's success is measured by the number of its programs, the visibility of its calendar, and the availability of the latest programs with currently popular jargon in their titles (such as "Entrepreneurial Management," "The Right-Brain Supervisor," and "Neuro-linguistic Programming in Interviewing"). Management's usually happy because it appears they've got a state-of-the-art training effort, the training department is happy because it can forcefeed the latest training community bilge-water jargon down the throats of personnel who are forced to attend, and then everyone goes back to work in an organization which isn't one whit different from how it was before. If an organization isn't going to deal with the basic issues we've addressed in earlier chapters and if it isn't implementing the type of training program we'll discuss below, it would be better to eliminate all in-house management development training and simply save the money and lost work time. The only legitimate purpose of an isolated training department is to provide essential technical training. Without a comprehensive organization change program in place, 99 percent of in-house management development training is a waste of money, plain and simple.

Training That Works

As we've just discussed, there's no point in wasting money on OMD training programs that aren't an integral part of an overall strategy of organizational change. Let's examine the types of training efforts that are appropriate to a sincere and comprehensive organizational change effort. Implementation of an effective organizational change effort means that, at a minimum, the supervisors must be taught the ten supervisory skills outlined in chapter 5 and the organization will be implementing many of the techniques suggested in chapter 7. Such a change effort should also involve a number of the recommendations concerning planning and compensation that were made in chapters 6 and 8.

Timing

It's absolutely essential that the training be started with the executives and that it move down the chain of command rapidly. If there's more than a three- to four-month delay between the start of the training effort with the executives and the beginning of training at the lower supervisory levels, much of the training's potential effectiveness is lost. It's critically important that the organization be suffused with good signals about new norms and goals. It's therefore essential that everyone be brought on board quickly so that they will understand what's going on, support the good behaviors when they see them, and be supported when they perform them.

The nontraining efforts involving communication practices, rituals, and ceremonies should begin no later than the start of the executives' entrance into the formal training program. These message efforts can be extremely effective in demonstrating to everyone that the organization is committed to the new changes. Changes in planning and compensation systems need not be implemented immediately when the organizational change effort starts. It's best if they are, but few organizations have the energy or resources for such wide-ranging and numerous changes all at once.

If formal interventions (described in chapter 10) are planned, it's best to schedule them after the knowledge training has begun, so that supervisors will have a clear idea about the necessity for the interventions.

Format and Types of Training

Knowledge Training

All employees need to know what's about to happen. Group meetings (the department meetings recommended in chapters 5 and 7) and the company newsletter should be used to announce that the organization is about to make some big changes. The supervisors (at all levels) require in-depth knowledge training about the ten functions of a supervisor—what they are and why they're important. They will also require knowledge training regarding how any new compensation, planning, or performance review programs will work.

This training can be accomplished in traditional classroom fashion. Finding people who know how to train this type of applied content instead of the usual pap is sometimes a problem. Don't assume just because you've got in-house training people or a favorite consultant that they can do what you need. It's also a good idea to expose all supervisors to an in-depth program which evaluates their supervisory style and demonstrates how and why employees need to be involved and given the opportunities to satisfy the needs outlined in chapter 2. The single best canned program of this type that I've seen is offered by Teleometrics International of Houston. By themselves, their programs aren't much more than a series of standalone seminars, but when used as part of the knowledge component of an organizational change effort they're excellent. If you decide to use them, have one of your senior managers take the seminar and then present it to your supervisors. Without the active leadership of a high-status manager, the attendees won't perceive as strong a message about the importance of the program to the overall change effort. This type of involvement by senior management is critical.

Skills Training

Some basic skills training in supervisory functions can be conducted through role playing in traditional classroom setting. If this is all that's done, it's a waste of time. In order to develop strong and lasting skills in coaching, providing feedback, conducting joint decision making, and so on, most supervisors will need extensive one-to-one coaching. Role playing between a content expert and the supervisor is the only technique that's going to develop these solid skills. Anyone who tells you anything different has never done followup studies of typical OMD knowledge and skills training. I recommend that videotaping be used in the role-playing sessions to increase the supervisor's awareness of his or her style. The typical supervisor requires at least six to eight hours of intensive one-to-one work. It should be conducted in half-hour to one-hour sessions, never longer. All supervisors, however skilled (don't let anyone evaluate themselves), must receive at least two hours of role-playing training. This will ensure that everyone has the same norms about what each supervisory function looks like so they can provide uniform coaching to their subordinates.

This type of one-to-one training can be done by in-house people (if they have the skills and knowledge) or a consultant. Beware of consultants who merely coach in interpersonal skills or "more effective relating." You're looking for someone who can teach supervisors to go through the step-by-step sequences of the ten supervisory functions under a wide array of simulated situations. You're not looking for supervisors who can nod their heads, smile, and say, "I see," when employees are talking to them. A number of consulting companies offer interpersonal skills training in which the emphasis is on teaching supervisors to reflect and mirror. (If the employee says, "This really makes me mad!" the supervisor says something like, "So, you're not happy about the change?") That's not supervisory training. If you've got someone who's a complete wreck in interpersonal relations and it's a problem, such a charm school might be appropriate. For organizational change efforts, it's a complete waste of time.

A major implementation problem with any type of intensive role-playing skills training is that higher-level executives excuse themselves from such training and proclaim themselves experts in the content. This sends signals to everyone that it's another rah-rah program. Even worse, the executives are then unable to provide direction to their subordinates because they don't have a clear idea of the proper behaviors which comprise each supervisory function. If you've got any reason to believe that this could happen in your organization, don't even bother trying to change anything. If the executives aren't concerned enough to spend a few hours in skills training (just to show the flag even if they don't need it), they won't have the persistence to stick with the even tougher demands of effective organizational change.

Practice and Feedback

This is where the implementation of change becomes hard and difficult work. The only way any change is going to stick is if it's practiced in the actual work environment. This means that supervisors must perform the ten supervisory functions as they do their work and then receive on-the-spot feedback. The supervisor's own supervisor can do some of this practice observation and review, but it's not going to be enough. Without the incentive provided by the fact that someone will be there to see if they do it, many supervisors won't do any of the ten functions or they may do them poorly. The most effective way to ensure that the skills are practiced is bird dogging.

A trainer is assigned to the supervisor for two to four hours per day and observes the supervisor closely as he or she performs the various supervisory functions. A schedule is established so that the supervisor performs a variety of the functions when the trainer is present. The trainer gives confidential feedback on the spot and makes recommendations. This is the only way good supervisory skills can be rapidly and consistently developed. Clearly, with any large number of supervisors, a number of these observers and feedback personnel will be required if all the supervisory personnel (at all levels) are to be trained within a limited time period. Outside consultants may be your only choice (but they'd better know what they're doing). This type of training won't work unless it starts at the top and everyone participates. As soon as one executive is exempted, there will be no end to the creative excuses dreamed up by the next level of management.

Reward

If the above training is in place, the organization is doing enough of the communication, ritual, and ceremony techniques (chapter 7), and there's at least an attempt made to control the biggest abuses of the existing planning and compensation systems, there should be plenty of rewards of all types available to supervisors who practice the correct behaviors. When supervisors see their bosses performing the same behaviors and if there's lot of talk and information about the behaviors and their purpose, employees will begin to form and value personal norms for behavior which are similar to those of the organization. Each employee will then begin to provide his or her own rewards internally by performing the behaviors which both they personally and the organization value. They'll also reward others for sticking to the norms by providing the subtle social signals of approval.

Training Isn't the Last Word

As you can see, traditional training methods aren't going to do more than provide the very basic knowledge training which is only the first step in an organizational change. After that, the bulk of the changes must be caused by system modifications (communication channels, planning changes), extensive coaching, and on-the-job coaching and feedback. Believe me; there is no other way. If you try a shortcut to save time and money, all you'll do is waste money and get nothing. Better not to spend a penny and keep things the way they are.

CHAPTER 10

Getting Started Tomorrow: What to Do and What to Expect

The transformation of your section, department, division, or entire organization from its present condition to the productivity of a *Millennium Management* environment will start tomorrow when you get to work. Whether you're a first-line supervisor with five hourly workers reporting to you or a company president with thousands of subordinates, nothing will change unless you do something different when you get back to work. Regardless of your level of authority or responsibility, this chapter will tell you what to do first, how to do it, and what to expect, in terms of results and resistance.

The manner and number of *Millennium Management* techniques which can be implemented by a supervisor are directly related to the supervisor's position in the organizational hierarchy. If you're a first-line supervisor, you can't expect to have much influence on the situation outside your areas of responsibility. In fact, any suggestions you might have about communication, compensation systems, plans, or company rituals would be viewed as inappropriate and out of line; you'd probably be told to mind your own business. Your main focus must be on the performance of the ten supervisory functions and any small-group facilitation techniques that are within your scope of authority. You're not going to be able to implement sweeping organizational policy changes. If you allow that consideration to stop you from doing anything in your section, then nothing will ever happen. It's unreasonable and not very

166

smart for an organization to expect its lower-level employees to want or be able to motivate large-scale changes. As we've seen throughout this book, change just doesn't happen that way. Yet, as a supervisor of only a small number of your organization's employees, you do have the power to make significant changes in your section or group. If you make those changes, your group will be more productive, everyone (including you) will be more satisfied and happy with their work, and your section will look like champions compared to everyone else. If that's not enough benefit to motivate you to do something, then there's really no hope for American business. You wouldn't be reading this book if you weren't looking for answers, so I'm confident that every supervisor who reads this will at least modify a few of his or her supervisory behaviors.

If a supervisor is higher in the organization, there's more potential for change. He or she has a number of supervisors to direct, many more employees to influence, and perhaps some influence over organizational policy and procedure. This means that the middle-management supervisor must not only do what is required of a supervisor in terms of the ten supervisory functions, but must also implement as many of the norm inoculation *Millennium Management* techniques as are within his or her scope of authority.

If the supervisor is an executive, even more can be done. The executive must supervise his or her managers, must practice norm inoculation techniques for his or her work group, and must implement organizationwide *Millennium Management* techniques which affect planning, compensation, and communication, rituals, and ceremonies. Only these executives can direct the entire transformation of an organization. As you might expect, it's the hardest job. But it's the only way to obtain changes that will transform the very fabric of an organization from that of a typical business to a vigorous, highly productive *Millennium Management* organization.

Each section of this chapter will also describe the types of difficulties and resistance that can be expected when the new programs first appear. There's no magic way to avoid the problems or make them disappear faster. Knowing what to expect and that the resistance is natural and normal will make it appear to be less momentous and easier to deal with.

Millennium Management Practices for All Supervisors

What to Do

The first emphasis for any supervisor must be on building a solid leadership role among his or her subordinates. This means you'll have to start practicing the ten *Millennium Management* supervisory functions. If you don't use them yourself, there's no point in trying to persuade anyone else to try them. If you're planning to do it on your own, without organizational support, you're not going to have the benefit of formal training in the ten supervisory functions or the assistance the organization's use of norm inoculation techniques would bring.

It is important for supervisors to know exactly how their time is being spent and to ensure that each employee gets a variety of attention in the ten supervisory function areas each week. You may want to keep a log of the time you spend on each area with each employee.

To start, simply go to the first employee and begin a coaching, problem-solving, or goal-setting session, depending on what's appropriate. The first time will probably be tough; you'll feel as if you're being insincere and phony (planning and calculating an employee interaction). But you're only attempting to put some structure into the typically chaotic supervisory process. Set a goal of doing at least five sessions of one type each day with various employees for the first week. If you can make yourself do them for five days, you'll be comfortable by the end of the week and it won't be such a chore.

The next action which should be implemented is to hold regular weekly or biweekly section or department meetings for all employees. Announce the first one tomorrow. They don't have to be more than five to ten minutes long (and shouldn't last longer than twenty minutes unless something very important must be presented). Use them to pass along any information you've learned about what the organization is doing or plans to do.

You should identify one or two hot items critical to the department's success and use these to focus the section's energy. Employees should be asked to provide input (both during section meetings and individually during one-on-one meetings) about what should be done to improve performance on these items and how progress should be tracked. Graphs and charts relating to the items should be posted where all employees in the group can see them every day (see chapter 7 on product/process boards). Progress made on the hot items should be a topic in all section meetings until the goal is reached or another topic takes its place.

As far as rules and policies permit, employees should be cross-trained on each other's jobs. This keeps their work more interesting (if routine is a problem), it allows them to comment more knowledgeably about other aspects of the section's work, and it assures you of more complete coverage if there are short-term staffing problems. It also requires workers to work more effectively as a team.

In your first meeting, announce that you'll be forming some special teams in the near future (if this is appropriate to your operation) which will help solve specific problems. Outline the problems and ask for volunteers. If you can swing it, try to arrange the employees' workloads so they can spend an hour or two per week on company time working on the problems. If time during the workday isn't possible (as on an assembly line), perhaps management would spring for an hour's worth of overtime once a week for a group to work on a special problem. The progress of this group could be used to sell more aggressive efforts to management in the future.

If there's a newsletter in your organization, send up a few items about the work your group is doing, particularly if someone's made a good suggestion or a problem has been solved. Ask a higher-level executive to drop by and congratulate your employees for something good they've done. Do whatever you can to promote your group or section and make it look like a winner.

What to Expect

If you're implementing *Millennium Management* practices by yourself, don't expect much support from the organization. And don't expect much initial assistance or cooperation from the employees. They'll probably be cynical and hardened as a result of prior participatory programs by management that turned out to be short-lived experiments in jargon and mottos. Your increased one-to-one contact with them will yield almost immediate returns in their friendliness, cooperation, and compliance with your requests, but they won't begin really to pitch in on their own initiative for at least two months. It will take that long for them to realize that you're sincerely interested in working with them and not on them. They'll be participating with enthusiasm in about four months.

Don't be disappointed if there's still a lot of grumbling and complaining, even after things are moving along nicely. Your section isn't the entire company, and the general atmosphere of the organization affects everyone in it. What you're trying to do, if you're an individual supervisor implementing *Millennium Management* techniques, is to make your job easier (in the long run), increase your section's productivity, and make your employees and yourself look like champions. No matter what any other section or the organization does, you'll accomplish these goals.

Millennium Management Implementation for Middle Managers

What to Do

A supervisor who directs other supervisors—a middle manager—faces a bigger challenge when implementing a *Millennium Management* approach within his or her section or department. Not only must the middle manager perform all of the functions outlined above, but he or she must motivate, lead, and direct subordinate supervisors to do the same thing. The tradeoff for the increased work required is the larger benefit that accrues to the organization (and the middle manager) by having many supervisors simultaneously applying

Millennium Management techniques. As chapter 3 pointed out, it's much easier to effect a change in group and organizational norms if more people are supporting the change. If a group of supervisors begins to implement *Millennium Management* techniques, they and their subordinates will send and receive positive signals from each other which will lead to faster and more complete changes. The problem is that, unlike the situation in which an individual supervisor goes it alone in implementing *Millennium Management* techniques, it takes more than a simple decision to get moving.

In order to get a group of people moving in a new and unfamiliar direction, it's necessary to impose a considerable amount of structure so that everyone will be pursuing the same goals with similar techniques. That's the only way to ensure that mutually reinforcing norms are established. The first decision you face is how to kick off the program. When leading a group of supervisors, it helps to formally establish the program with goals, fanfare, guidelines, and so on. Such an approach generates enthusiasm, quiets anxieties about peer pressure, and lends an aura of importance to the program. Much of your leeway in making this decision rests on your level of autonomy. If you're tied into a rigid set of policies and procedures which mandate expected and allowable behaviors specifically, you won't have the authority to pursue a number of options which can be quite effective.

The best way to launch an organizational change is to conduct an intervention. An intervention is a carefully designed approach which gathers data about an organization or group and then shares that information with the group in a controlled manner in an attempt to stimulate the group's insights and effectiveness. The optimal technique is to conduct an organizational survey of the department in question. The results are then used to stimulate discussion among the group members about how they can more work together effectively. Appendix A presents a forty-two-item organizational survey designed for this purpose. The survey is given to the members of the group, and the results are used to direct the group's attention to the areas that require improvement. The chronology of an intervention is as follows.

General Meeting

A meeting of the entire department is scheduled. The announced purpose is to explore ways to work together more effectively. If there are too many employees for one meeting, several can be held. At the meeting, the manager announces that he or she is interested in improving the productivity of the department and, at the same time, providing all employees with an opportunity to get more satisfaction from their jobs. It's useful to talk briefly about the general content of chapter 2. The survey is then introduced (see appendix A) as a means of gathering information which will be shared with employees in the next meeting and which will be used to guide an ongoing series of meetings in which employees and supervisors will explore ways to work more effectively.

It's a good idea to announce that there will be regular department meetings every four to six weeks to discuss progress, share information, and explore departmentwide issues. It's important to assure the employees that they'll get more chances to meet with you, because they may not trust their supervisors at this point. The surveys are then distributed and employees are asked to mail them back to the return point. At the end of this meeting it's also a good idea to distribute the departmental questionnaire included in appendix B. This feedback instrument solicits employees' input concerning issues they believe are limiting productivity. One way or another, their perceptions must be dealt with. In many organizations where surveys are not permitted, instruments such as the departmental questionnaire are deemed appropriate as they seem less threatening.

Instruments Scored

The organizational surveys are collected and scored. Appendix A provides complete instructions for this process. The departmental questionnaire, if used, will yield self-explanatory feedback.

Second Meeting

At this meeting, the general results of the survey are presented. It's important to be factual and honest but positive. You'll find that candor on your part, even in the face of bad results, will be positively received; so few employees believe that management will tell them the truth. A useful way of discussing the results is to use overhead transparencies or slides to present a graph of the survey results (as shown in appendix A), explaining their meaning and significance. After the general results are presented, the results of the departmental questionnaire should be presented and discussion encouraged. The goal is to lead the group to the point where the real issues surface and can be dealt with. If it's appropriate, solicit volunteers to work on committees to explore the areas of most concern. What you're after is to have the employees present proposals to you for how they'd like to resolve the areas of contention. You'll then have their participation and a firm basis for a decision. Remember, you're not looking for the employees to make decisions. Explain that you want to provide them with an opportunity to tell you what they want, to present their ideas and suggestions, and you want to involve them to the point where they have enough information to see both sides of an issue. Then, when you make your decision, everyone will have a clear understanding of why and how you arrived at it.

At this point in the meeting, it's a good idea to distribute the survey results form (appendix B) which presents the specific items of the survey on which the group did best and worst. If you used the organizational survey in appendix A, also distribute the item feedback form from appendix B, which will solicit feedback about the items mentioned on the survey results form.

These forms will result in a complete picture of the employees' concerns. This information will be used to direct the supervisors' efforts at participative management. After all earlier results are discussed and the new forms are distributed, the date of the next meeting should be announced.

Item Feedback Forms Collected

The item feedback forms are analyzed as they come back.

Third Meeting

At this meeting you've got to have some concrete proposals about how to proceed in resolving some of the issues that will have been raised. The most typical and effective steps are to announce that several departmental teams will be formed to work on various problems and that supervisors will be meeting with their employees on a regular and mandatory basis (every week). The employees will be ready and hopeful for changes but concerned that things will stall.

In order to ensure that things don't run aground, you must be working with the supervisors while the above actions are occurring. Among the things you should be doing at the same time are:

1. The ten supervisory functions must be introduced to the supervisors, and they must be prepared to start to use them. They needn't be expert in them, but they need to know what they are and they must be aware that the new approach is mandatory.

2. The plan for implementing *Millennium Management* techniques in the department must be developed. The manner in which employees will have input into the planning cycle must be determined. If you're planning to change the way you use the existing performance review system, that must be determined with the supervisors so that you all concur and so that it can be announced. (For example, you may decide to reward only high performers and begin to be as honest with appraisals as the system will allow.)

3. Methods and operations for introducing product/process boards, cross-training between groups, supervisory luncheons, employee attendance at meetings, and the manner in which problem-solving teams will operate must all be determined so that you can announce the measures at the final intervention meeting. Not all of these techniques will be appropriate or permissible for all managers, but as many as possible should be used.

4. Arrange for any appropriate training resources. Remember, as far as *Millennium Management* practices are concerned, almost all management development and supervisory skills training currently available

is a complete waste of time because it's not followed up and only teaches knowledge, not skills. If you can arrange for your supervisors to attend a comprehensive management style self-appraisal and knowledge seminar, that's a good first step. However, your supervisors will require much on-the-job skills training in the ten supervisory functions. You may not be able to handle the time demands (and you may not be skilled in the ten supervisory functions yourself). Unfortunately, few middle managers are free to commit the resources necessary to pay for such training. Don't allow yourself to be forced into using the existing training resources if they're not appropriate. If your existing training department has enthroned itself as subject matter experts by catering to jargon generation, avoid them and do what you can on your own.

What to Expect

Don't expect the supervisors to jump on board as soon as you announce your plan. Chances are they've been around to observe the flurry of short-lived activity as other managers in the past have seen the light. You've got to demonstrate by your actions (the ten supervisory functions, sharing of data, refusing to revert to the old ways, and so on) that you're serious and committed. The biggest danger is that they'll say they want to go along and will claim to be doing everything you ask but won't do it. I've seen this in dozens of environments. Their anxiety over appearing weak or soft with the employees will lead them to resist. Further, they won't want to expose their poorly developed supervisory skills to the ridicule of the employees. It never occurs to them that the employees will be so happy to be treated with respect and involved in the decision making that they won't be inclined to be critical. The first three months will be rough; you'll have to drag them along. That's why it's critical for you to maintain a high degree of visibility with the employees so they realize they haven't been cut adrift with a group of supervisors who are just going along in word alone. If the problem-solving teams are maintained, if the section meetings are mandatory, if you require minutes of the meetings, if the product/process boards are maintained, if the employees are as involved as you can allow, and if you practice the ten supervisory functions, you'll begin to get the supervisors on board.

Millennium Management at the Executive Level

What to do

Executives, those supervisors who direct relatively autonomous portions of organizations (if not the whole show), have the potential to effect dramatic transformations of their entire organizations. Yet, as is often the case, the greatest potential is accompanied by the biggest challenges. It's almost impossible for an executive to implement an effective and sweeping organizational change unless his or her company is faced with imminent and complete disaster. Most executives have little or no idea of what the actual situation is among the majority of employees. The executive's lieutenants never pass along, and often don't know themselves, the real state of the organization environment. And, typically, executive-level personnel tend to give scant attention to people factors and management styles as a productivity issue; "important" corporate discussions usually involve diversification, investments, ROI, the stock market, and other executive-level concerns.

The result is that most executives are led to believe that things are pretty good down among the rank and file. And they're not apt to question what their highly paid subordinates tell them. If you're an executive, ask yourself one question: If things are so good, why aren't you getting the type of productivity from your employees that you really believe, deep inside, they could give you? If you're happy with what you're getting, no problem. But you're not—you and I both know it—and you shouldn't be. Believe me, your organization is doing the same things to its employees as every typical organization I've discussed. If you want to change this sorry condition, you're going to have to be the one to break the mold. Every single eye in your entire organization is on you and you alone. If you do what has to be done, the others will begin to follow.

First of all, don't announce a great big new program to get things underway. That's the surest way to create cynicism. There have probably been many new programs over the last few years which never amounted to anything. Begin aggressively but without a lot of hoopla. Start by supervising and managing your subordinates and the operations at your location according to all of the recommendations made in the first two sections of this chapter. You'll have to supervise your staff according to the ten supervisory functions, not only to show them that you mean business but to teach them how to do it. If you don't know how to do it, bring in some help to train yourself, but make sure they know what they're doing. The last thing you need is the latest fad to ruin the enthusiasm of your senior people. Next, implement the middle-manager program among your staff. Do the survey and the interventions, telling them it's not because it's a great new program but just because you're interested in trying something new. You'll be surprised at the survey results. In fact, send a packet of surveys to the employees at one of your representative locations and have them administered and returned to you unscored. The results will be eye-opening. Once your own senior people see you using the surveys, dealing openly with the results, problem solving with subordinates, inviting input from the lower level, and so on, they'll quickly begin to jump on board. At first, they'll do it because you're doing it, but then they'll see the value of it. (If they don't, it's time to open up those slots for people with some imagination and management savvy.)

Once you've got the program up and running in your local organization, you've got several options. The one option you don't have is the one that's most tempting. You can't send out a memo, videotapes, laminated wallet cards, key chains, bumper stickers, and a few posters and expect anything to happen. Significant changes are going to require significant resources and effort. People are going to require direction, training, guidelines, and plenty of information. You can try it one plant, function, or region at a time, or go for the whole ball of wax in one shot. I prefer the targeted approach in which an implementation team is assigned to assist (not run) the program in each location. The team would train all levels of supervisors in the ten supervisory functions, familiarize them with your philosophy and required practice for company communication, rituals, and ceremonies (chapter 7), and assist them in the formation of a functioning *Millennium Management* operation. During the time that this effort is ongoing, it must be *the* program of importance at the facility, location, or region implementing it. If operational concerns are permitted to interfere or take precedence, everyone will quickly realize that it's just another rah-rah program.

Meanwhile, you've got to start putting together a corporate system of communication, rituals, and ceremonies that cuts through all the nonsense and starts talking tough about productivity, involvement, and hard work. For example, you might start to bring randomly selected employees to corporate meetings so they can report back to their units about what's happening at the head shed. You can start answering the tough questions in the company paper instead of listing whose daughter won the latest Miss Little Sweets contest. You can hold press conferences to communicate with the troops. Don't supersede local executives in this, as you're not the perceived leader at those levels, but lend the prestige which your presence brings.

Start looking at changes in the performance review and compensation system which put the value on performance and not longevity. The message has got to be that average performance doesn't win awards. Institute a formal system of top-down, bottom-up, top-down planning in which all supervisors are required to obtain the input of their subordinates. As far as you can, attempt to integrate the planning process and the setting of goals into the performance evaluation process. If that's not possible in any reasonable amount of time, put out some guidelines which make it clear that average performance means zero increases. Cut out the across-the-board bonuses and the differential perks for management. Start paying for performance and cut off the nonperformance gravy train.

What to Expect

The biggest danger is that people will pretend to go along but will just go through the motions. They'll be thinking that it's just another thirty-day wonder. You're going to have to keep the pressure on, both in terms of what you demand of them and in terms of the signals which you send. It's a good idea to bring some of the lower-level managers in to observe your own efforts at communication, intervention, and so on, once you've got them going. Don't bring them in before they're working well; they'll think you're snowing them, and they'll treat the entire program like a motto key chain. Remember, the only way the program will reach down into the depths of the company and do the job effectively is if your subordinates and their subordinates do it. You can't push the program hard enough on your own from your remote location to make it happen. You'll require the enthusiastic and wholehearted participation of all of your supervisors, all the way down the line, to make it happen. The only way you'll get that is to give them the very things we talked about in chapter 2: feeling of accomplishment, personal recognition, leadership, proper direction and training, and so on. If you give them these and the other employee needs, they'll implement *Millennium Management* in a way you never dreamed possible.

It's Up to You

There's a great sense of detachment in many work environments these days, a feeling that there's not really much any of us can do to affect the way things are. Many people hope to make it big by being successful in what they do, but few people have any real hope that they can change the way it is and make it better overall. *Millennium Management* has shown you a way that works if you want to change your work environment for the better. It works, it has worked, and it will always work, because it gives employees the best of what they want from work: the satisfaction and dignity that come from doing a job well and being recognized for it. In return, the employees will give the organization what it must have: success and profits. Whether you're a rookie supervisor or a seasoned corporate executive, the techniques we've discussed will make your job more fulfilling, your employees more satisfied and productive, and your organization more successful. But it's hard work, and nobody else will do it for you.

American business is in a tight spot, and there's no easy way out. *Millennium Management* isn't a magic wand. It can't even turn the tide of our economic defeats. That's out of our control now. All we can do is stem the tide, reduce our losses, and fight it out with the competition with every fiber of our intelligence and determination. *Millennium Management* supplies the best techniques for tapping the last great resource we've got: our people. You'll have to supply the determination. I hope you decide to do the right, hard thing for American business and yourself. Good luck!

APPENDIX A

An Instrument for Assessing Your Organization

This appendix presents an organizational assessment instrument which can be used to determine the relative organizational health of your department, section, or division. If you're working in a large organization, don't start distributing questionnaires in your area without checking with the people who make the policies about such things (unless you're an executive); many organizations don't want to know. The results of this survey can be used to guide an organizational change effort which deals with the reality of your organization's situation and not preconceived and generally incorrect notions of what's going on. The survey is also very useful for determining the effect of any management development programs or interventions. Simply give the survey before the program and then again in ten to twelve months (you won't get significant change earlier than that). If nothing changes, you probably wasted your money.

This appendix provides everything you need, including the survey itself and the information for scoring it. Since it's laborious to compute averages for each question, I've also included instructions for designing a Lotus 1-2-3 file which will perform all of the calculations for you and generate a graph to display your results.

The Survey

The survey is a forty-two-item questionnaire which asks respondents to answer each question by placing an X somewhere along a twenty-point scale. The items are fairly straightforward and are not intended to measure any hidden motivations or psychological traits. The questions are just what they appear to be—inquires into employee perceptions about the work environment.

Administration

The survey takes from five to fifteen minutes to complete, depending on the reading skills of the respondent. Most employees complete it in five to eight minutes. It's better if the survey is administered in a controlled setting (everyone in one place at one time), but that's often impractical. Employees can be given the test to do on the job as they get time or can be asked to take it home and bring it back when they're done. It's essential to tell them not to put their names on it. When distributing the surveys, explain briefly why the survey is being used ("To help us put together a training program") and assure everyone of the confidentiality and anonymity of the results: "We don't want any names or identifying information on the surveys which might tell us who filled it out. All we want to do is find out what the group thinks so we can use the information to try to make this a better place to work." Each questionnaire should be distributed with a self-sealing envelope which can be used to return the completed questionnaire to a certain location or via interoffice or regular mail (if the survey isn't administered and collected in a single location). I prefer to talk with each employee for a minute or so if I'm distributing the surveys individually. This increases the rate of return compared to what you can expect if you simply hand them out to groups.

Scoring

Each of the forty-two items has a good end and a bad end. Responses toward the good end of the twenty-point scale represent answers which indicate that proper *Millennium Management* practices are in use. Responses toward the bad end indicate that employees do not perceive that *Millennium Management* practices are in effect. The direction of the good end of each item is varied throughout the survey.

For purposes of scoring, each item is given a score between 1 and 20, depending on the interval in which the X is marked. If the X is on a line, score it as if it was in the higher of the two intervals. If there is no X for a question, don't score that question. If there is more than one X per item, don't score it. The good end of each item is the end which is scored high, with 20 as the value of the highest score. The bad end is the end which is scored low, with 1 as the value of the lowest score.

Figure A.1 indicates which end of each item is the good or high end

Question	Good end	Question	Good end	Question	Good end	Question	Good end
1	L	12	R	23	R	34	R
2	R	13	L	24	L	35	R
3	R	14	R	25	L	36	R
4	L	15	L	26	R	37	L
5	L	16	L	27	L	38	L
6	R	17	L	28	R	39	L
7	R	18	L	29	L	40	R
8	L	19	L	30	R	41	L
9	L	20	R	31	R	42	R
10	R	21	R	32	R		
11	L	22	R	33	L		

Figure A.1   Good or High-Scoring End of Survey Items

which rates the 20. *R* stands for the right side of the item as you look down at it on the survey, and *L* stands for the left side.

As you score each item, start counting intervals of the line from the end opposite the good end. For example, item number 2 is:

2.   How much trust and confidence do you have in your supervisors?

| Very little | | Some | | Moderate amount | | | A lot | | A great deal |

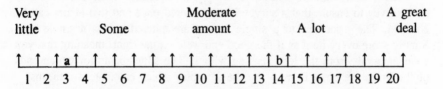

As shown by Figure A.1, the good end of item 2 is to the right (*R*). As shown above, the good end is toward "a great deal," or the right side of the question as it appears in the survey. The numbers beneath the response line do not appear with the survey items themselves but are the values assigned to an *X* placed in the interval directly above the number. Thus, an *X* placed where the *a* is shown would be scored as a 3, while an *X* shown in the interval indicated by the *b* would be scored as 14.

Item 5, shown below, is an item whose good end is to the left.

5.   How often do the supervisors around here, when they're solving problems, ask for employees' ideas and opinions?

| Almost always | | Frequently | | Half the time | | Sometimes | | Hardly ever |

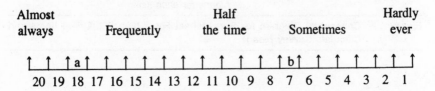

A response in the interval marked with the *a* would be scored 18 on this item, and a response in the interval marked with the *b* would be scored as 7.

If you're going to be calculating scores by hand, set up a table with the question numbers across the top, left to right, from 1 to 42. Figure A.2 displays this format. Each row will contain the responses of one survey. Before scoring, mark each survey with a control number and label the row with the control number to the left. Don't throw away the surveys until you've completed all the scoring.

As you can imagine, it's tedious to have to score each item by referring to Figure A.1 and then begin counting from 1 at the opposite end. It's also no fun to have to add up forty-two columns of numbers in order to develop group averages for each question. You can create a Lotus 1-2-3 file which will automatically orient each item's score in the proper direction, calculate item means, and generate a graph of the results. All you'll have to do is to enter the scores. You don't even have to worry about which end of the item is the good end. The computer will do all of the adjusting.

I'm going to assume that you are familiar with the operation of Lotus 1-2-3. The principles are exactly the same for almost any spreadsheet program, such as Multiplan, VP Planner, and so on. Figure A.2 presents a conceptual diagram of the spreadsheet.

The control number column is simply a sequential number assigned to each survey to ensure that a survey is only scored once and that errors can be checked. The responses to a single survey are entered across a single row. Simply score every item as if the good end were on the right, meaning that you count intervals from the left, starting with 1. The adjustments for which ends of the items are good is made by the formulas which calculate the means.

Figure A.3 presents the cell addresses and formulas which calculate the

Control number	Items
	1 2 3 4 5 6 7 ... 40 41 42
1	
2	Item responses, entered as if extreme lefthand interval was one.
3	
—	
N	
	M1 M2 M3 M4 M5 M6 M7 ... M40 M41 M42
	Means for each item

Figure A.2 Conceptual Diagram for Spreadsheet File Which Will Orient Items and Calculate Survey Means

Item	Cell address	Formula	Item	Cell address	Formula
1	B121	21-@AVG(B119 . . B2)	22	W121	@AVG(W119 . . W2)
2	C121	@AVG(C119 . . C2)	23	X121	@AVG(X119 . . X2)
3	D121	@AVG(D119 . . D2)	24	Y121	21-@AVG(Y119 . . Y2)
4	E121	21-@AVG(E119 . . E2)	25	Z121	21-@AVG(Z119 . . Z2)
5	F121	21-@AVG(F119 . . F2)	26	AA121	@AVG(AA119 . . AA2)
6	G121	@AVG(G119 . . G2)	27	AB121	21-@AVG(AB119 . . AB2)
7	H121	@AVG(H119 . . H2)	28	AC121	@AVG(AC119 . . AC2)
8	I121	21-@AVG(I119 . . I2)	29	AD121	21-@AVG(AD119 . . AD2)
9	J121	21-@AVG(J119 . . J2)	30	AE121	@AVG(AE119 . . AE2)
10	K121	@AVG(K119 . . K2)	31	AF121	@AVG(AF119 . . AF2)
11	L121	21-@AVG(L119 . . L2)	32	AG121	@AVG(AG119 . . AG2)
12	M121	@AVG(M119 . . M2)	33	AH121	21-@AVG(AH119 . . AH2)
13	N121	21-@AVG(N119 . . N2)	34	AI121	@AVG(AI119 . . AI2)
14	O121	@AVG(O119 . . O2)	35	AJ121	@AVG(AJ119 . . AJ2)
15	P121	21-@AVG(P119 . . P2)	36	AK121	@AVG(AK119 . . AK2)
16	Q121	21-@AVG(Q119 . . Q2)	37	AL121	21-@AVG(AL119 . . AL2)
17	R121	21-@AVG(R119 . . R2)	38	AM121	21-@AVG(AM119 . . AM2)
18	S121	21-@AVG(S119 . . S2)	39	AN121	21-@AVG(AN119 . . AN2)
19	T121	21-@AVG(T119 . . T2)	40	AO121	@AVG(AO119 . . AO2)
20	U121	@AVG(U119 . . U2)	41	AP121	21-@AVG(AP119 . . AP2)
21	V121	@AVG(V119 . . V2)	42	AQ121	@AVG(AQ119 . . AQ2)

Figure A.3   Spreadsheet Cell Locations and Formulas for Orienting Items and Calculating Means

means for a spreadsheet that will score up to 117 surveys. If you've got more than 117, simply enlarge the spreadsheet by moving the means row (121) further down the spreadsheet. The item numbers are also given so that you may adjust your formulas if you don't put the first item's answers in column B of the spreadsheet.

You'll note that all of the items are oriented so that their good ends are in the same direction by subtracting the average scores of the left side good items from 21. This results in a set of mean scores in which higher numbers always denote an environment which is more participatory and productive. This orientation of results makes it easy to assess the significance of a particular item's mean and to generate a graph of overall results which is easy and straightforward to understand.

Two additional formulas are necessary to assess overall results. They can be placed anywhere on the spreadsheet. The formulas, as they would appear if they were placed in the following cell locatons (right after the last item mean),

Cell Location	Formula	Purpose
AR121	@SUM(B121 .. AQ121)	Sums all of the item means.
AR122	+AR121/840	Converts the area covered by the items to a percentage of the total unit area which could be covered (which is 42 items times 20 intervals on each or 840).

Although it's not required for analysis purposes, it's useful to enter a row of numbers beneath the item means (on row 121) so that individual item scores can be easily located and reviewed on the monitor or on a printout. Because most spreadsheets' graphics capabilities are limited, it's also a good idea to enter a line of item numbers in which only every third number is included. This permits the generation of graphs (see examples later on this section) in which the X-axis labels don't overlap. For the spreadsheet we've been discussing, the cell locations and entries are shown in Figure A.4.

Cell location	Entry	Cell location	Entry	Cell location	Entry
B123	1	Q123	16	AF123	31
E123	4	T123	19	AI123	34
H123	7	W123	22	AL123	37
K123	10	Z123	25	AO123	40
N123	13	AC123	28		

Figure A.4   Cell Locations and X-axis Label Entries

Generating a Graph

Figure A.5 shows the necessary steps for generating and saving a bar graph of the means which will update itself automatically after additional surveys are entered. The next section displays several of these graphs. The following instructions are specific to Lotus 1-2-3 only and the spreadsheet design discussed in this section. It's assumed that the spreadsheet has been created and saved before the steps in Figure A.5 are implemented. *Return* indicates the return or enter key, and *Escape* indicates the escape or cancel key. All entries between quotes are typed labels. Steps shown in square brackets are instructions, not keyboard input. All other steps should be typed exactly as they appear.

Step	Command	Step	Command
1	/GNC	18	Escape
2	"name of graph"	19	Escape
3	Return	20	C
4	TBX	21	TF "Organizational Survey"
5	[HIGHLITE B123..AQ123]	22	Return
6	Return	23	TS "type group name"
7	A	24	Return
8	[HIGHLITE B121..AQ121]	25	Escape
9	Return	26	S "type name used in step 2"
10	OXT "Question Number"	27	Return
11	Return	28	Escape
12	TY "Rating"	29	Escape
13	Return	30	/FS
14	GBSYMLO (last is zero)	31	Return
15	Return	32	R
16	MU20 (last is zero)	33	/GV
17	Return		

Figure A.5 Lotus 1-2-3 Commands for Generating Bar Graph of the *Millennium Management* Organizational Survey

Interpreting the Results

Figure A.6 displays a graph of item means for a large group ($N = 67$) of office workers in the loan processing department of a large bank. The first thing to look at is the amount of dark area covered by the bars. The larger the dark area, the healthier the organization or group. The two formulas that were mentioned earlier (located in cells AR121 and AR122) calculate this area exactly. In the case of Figure A.6, the area covered is 65 percent of the entire graph. This is indicative of a fairly healthy organization. General guidelines for assessing the significance of the total area covered by the graph are as follows:

Area covered	Meaning
Less than 25%	An abusive environment in which employees are totally withdrawn from the organization and in which there's apt to be considerable friction and hostility. Don't expect any help from the employees here (and dive for cover if the lights go out!).
25 to 50%	An environment in which the employees are frustrated, somewhat withdrawn, and suspicious of management's intentions. The work gets done, but there's little energy or concern for fighting the system.

(continued next page)

Area covered	Meaning
	The employees perceive that their norms and goals are markedly different from those of the organization. Most traditional and mature businesses in the United States will score in this range.
50 to 65%	Employees feel somewhat involved in the process and strive to make the system work. Nowhere near a *Millennium Management* environment but could get there with a year of aggressive effort.
65 to 75%	A very healthy participative environment in which the employees perceive that their informal norms and goals are very similar to those of the organization. Just about a *Millennium Management* environment.
Over 75%	A *Millennium Management* situation or very close to it. There are few organizations or groups that score above 75%. Anything over 75% is indicative of an extremely participatory work environment in which employees and supervisors are able to communicate clearly and accurately with each other on all issues.

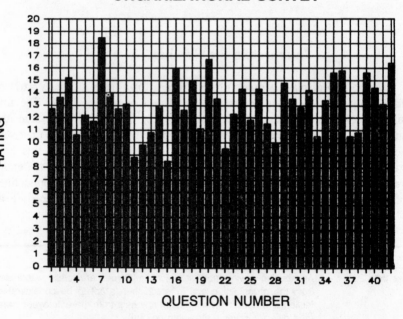

ORGANIZATIONAL SURVEY

Figure A.6 Graph of *Millennium Management* Organizational Survey of Group of Office Workers in a Bank Showing a Relatively Healthy Organizational Environment

Analysis of individual items is useful for gaining insight into the specific perceptions of the employees and for planning an intervention which attempts to open up communications. (Appendix B presents suggested materials for conducting such an intervention.) For example, the graph in Figure A.6 demonstrates for question 2 ("How much trust and confidence do you have in your supervisors?") that the group answered at an average of a little more than 13.5. On the twenty-point scale, that's just about under the "A lot" label on the response line.

You'll note that on item 15 ("How often does management run things by issuing orders without first asking employees for information?") the group scored its lowest mean, about 8.5. That's just between "Frequently" and "Half the time" on the response line and not indicative of a healthy management practice. This is one area in which the management of this group could effect significant improvements.

There are a number of items which are "employee good" items; that is, they're items in which the employees rate themselves and their peers on how much they want to help, how much they try to do the job, and so on. These items are 10, 11, 14, 18, 20, 32, 34, 35, and 36.

In a fairly healthy profile such as that shown in Figure A.6, there's little difference between the means of the "employee good" items and the rest of the items; the peaks of the items don't tower above the other items' means. In poor environments (where the area covered is less than 50 percent), these "employee good" items are generally the only bright spots. Figure A.7 displays such an environment. Figure A.7 is based on ninety-six blue-collar workers in a metal fabrication plant. The area covered by this graph was 38 percent, very low for a large, supposedly progressive organization. You can see that "employee good" items 11, 14, 18, 20, 32, 34, 35, and 36 are all among the peaks. Without them, the average area covered would have been pathologically poor, in the neighborhood of 25 percent.

Sample Size and Selection

It's always better to sample as many employees as possible. Yet it's not necessary to get everyone or even most employees. If you distribute surveys to all employees and get back 10 percent, you'll have enough to use. Of course, fewer than an absolute number of five may be a problem. I've never noticed any substantial changes (other than reductions in variances about the mean and other statistical characteristics) in the graph obtained from the first ten surveys from a sample and the graph of the total sample. It appears as if there's always a fairly uniform perception among most employees of what the environment is like. Be wary of interpreting results from many departments. Don't combine data.

ORGANIZATIONAL SURVEY

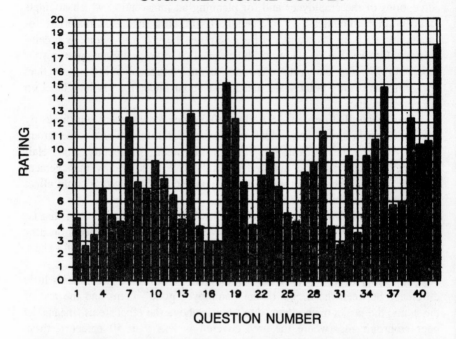

Figure A.7 Graph of *Millennium Management* Organizational Survey of Group of Metal Fabrication Workers in an Unhealthy Organizational Environment

I recommend that you make any survey voluntary. And don't expect candid answers from very small groups in which the supervisor will have a good idea of what individuals said.

THE MILLENNIUM MANAGEMENT ORGANIZATIONAL SURVEY

Instructions

General directions: This survey asks you to rate your organization on a variety of characteristics. Answer the questions based on what you know rather than what other people say. Your responses are completely confidential, so please be candid.

Rate each item by placing a single X on the line below each statement. Treat the line as a continuous variable, with one end representing a lot of the quality or condition and the opposite end representing very little or none. The five statements above each line provide an estimate of what the various parts of the line stand for. Answer each question with only one X. An example is shown and explained below.

Example: The sample item below asks for an opinion about the physical comfort of someone's work area. If you were answering the question, you would place one X somewhere on the line. If you felt that your work area was just about as comfortable and relaxing as it could be, you'd put your X on the line somewhere under "Excellent," perhaps where the "X1" is shown. If you felt that it was absolutely the best it could be, you would place your X all the way to the right, where the "X2" is shown. If you felt that your work environment was about average, you might put an X somewhere under the "Fair" location, about where the "X3" is shown. If you felt that your work area was pretty awful in regard to comfort and relaxation, but not absolutely the worst it could be, you might place your X about where the "X4" is shown. The two empty spots to the left of the "X4" demonstrate that you didn't think it was the worst it could be even though you felt that it was terrible. There are 20 spots along each line in which you can place your response. Always place only one X on each line, and always place it between two of the arrows.

Sample item: How comfortable and relaxing is your work area?

Terrible	Poor	Fair	Good	Excellent

X4 ↑ ↑ ↑ ↑ ↑ ↑ ↑ ↑ ↑ ↑X3↑ ↑ ↑ ↑ ↑ ↑ ↑ ↑X1↑ X2

You'll notice as you respond to the items in the survey that the "good" and "bad" ends of the line are not always on the same side. Sometimes the "Excellent" is on the right, and sometimes it's on the left. Let the short statements above each line be your guide when you are determining where to place your response.

When you have completed the survey, place it in the envelope which came with it and return it to ＿＿＿＿＿＿＿＿＿＿＿＿ .

Thank you for your help.

1. How much trust and confidence do you feel supervisors have in the employees around here?

| A great deal | A lot | A moderate amount | Some | Very little |

↑↑ ↑ ↑ ↑ ↑↑ ↑ ↑ ↑ ↑↑ ↑ ↑ ↑ ↑ ↑ ↑↑ ↑ ↑ ↑↑ ↑

2. How much trust and confidence do you have in your supervisors?

| Very little | Some | A moderate amount | A lot | A great deal |

↑↑ ↑ ↑ ↑ ↑↑ ↑ ↑ ↑↑ ↑ ↑ ↑↑ ↑ ↑ ↑ ↑↑ ↑ ↑ ↑↑ ↑

3. How often do the supervisors around here display supportive behaviors toward the employees (being friendly, watching out for them, etc.)?

| Hardly ever | Sometimes | Half the time | Frequently | Almost always |

↑↑ ↑ ↑ ↑ ↑↑ ↑ ↑ ↑↑ ↑ ↑ ↑↑ ↑ ↑ ↑ ↑↑ ↑ ↑ ↑↑ ↑

4. To what extent do the supervisors act as if they want employees to be candid with them when discussing problems about their jobs?

| A great deal | A lot | A moderate amount | Some | Very little |

↑↑ ↑ ↑ ↑ ↑↑ ↑ ↑ ↑ ↑↑ ↑ ↑ ↑↑ ↑ ↑ ↑↑ ↑ ↑ ↑↑ ↑

5. How often do the supervisors around here, when they're solving problems, ask for employees' ideas and opinions?

| Almost always | Frequently | Half the time | Sometimes | Hardly ever |

↑↑ ↑ ↑ ↑ ↑↑ ↑ ↑ ↑↑ ↑ ↑ ↑↑ ↑ ↑ ↑ ↑↑ ↑ ↑ ↑↑ ↑

6. How often do supevisors use employees' pride and self-esteem to motivate them to do a good job?

| Hardly ever | Sometimes | Half the time | Frequently | Almost always |

↑↑↑↑↑↑↑↑↑↑↑↑↑↑↑↑↑↑↑↑↑↑↑↑↑

7. How often do supervisors use threats, fear, and disciplinary actions to motivate employees to work harder?

| Almost always | Frequently | Half the time | Sometimes | Hardly ever |

↑↑↑↑↑↑↑↑↑↑↑↑↑↑↑↑↑↑↑↑↑↑↑↑↑

8. How much hostility and conflict is there between what management wants and what employees want?

| Very little | Some | A moderate amount | A lot | A great deal |

↑↑↑↑↑↑↑↑↑↑↑↑↑↑↑↑↑↑↑↑↑↑↑↑↑

9. To what extent are management and employees working effectively toward common goals?

| A great deal | A lot | A moderate amount | Some | Very little |

↑↑↑↑↑↑↑↑↑↑↑↑↑↑↑↑↑↑↑↑↑↑↑↑↑

10. How much responsibility do the employees feel to help the organization reach its goals?

| Very little | Some | A moderate amount | A lot | A great deal |

↑↑↑↑↑↑↑↑↑↑↑↑↑↑↑↑↑↑↑↑↑↑↑↑↑

11. How much do the employees like and respect one another around here?

A great deal	A lot	A moderate amount	Some	Very little

↑↑↑↑↑↑↑↑↑↑↑↑↑↑↑↑↑↑↑↑↑↑↑↑↑

12. How much satisfaction do the employees get from working here?

Very little	Some	A moderate amount	A lot	A great deal

↑↑↑↑↑↑↑↑↑↑↑↑↑↑↑↑↑↑↑↑↑↑↑↑↑

13. How much open and accurate communication is there between groups and departments?

A great deal	A lot	A moderate amount	Some	Very little

↑↑↑↑↑↑↑↑↑↑↑↑↑↑↑↑↑↑↑↑↑↑↑↑↑

14. To what extent do employees try to communicate information to management about problems and possible solutions?

Very little	Some	A moderate amount	A lot	A great deal

↑↑↑↑↑↑↑↑↑↑↑↑↑↑↑↑↑↑↑↑↑↑↑↑↑

15. How often does management run things by issuing orders without first asking employees for information?

Hardly ever	Sometimes	Half the time	Frequently	Almost always

↑↑↑↑↑↑↑↑↑↑↑↑↑↑↑↑↑↑↑↑↑↑↑↑↑

16. How often do supervisors willingly share information with employees?

| Almost always | Frequently | Half the time | Sometimes | Hardly ever |

17. How much do employees around here believe what management says?

| A great deal | A lot | A moderate amount | Some | Very little |

18. How good is the information supervisors and management get from employees?

| Excellent | Good | Fair | Poor | Terrible |

19. How responsible do employees feel for trying to tell management what's really going on?

| A great deal | A lot | A moderate amount | Some | Very little |

20. How often is information deliberately distorted by someone passing it from employees to management?

| Almost always | Frequently | Half the time | Sometimes | Hardly ever |

21. How much accurate information gets from employees to upper management?

| Very
little | Some | A moderate
amount | A lot | A great
deal |

↑ ↑

22. How much need is there for additional systems (such as suggestion programs) to get accurate information to management?

| A great
deal | A lot | A moderate
amount | Some | Very
little |

↑ ↑

23. How good is the information which passes between different departments and work groups around here?

| Terrible | Poor | Fair | Good | Excellent |

↑ ↑

24. How would you rate the friendliness between supervisors and employees?

| Excellent | Good | Fair | Poor | Terrible |

↑ ↑

25. To what extent do managers and supervisors understand the problems faced by employees?

| A great
deal | A lot | A moderate
amount | Some | Very
little |

↑ ↑

26. How much cooperative teamwork is there in general?

| Very little | Some | A moderate amount | A lot | A great deal |

↑ ↑

27. To what extent does management think employees have a say in determining how employees do their jobs?

| A great deal | A lot | A moderate amount | Some | Very little |

↑ ↑

28. How much influence would employees say they have in determining how employees do their jobs?

| Very little | Some | A moderate amount | A lot | A great deal |

↑ ↑

29. How much decision-making authority and responsibility has management given to supervisors around here?

| A great deal | A lot | A moderate amount | Some | Very little |

↑ ↑

30. To what extent do the decision makers know the real story about the things they're deciding on?

| Very little | Some | A moderate amount | A lot | A great deal |

↑ ↑

31. How often, before making a decision, does management get together with the people who know most about the topic?

Hardly ever	Sometimes	Half the time	Frequently	Almost always

↑ ↑

32. To what extent are employees committed to making management's programs work?

Very little	Some	A moderate amount	A lot	A great deal

↑ ↑

33. To what extent does management use teamwork and group decision making to set goals?

A great deal	A lot	A moderate amount	Some	Very little

↑ ↑

34. How hard do employees work to meet the performance goals set by management?

Very little	Some	A moderate amount	A lot	A great deal

↑ ↑

35. How much do employees resist or reject the established goals of management?

A great deal	A lot	A moderate amount	Some	Very little

↑ ↑

36. To what extent are employees concerned about seeing that work gets done on time and correctly?

Very little	Some	A moderate amount	A lot	A great deal

↑ ↑

37. To what extent are employees involved in reviewing information on production, quality, costs, and efficiency so they can do their jobs better?

A great deal	A lot	A moderate amount	Some	Very little

↑ ↑

38. How often is information concerning production, quality, cost, and efficiency used in a manner which encourages teamwork and problem solving?

Almost always	Frequently	Half the time	Sometimes	Hardly ever

↑ ↑

39. How often is production, quality, cost, and efficiency information used to punish, coerce, and/or intimidate employees?

Hardly ever	Sometimes	Half the time	Frequently	Almost always

↑ ↑

40. How much of the training you need to do a good job have you received?

Very little	Some	A moderate amount	A lot	A great deal

↑ ↑

41. To what extent are you satisfied with this organization as a place to work?

| A great deal | A lot | A moderate amount | Some | Very little |

↑ ↑

42. How much better do you think this organization could be if everyone pulled together as much as they could if they really wanted to?

| Very little | Some | A moderate amount | A lot | A great deal |

↑ ↑

APPENDIX B

Materials for Starting an Organizational Change Intervention

This appendix provides three forms which can be used to kick off an organizational change intervention. (The Millennium Management Organizational Survey—MMOS—is a central part of many interventions and is treated separately in appendix A.) Chapter 10 discusses a number of general issues related to planning and operating an organizational change effort. You should read chapter 10 before using any of these forms.

The first form is the departmental questionnaire. This solicits input from employees about a wide range of issues that are central to their involvement and participation. The departmental questionnaire can be distributed by itself or in conjunction with the MMOS. Participation should be voluntary and confidential. Provide each respondent with a self-sealing envelope so that the results can be sent back or dropped off without fear of having their answers matched to themselves.

The departmental questionnaire is best distributed after its purpose has been explained to a group in a meeting especially held for that purpose. Such a meeting eliminates any confusion about what it is and why it's being used.

When all the results are returned (in a week or so), the results should be presented to the group as a whole and used as the basis for further large-group discussion, small work-group (supervisor and subordinates) meetings, and the formation of task forces to attack various issues.

The second two forms are used in conjunction with the MMOS. The first is the MMOS item result form. This form (an example is shown from the MMOS given to the group which generated the graph in Figure A.6) is used to provide detailed information to employees about specific items on the MMOS. This form stimulates their thinking about specific items. It should be distributed at the first group meeting when the results of the survey are presented.

The last form is the MMOS item feedback form. This should be distributed at the end of the meeting in which the MMOS results are discussed (the same meeting in which the MMOS item result form is distributed).

The collected item feedback forms, if used, and the departmental questionnaire should provide a significant amount of information about the specific things that need to be changed if your organization is to improve its productivity.

DEPARTMENTAL QUESTIONNAIRE

You are scheduled to attend a departmental meeting with the management of your deparment in the near future. The meeting will be a frank discussion of what both you and your supervisors can do to increase the effectiveness of your department. The focus of the sessions will be on setting realistic behavioral goals for both managers and subordinates. In order to save valuable time and better utilize the meeting time, please complete this questionnaire and the other materials which accompanied it and then return them via interoffice mail to _____ . Your individual responses are completely confidential. However, the overall group responses will be discussed candidly and directly at the meeting and will be used to set objectives and goals. Please think carefully about your responses.

1. What restraints, if any, are there in your individual work group and/or your department which prevent you from doing a better job? Be specific.

_____

_____

_____

2. Do you believe that the management of your department is truly interested in encouraging you to participate in departmental decision making?

　　　　　　Yes _____　　　　　No _____

3. If no, cite an example which demonstrates a lack of participatory decision making in your department.

_____

_____

_____

4. What's the biggest challenge facing your individual work group and/or department these days?

_____

_____

_____

5. What do you think needs to be done to meet this challenge?

_____

_____

_____

6. Do you feel that you have an adequate knowledge of where your individual work group and/or your department as a whole is going in the next five years and how it plans to get there?

Yes _____   No _____

If yes, where did you find or obtain the information which keeps you informed?

_____

_____

_____

If no, what additional information or modes of communication would you like to have or see?

_____

_____

_____

7. What one single thing could your immediate supervisor do to make you more effective in your job?

_____

_____

_____

8. What one single thing could your immediate supervisor stop doing which would make you more effective on your job?

_____

_____

_____

9. List the three things you dislike most about the way your individual work group and/or your department currently operates. List them in order, using number 1 for the thing you dislike the most.

   1. _____

   2. _____

   3. _____

10. List the three things you like most about the manner in which your individual work group and/or your department currently operates. List them in order, with 1 being the item you like most.

   1. _____

   2. _____

   3. _____

Do you have any other observations or comments you would like included as material in the planning of the meeting?

_____

_____

_____

_____

_____

Please return this questionnaire to _____ .

Thank you for your help!

SURVEY RESULTS

Group: Loan Processing

Directions: Your group/department recently took the forty-two-item Organizational Survey. This analysis summarizes the principal findings of the survey results. Page 3 presents a listing of the survey questions which were ranked most favorably by your group as a whole. Note that some of the questions yield favorable results if they are answered negatively. For example, in regard to item number 7, "How often do supervisors use threats, fear, and disciplinary actions to motivate employees to work harder?" it's better if the answer is "hardly ever" rather than "almost always." Other questions are scored favorably if they are answered "a great deal" or "almost always." Item 2, "How much trust and confidence do you have in your supervisors?" is one of these questions.

Page 4 presents a similar listing of the ten questions which were answered least favorably by your group. As with the favorable questions, unfavorable answers can be answered in either direction ("always" or "a great deal" versus "hardly ever" or "very little").

After you review each list of items, think about what you, your coworkers, and your supervisors would have to do to improve the situation in your department in terms of the unfavorable questions. Also consider what all of you could do to improve on the already favorable items. You'll be meeting to discuss these issues with your supervisors and colleagues in the near future.

The graph on page 2 summarizes the overall findings for your group on all of the questions. The numbers along the bottom are the question numbers. The ratings are the average ratings of your group on the twenty-point scale for each item. For ease in interpreting the graph, the results were statistically adjusted to always show a favorable response as being a higher number. Therefore, it's better to have higher scores on each item (bigger bars or dark areas).

Results in many other organizations have demonstrated that the most productive departments, sections, plants, and/or companies always have the majority of their scores above the middle of the graph (higher than 10); the higher the better. Scores which average above 15 on all questions are hardly ever found in larger companies. If your group sincerely works on eliminating the barriers and misunderstandings which created your unsatisfactory questions, you'll be well on your way to dramatically improving every aspect of your department's productivity and your satisfaction with your job.
Good luck!

ORGANIZATIONAL SURVEY

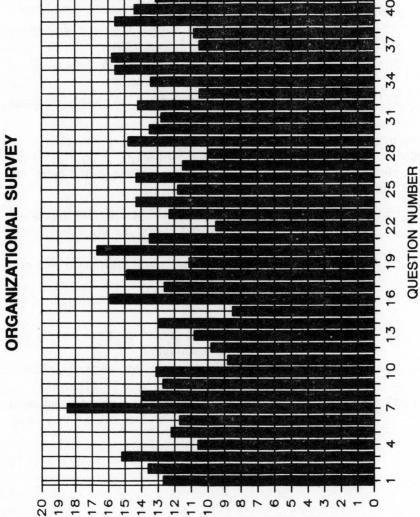

RATING

QUESTION NUMBER

MOST FAVORABLE QUESTIONS

The following items are favorable because they were answered more often in the direction of "very little" or "hardly ever." You should strive to even further reduce the occurrence of these observations even further.

7. How often do supervisors use threats, fear, and disciplinary actions to motivate employees to work harder?

20. How often is information deliberately distorted by someone passing it from employees to management?

35. How much do employees resist or reject the established goals of management?

The following items are favorable because they were answered more often in the direction of "excellent," "almost always," or "a great deal." You should work at increasing the frequency or quality of the behaviors or attitudes discussed in the following questions.

3. How often do the supervisors around here display supportive behaviors toward the employees (being friendly, watching out for them, etc.)?

16. How often do supervisors willingly share information with employees?

18. How good is the information supervisors and management get from employees?

36. To what extent are employees concerned about seeing that work gets done on time and correctly?

39. How often is production, quality, cost, and efficiency information used to punish, coerce, and/or intimidate employees?

42. How much better do you think this organization could be if everyone pulled together as much as they could if they really wanted to?

MOST UNFAVORABLE QUESTIONS

The following items were unfavorable because they were answered more often in the direction of "very little," "hardly ever," or "terrible." You should strive to reverse the situations which led to these ratings.

4. To what extent do the supervisors act as if they want employees to be candid with them when discussing problems about their jobs?

11. How much do the employees like and respect one another around here?

12. How much satisfaction do the employees get from working here?

13. How much open and accurate communication is there between groups and departments?

28. How much influence would employees say they have in determining how employees do their job?

33. To what extent does management use teamwork and group decision making to set goals?

37. To what extent are employees involved in reviewing information on production, quality, costs, and efficiency so they can do their jobs better?

38. How often is information concerning production, quality, cost, and efficiency used in a manner which encourages teamwork and problem solving?

The following items are unfavorable because they were answered more often in the direction of "almost always" or "a great deal." You should work at decreasing the incidence of situations which led to these undesirable ratings.

15. How often does management run things by issuing orders without first asking employees for information?

22. How much need is there for additional systems (such as suggestion programs) to get accurate information to management?

ITEM FEEDBACK FORM

You recently took the Organizational Survey. We'd like to ask you to take a few more moments to provide us with specific feedback about how we might be able to work toward eliminating some of our problems.

While the average responses of the entire group are useful, they don't do much to help us change specific day-to-day problems. What we'd like you to do is review the items shown on the Survey Results Form. For those items which are most important to you (because things aren't working out as well as you'd prefer), cite a specific example of a way in which we could do things differently on one of our projects, day-to-day activities, or work flows so that you'd be able to answer the question more favorably if it were asked in the future. Your specific feedback about concrete issues will enable us to be more responsive about the things we need to change.

Directions: Photocopy the following page as required. Don't put your name on it.

Example: Shown below is an example which demonstrates the proper way to fill out the attached Item Feedback Form.

Item: Question 15—"How often does management run things by issuing orders without first asking employees for information?"

Specific Problem Example: I would have preferred to be asked about the possible changes to the TX-14 report before the changes were authorized. Now I'm stuck with it, and it's too late to do anything. I suggest that when new systems are planned we hold a departmental meeting and set up a group to coordinate all of the employees' input.

Photocopy the attached sheet before you complete it so you'll have enough space to reply to all of the items you feel are important. If you need more room for a specific item, please use the back of the sheet or attach other sheets if you prefer. Thanks again for your help.

SURVEY FEEDBACK SHEET

Item: _____

_____

_____

Specific Problem Example: _____

_____

_____

_____

Item: _____

_____

_____

Specific Problem Example: _____

_____

_____

_____

Item: _____

_____

_____

Specific Problem Example: _____

_____

_____

_____

Photocopy as required and return in sealed envelope to _____ .

Thanks for your help!

Index